2014 SUPPLEMENT

BANKRUPTCY

CASES, PROBLEMS, AND MATERIALS

FOURTH EDITION

by

BARRY E. ADLER
Bernard Petrie Professor of Law and Business
New York University School of Law

DOUGLAS G. BAIRD
Harry A. Bigelow Distinguished Service Professor of Law
University of Chicago Law School

THOMAS H. JACKSON
Distinguished University Professor and President Emeritus
University of Rochester

FOUNDATION
PRESS

© 2013 by LEG, Inc. d/b/a West Academic Publishing
© 2014 LEG, Inc. d/b/a West Academic
    444 Cedar Street, Suite 700
    St. Paul, MN 55101
    1-877-888-1330

Printed in the United States of America

ISBN: 978-1-62810-086-0

Mat #41648365

TABLE OF CONTENTS

Below is the table of contents to the Fourth Edition along with references to those sections of that edition addressed by this update supplement. Page references are first to the Fourth Edition, then, in **boldface italics**, to this supplement; so, e.g., "41, *1*" refers to material that begins on page 41 of the casebook and on page *1* of this supplement.

Where new cases are added by this supplement, the reference in the table of contents to the cases and to the corresponding page number in this supplement both appear in **boldface italics**.

Also indicated by **boldface italics** is a reference to the section of this supplement devoted to **corrections** of the Fourth Edition. An asterisk ("*") in the table of contents indicates that there is a correction within the indicated page range of the casebook. As indicated below, corrections appear beginning on **page 170** of this supplement.

Part Three
Disposition of the Case

Corrections

PREFACE TO THE 2014 SUPPLEMENT

Since publication of the Fourth Edition there have been important developments in the world of bankruptcy. One such development is the enhanced prominence of going-concern asset sales. A second development is the increased significance of safe harbors from bankruptcy for transactions in derivatives. Each of these developments was highlighted by the financial meltdown of 2008-09 and the ensuing recession. Also related to these events is the Dodd-Frank Financial Reform Act of 2010. Although this Act is not part of the bankruptcy law, as it creates an alternative resolution authority to address the failure of important financial institutions, it is nevertheless of interest to bankruptcy lawyers. These events are addressed in this update supplement, which also addresses other developments since publication of the Fourth Edition.

In addition, this supplement identifies and provides corrections for some minor errors in the Fourth Edition. One should refer to these corrections while using the book.

This supplement supersedes the 2010, 2012, and 2013 versions, the material in which is incorporated and made current. The Fifth Edition of the casebook will follow shortly and should be available for adoption in spring or fall 2015.

B.E.A.
D.G.B.
T.H.J.

July 2014

EDITORS' NOTE ON CITATIONS AND CONVENTIONS

The term "Bankruptcy Code" refers to the current code as enacted in 1978 and as amended thereafter. (The law applicable before 1978 is called "the 1898 Act.") The Bankruptcy Abuse Prevention and Consumer Protection Act of 2005 is called "the Bankruptcy Reform Act of 2005" or simply "the Reform Act of 2005" or "the 2005 Reform Act." Generally, ellipses have been used to indicate deletion of material within a paragraph, while deletion of material through the end of a paragraph or more is indicated by three asterisks. However, citations and footnotes are omitted without any notation.

II. BANKRUPTCY AS COLLECTIVE DEBT COLLECTION REMEDY

[The material on "The Bankruptcy Forum" in chapter 2C, which begins on *page 41*, should be supplemented by the following.]

In Stern v. Marshall, 131 S.Ct. 2594 (2011), the Supreme Court held that a bankruptcy judge lacks the constitutional authority to issue a final judgment on a common law counterclaim to a claim in bankruptcy even though 28 U.S.C. §157(b), which defines core proceedings, purports to provide the bankruptcy court just such authority. The question remains whether *Stern* will meaningfully change the relationship between the bankruptcy and district courts.

Take, for example, a fraudulent conveyance claim brought by a debtor in bankruptcy. As explained in chapter 8 of the casebook, although fraudulent conveyances are expressly governed by the Bankruptcy Code, they also give rise to traditional claims under state law. Consequently, one might read *Stern* to prohibit a bankruptcy court's issuance of a final order in fraudulent conveyance claim even though the claim is a core proceeding under the statute.

The prohibition established by *Stern* may not be important as a practical matter, however, because in a subsequent case, Executive Benefits Insurance Agency v. Arkison, 134 S.Ct. 2165 (2014), the Supreme Court held that where a final order in a core proceeding is beyond the constitutional power of a bankruptcy court, the statutory authority to issue such an order includes the lesser authority to submit proposed findings of fact and conclusions of law for de novo review by the district court. See 28 U.S.C. §157(c)(1). The Court reached this conclusion even though there is no express statutory authority for a bankruptcy court to submit proposed findings and conclusions in a core proceeding.

Arkison left open the question whether parties can consent to final adjudication with respect to issues that are either constitutionally or statutorily noncore. The Court will revisit this issue in its next term. See Wellness International Network, Ltd. v. Sharif, 727 F.3d 751 (7th Cir. 2013), cert. granted, 2014 WL 497634 (July 1, 2014).

III. COMMENCEMENT OF THE CASE

[The material on "Eligibility for Bankruptcy" in chapter 3A, which begins on ***page 56***, should be supplemented by the following.]

The most important recent development in insolvency law is not a bankruptcy development at all. The Dodd-Frank Act of 2010 permits the Secretary of the Treasury to appoint the FDIC as receiver for a troubled financial institution the failure of which poses a threat to systemic liquidity. Prior to Dodd-Frank, these systemically important financial institutions would file for bankruptcy protection in the event of failure, as did Lehman and as would have AIG but for government intervention. In the aftermath of the financial crisis of 2008-09, however, it was widely believed that the bankruptcy process could not effectively address systemic risk should another crisis drive such firms to distress in the future. Thus, the decision was made to apply FDIC receivership more broadly, a process that has long been used to liquidate or transfer the businesses of failed deposit-taking institutions. (The non-deposit-taking financial companies remain eligible for bankruptcy unless their failure poses a systemic risk.)

A key component of FDIC receivership for these newly eligible firms—under the Act's orderly liquidation authority—is the creation of an orderly liquidation fund, which is to be financed by Treasury loans. This fund can serve, in essence, as an instantaneous source of DIP finance, which if used appropriately can be a source of payments necessary to prevent or limit a broad liquidity crisis. In principle, the fund (and thus the Treasury) is to be repaid from the debtor's assets, which will be possible, however, only if the payments needed to avoid systemic collapse are relatively small compared to the value of the debtor's assets. If the fund cannot be repaid directly from the debtor's available assets, it is to be reimbursed by creditors paid more than the amount to which they would be entitled under bankruptcy or through an industry assessment. The former raises the question of whether receivership will effectively stem a system wide crisis—with recipients of early payments concerned about a claw back—while the latter presents the possibility of a moral hazard problem—with healthy firms subsidizing those that fail.

Though there are exceptions, including the existence of the orderly liquidation fund, the FDIC receivership of financially important, non-deposit-taking institutions would largely replicate the bankruptcy process. For example, secured debt, contingent claims, preferential payments, and fraudulent conveyances are treated under the ordinary liquidation authority largely as they would be treated under bankruptcy law. But not all provisions are the same under the FDIC receivership model as under bankruptcy law. For example, the settlement of qualified financial contracts such as swap and repurchase agreements is subject to a stay of up to one business day after the commencement of an FDIC receivership but not subject to the stay at all under bankruptcy law, a potentially significant discrepancy inasmuch as the purpose of the FDIC receivership is to permit a rapid settlement of claims at a time of crisis. (That said, the unfettered settlement of qualified contracts during the last crisis did not prevent the contagion of failure and may have contributed to the panic's spread.) And setoffs, which are generally honored under the Bankruptcy Code, are subject to alteration under FDIC receivership.

Also, while the order of payments to creditors under the orderly liquidation authority generally follows state law priorities as under the Bankruptcy Code, under the Act, the FDIC would be able to cherry-pick among obligations (paying some out of priority order or treating obligations with similar priorities differently) subject to the proviso that no creditor receives less than what it would have received in a liquidation under the Bankruptcy Code.

The details of how the orderly liquidation authority will work in practice should it be called on are left for another day (and the next crisis). The changes from bankruptcy law, however, for the few, albeit important, firms to which the new law will apply are likely to be limited.

A more modest development on bankruptcy eligibility appears in In re General Growth Properties, Inc., 409 B.R. 43 (S.D.N.Y. 2009), where the court discusses Illinois Land Trusts and more generally the conditions under which trusts are eligible bankruptcy debtors, the same issues raised by *Treasure Island*. Other issues raised by *General Growth Properties* are presented in connection with chapters 3B and 10B below.

[The material on "Filing a Bankruptcy Petition" in chapter 3B, which begins on ***page 66***, should be supplemented by the following. The following can also be covered in connection with the material on "Judicial Subordination" in chapter 10B, which begins on ***page 538***.]

"Special Purpose" or "Bankruptcy Proof" entities have become increasingly common, at least in the aspirations of those who create these companies. Courts do not lightly ignore the formal separation of such an entity from affiliated companies. An entity's "status as an independent economic unit [can be] the entire basis on which [a] lender chooses to extend credit." In re Doctors Hospital of Hyde Park, Inc., 507 B.R. 558, 721 (N.D. Ill. 2013). And at least some courts honor provisions in governance documents that restrict a debtor's right to file for bankruptcy. See DB Capital Holdings, LLC, 463 B.R. 142 (10th Cir. BAP 2010) (distinguishing a debtor's covenant not to file for bankruptcy). But separateness and bankruptcy resistance are not always absolute. In the next case, *General Growth Properties*, foundational corporate documents reflect a determined effort to keep the constituent parts of a complex affiliated business organization out of bankruptcy and insulated from the financial failure of the affiliate as a whole. Under pressure applied by the financial crisis of 2008-09, this effort failed. Consider why. Consider too the court's statement that although the bankruptcy petitions of the constituent firms would be upheld over the objection that they were filed in bad faith, this result did not amount to a substantive consolidation of the bankruptcy cases. As a formal matter, this statement is undoubtedly correct, but one might question whether as a practical matter the creditors of the healthy constituents might not ultimately subsidize those of their weaker counterparts.

IN RE GENERAL GROWTH PROPERTIES, INC.

United States Bankruptcy Court, S.D.N.Y., 2009
409 B.R. 43

GROPPER, BANKRUPTCY JUDGE

Before the Court are five motions (the "Motions") to dismiss certain of the Chapter 11 cases filed by one or more debtors (the "Subject Debtors") that are owned directly or indirectly by General Growth Properties, Inc. ("GGP"). One of the Motions was filed by ING Clarion Capital Loan Services LLC ("ING Clarion"), as special servicer to certain secured lenders; one of the Motions was filed by Helios AMC, LLC ("Helios"), as special servicer to other secured lenders; and three of the Motions were filed by Metropolitan Life Insurance Company and KBC Bank N.V. (together, "Metlife", and together with ING Clarion and Helios, the "Movants"). Each of the Movants is a secured lender with a loan to one of the Subject Debtors. The primary ground on which dismissal is sought is that the Subject Debtors' cases were filed in bad faith. … The above-captioned debtors (the "Debtors") and the Official

Committee of Unsecured Creditors appointed in these cases (the "Committee") object to the Motions. Based on the following findings of fact and conclusions of law, the Motions are denied.

BACKGROUND

GGP, one of the Debtors, is a publicly-traded real estate investment trust ("REIT") and the ultimate parent of approximately 750 wholly-owned Debtor and non-Debtor subsidiaries, joint venture subsidiaries and affiliates (collectively, the "GGP Group" or the "Company"). The GGP Group's primary business is shopping center ownership and management; the Company owns or manages over 200 shopping centers in 44 states across the country. These include joint venture interests in approximately 50 properties, along with non-controlling interests in several international joint ventures. The GGP Group also owns several commercial office buildings and five master-planned communities, although these businesses account for a smaller share of its operations. The Company reported consolidated revenue of $3.4 billion in 2008. The GGP Group's properties are managed from its Chicago, Illinois headquarters, and the Company directly employs approximately 3,700 people, exclusive of those employed at the various property sites.

I. *Corporate Structure*

The corporate structure of the GGP Group is extraordinarily complex, and it is necessary to provide only a broad outline for purposes of this opinion. GGP is the general partner of GGP Limited Partnership ("GGP LP"), the company through which the Group's business is primarily conducted. GGP LP in turn controls, directly or indirectly, GGPLP, LLC, The Rouse Company LP ("TRCLP"), and General Growth Management, Inc. ("GGMI"). GGPLP LLC, TRCLP and GGMI in turn directly or indirectly control hundreds of individual project-level subsidiary entities, which directly or indirectly own the individual properties. The Company takes a nationwide, integrated approach to the development, operation and management of its properties, offering centralized leasing, marketing, management, cash management, property maintenance and construction management.

II. *Capital Structure*

As of December 31, 2008, the GGP Group reported $29.6 billion in assets and $27.3 billion in liabilities. At that time, approximately $24.85 billion of its liabilities accounted for the aggregate consolidated outstanding indebtedness of the GGP Group. Of this, approximately

$18.27 billion constituted debt of the project-level Debtors secured by the respective properties, $1.83 billion of which was secured by the properties of the Subject Debtors. The remaining $6.58 billion of unsecured debt is discussed below.

A. *Secured Debt*

The GGP Group's secured debt consists primarily of mortgage and so-called mezzanine debt. The mortgage debt is secured by mortgages on over 100 properties, each of which is typically owned by a separate corporate entity. The mortgage debt can in turn be categorized as conventional or as debt further securitized in the commercial mortgage-backed securities market.

(i) Conventional Mortgage Debt

The conventional mortgage debt is illustrated, on this record, by three of the mortgages held by Metlife. Each of the three mortgages was an obligation of a separate GGP subsidiary. There is no dispute that some of the Subject Debtors that issued the Metlife mortgages were intended to function as special purpose entities ("SPE"). SPE's typically contain restrictions in their loan documentation and operating agreements that require them to maintain their separate existence and to limit their debt to the mortgages and any incidental debts, such as trade payables or the costs of operation. Metlife asserts, without substantial contradiction from the Debtors, that SPE's are structured in this manner to protect the interests of their secured creditors by ensuring that "the operations of the borrower [are] isolated from business affairs of the borrower's affiliates and parent so that the financing of each loan stands alone on its own merits, creditworthiness and value … ." In addition to limitations on indebtedness, the SPE's organizational documents usually contain prohibitions on consolidation and liquidation, restrictions on mergers and asset sales, prohibitions on amendments to the organizational and transaction documents, and separateness covenants. Standard and Poor's, Legal Criteria for Structured Finance Transactions (April 2002).

The typical SPE documentation also often contains an obligation to retain one or more independent directors (for a corporation) or managers (for an LLC). The Metlife loans did not contain any such requirement, but for example, the Amended and Restated Operating Agreements of both Faneuil Hall Marketplace, LLC ("FHM") and Saint Louis Galleria LLC ("SLG"), in a section entitled "Provisions Relating to Financing," mandate the appointment of "at least two (2) duly appointed Managers (each an 'Independent Manager') of the

Company … ." The Company's view of the independent directors and managers is that they were meant to be unaffiliated with the Group and its management. It appears that some of the secured lenders believed they were meant to be devoted to the interests of the secured creditors, as asserted by a representative of Helios. In any event, this aspect of the loan documentation is discussed further below.

Although each of the mortgage loans was typically secured by a separate property owned by an individual debtor, many of the loans were guaranteed by other GGP entities. One of the Metlife loans, for example, was guaranteed. Moreover, many loans were advanced by one lender to multiple Debtors. For example, in July 2008, the GGP Group received a loan from several lenders led by Eurohypo AG, New York Branch, as administrative agent, the outstanding principal of which totaled $1.51 billion as of the Petition Date (the "2008 Facility"). GGP, GGP LP and GGPLP, LLC are guarantors, and 24 Debtor subsidiaries are borrowers under the 2008 Facility, which is secured by mortgages and deeds of trust on 24 properties. The loan was set to mature on July 11, 2011, but was in default as of the Petition Date due to a cross-default provision triggered by the default of another multi-Debtor loan called the 2006 Facility. One of the last financings the Debtors were able to obtain before bankruptcy, in December 2008, was a group of eight non-recourse mortgage loans with Teachers Insurance and Annuity Association of America, in the total amount of $896 million, and collateralized by eight properties (the "Teachers Loans").

The typical mortgage loan for the GGP Group members had a three to seven-year term, with low amortization and a large balloon payment at the end. Some of the mortgage loans had a much longer nominal maturity date, but these also had an anticipated repayment date ("ARD"), at which point the loan became "hyper-amortized," even if the maturity date itself was as much as thirty years in the future. Consequences of failure to repay or refinance the loan at the ARD typically include a steep increase in interest rate, a requirement that cash be kept at the project-level, with excess cash flow being applied to principal, and a requirement that certain expenditures be submitted to the lender for its approval. The Debtors viewed the ARD as equivalent to maturity and the consequences of a loan becoming hyper-amortized as equivalent to default, and historically sought to refinance such loans so as to avoid hyper-amortization.

(ii) Commercial Mortgage-Backed Securities

Many of the GGP Group's mortgage loans were financed in the commercial mortgage-backed securities ("CMBS") market, represented on these Motions by each of the loans serviced by ING Clarion and Helios, as special servicers. In a typical CMBS transaction, multiple mortgages are sold to a trust qualified as a real estate mortgage conduit ("REMIC") for tax purposes. The REMIC in turn sells certificates entitling the holders to payments from principal and interest on this large pool of mortgages. The holders of the CMBS securities typically have different rights to the income stream and bear different interest rates; they may or may not have different control rights.

The REMIC is managed by a master servicer that handles day-to-day loan administration functions and services the loans when they are not in default. A special servicer takes over management of the REMIC upon a transfer of authority. Such transfers take place under certain limited circumstances, including: (i) a borrower's failure to make a scheduled principal and interest payment, unless cured within 60 days, (ii) a borrower's bankruptcy or insolvency, (iii) a borrower's failure to make a balloon payment upon maturity, or (iv) a determination by the master servicer that a material and adverse default under the loan is imminent and unlikely to be cured within 60 days. While a master servicer is able to grant routine waivers and consents, it cannot agree to an alteration of the material terms of a loan or mortgage. A special servicer has the ability to agree to modify the loan once authority has been transferred, but often only with the consent of the holders of the CMBS securities, or in some cases the holders of certain levels of the debt.

(iii) Mezzanine Debt

The Debtors are also obligors on so-called mezzanine loans from at least four lenders, of which one, Metlife, is a Movant on these motions to dismiss. In these transactions generally, and in the Metlife mezzanine loan in particular, the lender is the holder of a mortgage on the property held by one of the Subject Debtors. The lender makes a further loan, ordinarily at a higher interest rate, to a single-purpose entity formed to hold the equity interest in the mortgage-level borrower. The loan to the single-purpose entity is secured only by the stock or other equity interest of the mortgage level borrower. The single-purpose entity typically has no other debt and its business is limited to its equity interest in the property-owning subsidiary.

B. *Unsecured Debt*

In addition to secured debt, members of the GGP Group were obligated on approximately $6.58 billion of unsecured debt as of the Petition Date. Other than trade debt incurred by some of the project-level Debtors, most of this debt was an obligation of one or more of the holding companies, generally at the top levels of the corporate chart. The principal components of this debt were as follows:

Under an indenture dated April 16, 2007, GGP LP issued $1.55 billion of 3.98% Exchangeable Senior Notes (the "GGP LP Notes"). The notes are senior, unsecured obligations of GGP LP and are not guaranteed by any entity within the GGP Group. The outstanding principal was $1.55 billion as of the Petition Date, with interest payable semi-annually in arrears.

Under an indenture dated February 24, 1995, TRCLP issued five series of public bonds (collectively, the "1995 Rouse Bonds"), which were unsecured obligations of TRCLP, not guaranteed by any other entity in the GGP Group. Four of the five series remain outstanding. Additionally, under an indenture dated May 5, 2006, TRCLP and TRC Co-Issuer, Inc., issued one series of private placement bonds, in the face amount of $800 million (the "2006 Rouse Bonds"). The 2006 Rouse Bonds are unsecured obligations of TRCLP and TRC Co-Issuer, Inc. and are not guaranteed by any other entity in the GGP Group. The total aggregate outstanding amount due on the Rouse Bonds as of the Petition Date was $2.245 billion. TRCLP was unable to pay the outstanding balance of one series of the Rouse Bonds upon maturity in March 2009 and received a notice of default. This default in turn triggered defaults for each of the other series of Rouse Bonds.

In February 2006, GGP, GGP LP and GGPLP, LLC became borrowers under a term and revolving credit facility with Eurpohypo AG, New York Branch serving as administrative agent (the "2006 Facility"). The 2006 Facility is guaranteed by Rouse LLC, with GGP LP pledging its equity interest in GGPLP, LLC, TRCLP and Rouse LLC and Rouse LLC pledging its general partnership interest in TRCLP to secure the obligations under the 2006 Facility. Each of the borrower, guarantor and pledgor entities is a Debtor, the current outstanding balance on the term loan is approximately $1.99 billion, and the outstanding balance on the revolving loan is $590 million. The facility was not scheduled to mature until February 24, 2010, but fell into default in late 2008 through a cross-default provision triggered by the default of one of the GGP Group's property-level mortgage loans.

On February 24, 2006, GGP LP issued $206.2 million of junior subordinated notes to GGP Capital Trust I ("the Junior Subordinated Notes"). GGP Capital Trust I, a non-Debtor entity, subsequently issued $200 million of trust preferred securities ("TRUPS") to outside investors and $6.2 million of common equity to GGP LP. The Junior Subordinated Notes are unsecured obligations of GGP LP, one of the Debtors, and are not guaranteed by any entities within the GGP Group. The current outstanding principal amount on the notes is $206.2 million and the notes mature on April 30, 2036. The Junior Subordinated Notes are subordinate in payment to all indebtedness of GGP LP, other than trade debt.

C. *Other Debt*

The GGP Group had entered into five interest-rate swap agreements as of December 31, 2008. The total notional amount of the agreements was $1.08 billion, with an average fixed pay rate of 3.38% and an average variable receive rate of LIBOR. The Company made April 2009 payments to only one of the counterparties, and two of the swaps have been terminated. Additionally, as of December 31, 2008, the Company also had outstanding letters of credit and surety bonds in the amount of $286.2 million.

With respect to the Company's joint venture interests, GGP LP is the promissor on a note in the principal amount of $245 million, payable to the Comptroller of the State of New York, as trustee for the New York State Common Retirement Fund, and due on February 28, 2013. It is secured by a pledge of GGP LP's member interest in the GGP/Homart II LLC joint venture. Additionally GGP LP is the promissor on a note in the amount of $93,712,500, due on December 1, 2012, payable to Ivanhoe Capital, LP, and secured by a pledge of GGP LP's shares in the GGP Ivanhoe, Inc. joint venture.

D. *Equity*

GGP had 312,352,392 shares of common stock outstanding as of March 17, 2009. GGP is required, as a REIT, to distribute at least 90% of its taxable income and to distribute, or pay tax on, certain of its capital gains. During the first three quarters of 2008, GGP distributed $476.6 million, or $1.50 per share, to its stockholders and GGP LP unitholders, but it suspended its quarterly dividends as of the last quarter of 2008.

III. *The Events of 2008-2009*

Historically, the capital needs of the GGP Group were satisfied through mortgage loans obtained from banks, insurance companies and, increasingly, the CMBS market. As noted above, these loans were generally secured by the shopping center properties and structured with three to seven-year maturities, low amortization rates and balloon payments due at maturity. There is no dispute that the Company's business plan was based on the premise that it would be able to refinance the debt. The testimony of Thomas Nolan, the President and Chief Operating Officer of GGP, is that "[t]his approach was standard in the industry, so for many years, it has been rare to see commercial real estate financed with longer-term mortgages that would fully amortize."

However, in the latter half of 2008, the crisis in the credit markets spread to commercial real estate finance, most notably the CMBS market. This in turn affected the ability of the GGP Group to refinance its maturing debt on commercially acceptable terms. The GGP Group attempted to refinance its maturing project-level debt or obtain new financing, contacting dozens of banks, insurance companies and pension funds. It also contacted national and regional brokers and retained the investment banking firms of Goldman Sachs and Morgan Stanley to attempt to securitize and syndicate the loans. Despite these efforts, the only refinancing the GGP Group was able to obtain during this period was with Teachers Insurance, which is described above.

The GGP parent entities also attempted to find refinancing for their own mostly unsecured debt, but efforts to raise debt or equity capital were similarly unsuccessful. GGP hired an investment banking firm that specializes in the restructuring of debt, Miller Buckfire & Co., LLC ("Miller Buckfire"), to attempt to renegotiate the debt, but the lenders were unwilling to consent to additional forbearance, which in turn led to defaults and cross-defaults. Furthermore, the GGP Group was generally unable to sell any of its assets to generate the cash necessary to pay down its debts, as potential purchasers were themselves unable to acquire financing.

The Debtors claim that the CMBS structure caused additional roadblocks to the Company's attempts to refinance its debt or even talk to its lenders. In January 2009, the GGP Group contacted the master servicers of those loans that were set to mature by January 2010, seeking to communicate with the special servicers regarding renegotiation of the loan terms. The response from the master servicers was that the Company could not communicate with the special servicers until the loans were transferred, and that the loans had to be much closer to maturity to be transferred. The GGP Group subsequently attempted to communicate with the master servicers regarding only those loans set to mature through May 2009, but received the same response. The Debtors then attempted to contact the special servicers directly, only to be referred back to the master servicers. Finally, in February 2009, the GGP Group attempted to call a "summit" of special servicers to discuss those loans due to mature through January 2010, but only one servicer was willing to attend and the meeting was cancelled.

Unable to refinance, the Company began to tap more heavily into its operating cash flow to pay both its regular expenses and financial obligations. This in turn left the Company short of cash to meet prior commitments towards development and redevelopment costs. As additional mortgage loans began to mature, the Company's liquidity problems grew worse. For example, two large loans from Deutsche Bank matured on November 28, 2008. In return for brief extensions of the maturity date, Deutsche Bank required the Debtors to increase the rate of interest 3.75%, from LIBOR plus 225 basis points to LIBOR plus 600 basis points, 75 basis points over the prior default interest rate. Additionally, Deutsche Bank required excess cash flow from the properties to be escrowed in a lockbox account and applied entirely to the relevant properties, with surplus used to amortize the principal on the relevant loan.

Based on the state of the markets, the GGP Group began to contemplate the necessity of a Chapter 11 restructuring. Several of the loans went into default and one of the lenders, Citibank, commenced foreclosure proceedings on a defaulted loan on March 19, 2009. On April 16, 2009, 360 of the Debtors filed voluntary petitions under Chapter 11 of the Bankruptcy Code. An additional 28 of the Debtors filed for protection on April 22, 2009, for a total of 388 Debtors in the above-captioned Chapter 11 cases.

Upon filing, the Debtors did not dispute that the GGP Group's shopping center business had a stable and generally positive cash flow and that it had continued to perform well, despite the current financial crisis. Specifically, they stated "[t]he Company's net operating income ('NOI'), a standard metric of financial performance in the real estate and shopping center industries, has been increasing over time, and in fact increased in 2008 over the prior year despite the challenges of the general economy." Despite this, faced with approximately $18.4 billion in outstanding debt that matured or would be maturing by the end of

2012, the Company believed its capital structure had become unmanageable due to the collapse of the credit markets.

The Debtors filed several conventional motions on the Petition Date. The only motion that was highly contested was the Debtors' request for the use of cash collateral and approval of debtor-in-possession ("DIP") financing. By the time of the final hearing on May 8, 2009, numerous project-level lenders had objected, based on concerns that the security of their loans would be adversely affected. Many of these parties argued that it would be a violation of the separateness of the individual companies for the Debtors to upstream cash from the individual properties for use at the parent-level entity. After hearing extensive argument, the Court ruled that the SPE structure did not require that the project-level Debtors be precluded from upstreaming their cash surplus at a time it was needed most by the Group. The final cash collateral order, entered on May 14, 2009, however, had various forms of adequate protection for the project-level lenders, such as the payment of interest at the non-default rate, continued maintenance of the properties, a replacement lien on the cash being upstreamed from the project-level Debtors and a second priority lien on certain other properties. DIP financing was arranged, but the DIP lender did not obtain liens on the properties of the project-level Debtors that could arguably adversely affect the lien interests of the existing mortgage lenders, such as the Movants.

At an early stage in the cases it became clear that several lenders intended to move to dismiss, and the Court urged all parties who intended to move to dismiss any of the cases to coordinate their motions. Six motions were filed (three by Metlife), with one party subsequently withdrawing its motion. ING Clarion and Helios, which hold CMBS debt, argued that their cases should be dismissed because they were filed in bad faith in that there was no imminent threat to the financial viability of the Subject Debtors. ING Clarion also contended that Lancaster Trust, one of the Subject Debtors, was ineligible to be a debtor under the Bankruptcy Code. Metlife, which holds conventional mortgage debt, similarly argued that the Subject Debtors were not in financial distress, that the cases were filed prematurely and that there was no chance of reorganization as there was no possibility of confirming a plan over its objection.

DISCUSSION

I. *Bad Faith Dismissal*

The principle that a Chapter 11 reorganization case can be dismissed as a bad faith filing is a judge-made doctrine. In the Second Circuit, the leading case on dismissal for the filing of a petition in bad faith is *C-TC 9th Ave. P'ship v. Norton Co. (In re C-TC 9th Ave. P'ship)*, 113 F.3d 1304 (2d Cir.1997). Under [this decision], grounds for dismissal exist if it is clear on the filing date that "there was no reasonable likelihood that the debtor intended to reorganize and no reasonable probability that it would eventually emerge from bankruptcy proceedings." 113 F.3d at 1309-10. One frequently-cited decision by Chief Judge Brozman of this Court has restated the principle as follows: "[T]he standard in this Circuit is that a bankruptcy petition will be dismissed if *both* objective futility of the reorganization process *and* subjective bad faith in filing the petition are found." *In re Kingston Square Assocs.*, 214 B.R. 713, 725 (Bankr. S.D.N.Y. 1997).

No one factor is determinative of good faith, and the Court "must examine the facts and circumstances of each case in light of several established guidelines or indicia, essentially conducting an 'on-the-spot evaluation of the Debtor's financial condition [and] motives.'" *In re Kingston Square,* 214 B.R. at 725. "It is the totality of circumstances, rather than any single factor, that will determine whether good faith exists." *In re Kingston Square,* Id. at 725. Case law recognizes that a bankruptcy petition should be dismissed for lack of good faith only sparingly and with great caution.

C-TC 9th Ave. P'ship, like many of the other bad faith cases, involved a single-asset real estate debtor, where the equity investors in a hopelessly insolvent project were engaged in a last-minute effort to fend off foreclosure and the accompanying tax losses. Thus, many of the following factors listed by the C-TC Court as evidencing bad faith were characteristics of this type of case:

> (1) the debtor has only one asset; (2) the debtor has few unsecured creditors whose claims are small in relation to those of the secured creditors; (3) the debtor's one asset is the subject of a foreclosure action as a result of arrearages or default on the debt; (4) the debtor's financial condition is, in essence, a two party dispute between the debtor and secured creditors which can be resolved in the pending state foreclosure action; (5) the timing of the debtor's filing evidences an intent to delay or frustrate the legitimate efforts of the debtor's secured

creditors to enforce their rights; (6) the debtor has little or no cash flow; (7) the debtor can't meet current expenses including the payment of personal property and real estate taxes; and (8) the debtor has no employees.

113 F.3d at 1311. Relatively few of these factors are relevant to the cases at bar, and two of the Movants, ING Clarion and Helios, expressly disavowed reliance on the *C-TC* bad faith formulation at the hearing on the Motions, conceding in effect that there was a reasonable likelihood that the Debtors intended to reorganize and could successfully emerge from bankruptcy. These Movants instead argue that the filings, when examined from the perspective of the individual Debtors, were premature. The third Movant, Metlife, did not expressly disavow reliance on the *C-TC* formulation. However, its contentions were not based on the argument that the debtors did not intend to reorganize. Metlife argued that the Debtors could never confirm a plan over its objection, implying that Metlife would never agree to a plan proposed by the Debtors. Then, having staked out a position that the Debtors might characterize as evidence of bad faith, Metlife contended that the Subject Debtors' subjective bad faith was evidenced by the prematurity of the filing and various actions taken by the Debtors that are further analyzed below.

A. *Objective Bad Faith: Prematurity*

All three Movants support their contention that the Chapter 11 filings of these Debtors were, in effect, premature by reliance on the few cases that have dismissed Chapter 11 petitions where the debtor was not in financial distress at the time of filing, where the prospect of liability was speculative, and where there was evidence that the filing was designed to obtain a litigation advantage. The leading decision is *In re SGL Carbon Corp.*, 200 F.3d 154 (3d Cir.1999), in which the debtors filed Chapter 11 petitions for the express purpose of protecting themselves from antitrust litigation. At the same time they published a press release touting their financial health, as well as their denial of any antitrust liability. The Third Circuit held that "the mere possibility of a future need to file, without more, does not establish that a petition was filed in 'good faith.' " *Id.* at 164. The principle of *SGL Carbon* was followed by this Court in *In re Schur Mgmt. Co.*, 323 B.R. 123 (Bankr. S.D.N.Y. 2005), where two debtors filed for bankruptcy to avoid a possible judgment from a personal injury suit in which they denied all liability and which had yet to go to trial. In *Schur Mgmt.*, this Court noted that "[i]t would be sheer speculation to guess as to the amount of a judgment, whether it would be imposed on one or both debtors and whether it would impair healthy companies with only $14,075 in aggregate liabilities and a net positive cash flow." 323 B.R. at 127.

In *SGL Carbon* and *Schur Mgmt.,* the prospect of any liability from pending litigation was wholly speculative. By contrast, the Subject Debtors here carry an enormous amount of fixed debt that is not contingent. Movants argue nevertheless that none of the Subject Debtors had a mortgage with a maturity date earlier than March 2010, and that the Subject Debtors should have waited until much closer to the respective maturity dates on their loans to file for bankruptcy. Movants contend in effect that the prospect of liability was too remote on the Petition Date for the Subject Debtors, and that the issue of financial distress and prematurity of filing cannot be examined from the perspective of the group but only on an individual-entity basis. Accepting for the moment this latter proposition, the question is whether the Subject Debtors were in actual financial distress on the Petition Date and whether the prospect of liability was too remote to justify a Chapter 11 filing.

(i) The Financial Distress of the Individual Project Debtors

The record on these Motions demonstrates that the individual debtors that are the subject of these Motions were in varying degrees of financial distress in April 2009. Loans to four of the Subject Debtors had cross-defaulted to the defaults of affiliates or would have been in default as a result of other bankruptcy petitions. Of the loans to the remaining sixteen Subject Debtors, one had gone into hyper-amortization in 2008. Interest had increased by 4.26%. Five of the Subject Debtors had mortgage debt maturing or hyper-amortizing in 2010, two in 2011, and one in 2012. The remaining seven Subject Debtors were either guarantors on maturing loans of other entities or their property was collateral for a loan that was maturing, or there existed other considerations that in the Debtors' view placed the loan in distress, such as a high loan-to-value ratio.

The Debtors' determination that the Subject Debtors were in financial distress was made in a series of Board meetings following substantial financial analysis. The Debtors established that in late 2008 they hired a team of advisors to assist in the evaluation of either an in-court or an out-of-court restructuring. The team included Miller Buckfire as restructuring advisor, AlixPartners LLP as financial advisor, and both Weil Gotshal & Manges and Kirkland & Ellis as legal advisors. The process of evaluating the Company's restructuring options took approximately six weeks and encompassed a total of seven Board meetings and three informational sessions. During these meetings, the Boards discussed general considerations applicable to the project-level companies, as well as specific facts relating to the individual properties, with both GGP personnel and the financial, restructuring and legal advisors available. The Boards specifically focused on: "the collapse of the commercial real estate financing market; the challenges facing the CMBS market and the practical difficulties of negotiating with CMBS servicers to meaningfully modify loan terms; integration of the project entities with GGP Group and requirements for securing DIP financing; and the consequences of filing an entity for bankruptcy individually, outside a coordinated restructuring with other GGP entities." The Boards also concentrated on three of the above-referenced filing factors: "(i) defaults or cross-defaults with other loans; (ii) loans that were maturing in the next three to four years; and (iii) other financial considerations indicating that restructuring would be necessary, including a loan-to-value ratio above 70 percent."

In addition to these general considerations, the Boards discussed each project-level entity individually. For each entity, Robert Michaels, the Vice Chairman of GGP, "provided an overview of its financial and operational considerations, including the property's performance, outlook, and projected capital needs. In addition, for each entity, the Boards received written materials consisting of a fact sheet on the property, an income statement, and a draft board resolution." In these meetings, the Debtors divided the various property-level entities into separate groups to evaluate whether to file each individual entity. On April 15, 2009 the Boards separately voted to put most of the project-level Debtors into bankruptcy. Certain Subject Debtors acted by written consent of the directors or managers. Fourteen entities were left out of the filing, as none of the ten filing factors was applicable.[26]

---

[26] The entities were separated into Groups A through G. Ten factors were used to consider whether to file an entity for bankruptcy, although other considerations were applied depending on the facts and circumstances related to the entity. The ten factors included: (1) the Company is a borrower or guarantor under a credit facility that is currently in default and for which no forbearance has been obtained; (2) the Company is a borrower or guarantor under a credit facility that is currently in a forbearance period that can be terminated at the Lender's discretion; (3) the default of General Growth Properties, Inc. or another entity within the General Growth Properties structure and/or a bankruptcy filing by an entity guaranteeing the Company's debt triggers an Event of Default under the Company's existing loan; (4) the Company owns a property which is subject to an existing cash trap that has been implemented;

Movants contend that, in the name of the "doctrine" of "prematurity," the Debtors had a good faith obligation to delay a Chapter 11 filing until they were temporally closer to an actual default. For the following reasons, these Debtors were justified in filing Chapter 11 petitions when they did.

We start with the statute. Chapter X of the former Bankruptcy Act expressly required that a petition be filed in good faith, providing that "[u]pon the filing of a petition by a debtor, the judge shall enter an order approving the petition, if satisfied that it complies with the requirements of this chapter and has been filed in good faith, or dismissing it if not so satisfied." Bankruptcy Act of 1898 § 141, 11 U.S.C. § 541 (1976) (repealed 1978). Neither Chapter XI nor XII contained a similar good faith requirement, and the good faith provisions were one of the many parts of Chapter X that debtors avoided by filing under Chapter XI and that Congress rejected when it structured Chapter 11 of the Bankruptcy Reform Act of 1978.

Indeed, when Congress adopted the Bankruptcy Abuse Prevention and Consumer Protection Act of 2005 ("BAPCPA"), it significantly strengthened the provisions of §1112, requiring the Court to dismiss or convert an abusive Chapter 11 case. BAPCPA added several factors to the prior list of grounds for dismissal. Significantly, it did not provide expressly that a Chapter 11 case should be dismissed for bad faith in filing, and all of the listed grounds for dismissal relate to a debtor's conduct *after* the filing, not before. Similarly, in 2005 Congress added several provisions designed to shorten Chapter 11 cases, but it omitted any requirement that the Court hold an initial hearing on a Chapter 11 debtor's *bona fides* or good faith.

The Code's omission of any such hearing, which would doubtless invite significant litigation at the start of every Chapter 11 case, is nevertheless consistent with another of the Code's innovations, ordinarily leaving the debtor in possession and not appointing a trustee. These

---

(5) the Company is a borrower or guarantor under a loan that matures within the next three to four years; (6) the Company is part of a project in which one or more subsidiaries or affiliates are under consideration for filing to facilitate a restructuring; (7) the Company is the general partner of a partnership that is under consideration for filing; (8) the Company is subject to multiple other filing considerations, including a loan which has a loan-to-value ratio in excess of 70%; (9) the Company holds unencumbered assets and is filing to facilitate the inclusion of such assets as part of an overall corporate restructuring; (10) the Company may be part of a non-core asset disposition process that could be facilitated by a section 363 sale in bankruptcy.

provisions carry out the goal of the 1978 Bankruptcy Code to incentivize a debtor to file earlier rather than later, so as to preserve the value of the estate.

In light of the statute, this Court declines the invitation to establish an arbitrary rule, of the type desired by Movants, that a debtor is not in financial distress and cannot file a Chapter 11 petition if its principal debt is not due within one, two or three years. The Movants did not establish that the Debtors' procedures for determining whether to file the individual Subject Debtors were unreasonable or that the Debtors were unreasonable in concluding that the disarray in the financial market made it uncertain whether they would be able to refinance debt years in the future. There was no evidence to counter the Debtors' demonstration that the CMBS market, in which they historically had financed and refinanced most of their properties, was "dead" as of the Petition Date, and that no one knows when or if that market will revive. Indeed, at the time of the hearings on these Motions, it was anticipated that the market would worsen, and there is no evident means of refinancing billions of dollars of real estate debt coming due in the next several years. The following testimony of Allen Hanson, an officer of Helios, is telling: "Q. Helios is aware that there are debt maturities that will occur in 2009, 2010, 2011 and 2012 that the CMBS market will not be able to handle through new CMBS issuances, correct? A. Based on the circumstances we see today, yes."

For example, CMBS issuances dropped by 97% when the first nine months of 2008 are compared with the same period for 2007. Furthermore, CMBS issuances for the fourth quarter of 2008 were 98% lower than in the fourth quarter of 2007.

It is well established that the Bankruptcy Code does not require that a debtor be insolvent prior to filing. In *U.S. v. Huebner,* 48 F.3d 376, 379 (9th Cir.1994), the Court noted a corollary that is equally applicable here: "The Bankruptcy Act does not require any particular degree of financial distress as a condition precedent to a petition seeking relief." Many other cases have denied motions to dismiss, despite the fact that the subject debtors were able to meet current expenses. In *In re Century/ML Cable Venture,* 294 B.R. 9 (Bankr. S.D.N.Y. 2003), for example, the Court denied a motion to dismiss because, despite being able to meet current expenses, the debtor had "a huge financial liability which it does not have the ability to pay out of current cash flow, and without a substantial liquidation of its assets." 294 B.R. at 35-36.

The foregoing is not to assert that every stand-alone company with ample cash flow would necessarily act in good faith by filing a Chapter 11 petition three years before its only debt came due. However, contrary to Movants' contentions, the Court is not required in these cases to examine the issue of good faith as if each Debtor were wholly independent. We turn to the interests of the Group as a whole.

(ii) The Interests of the Group

Movants argue that the SPE or bankruptcy-remote structure of the project-level Debtors requires that each Debtor's financial distress be analyzed exclusively from its perspective, that the Court should consider only the financial circumstances of the individual Debtors, and that consideration of the financial problems of the Group in judging the good faith of an individual filing would violate the purpose of the SPE structure. There is no question that the SPE structure was intended to insulate the financial position of each of the Subject Debtors from the problems of its affiliates, and to make the prospect of a default less likely. There is also no question that this structure was designed to make each Subject Debtor "bankruptcy remote." Nevertheless, the record also establishes that the Movants each extended a loan to the respective Subject Debtor with a balloon payment that would require refinancing in a period of years and that would default if financing could not be obtained by the SPE or by the SPE's parent coming to its rescue. Movants do not contend that they were unaware that they were extending credit to a company that was part of a much larger group, and that there were benefits as well as possible detriments from this structure. If the ability of the Group to obtain refinancing became impaired, the financial situation of the subsidiary would inevitably be impaired.

The few cases on point support the Debtors' position that the interests of the group can and should be considered. In *Heisley v. U.I.P. Engineered Prods. Corp. (In re U.I.P. Engineered Prods. Corp.),* 831 F.2d 54 (4th Cir.1987), the Court addressed the propriety of Chapter 11 filings by solvent subsidiaries of a parent corporation that had filed its own Chapter 11 case shortly before the subsidiaries filed. Creditors sought to dismiss the subsidiaries' cases, arguing that the timing of the filings and the subsidiaries' admitted solvency evidenced an abuse of the bankruptcy process. The Court found otherwise, stating that is was irrelevant whether the subsidiaries could independently demonstrate good faith for their filings. Rather, the question was whether the wholly-owned subsidiaries "should have been included in their parent company's bankruptcy estate, when the parent company had filed in good faith for Chapter 11 reorganization." *Id.* at 56. The Court found that it was "clearly sound business practice for [the parent] to seek Chapter 11 protection for its wholly-owned subsidiaries when those subsidiaries were crucial to its own reorganization plan." *Id.* The Court explained that the nature of a corporate family created an "'identity of interest' … that justifies the protection of the subsidiaries as well as the parent corporation." *Id.* The Fourth Circuit also relied on the pre-Code case of *Duggan v. Sansberry,* 327 U.S. 499 (1946), which stated that it was Congress' intent "ordinarily to allow parent and subsidiary to be reorganized in a single proceeding, thereby effectuating its general policy that the entire administration of an estate should be centralized in a single reorganization court." *Id.* at 510-11. * * *

Movants do not contend that the parent companies acted in bad faith in filing their own Chapter 11 petitions. The parent companies depended on the cash flow from the subsidiaries, but much of the project-level debt was in default: from January 1, 2009 through the second week of April 2009, $1.1 billion of the GGP Group project-level debt had matured, none of which the Company had been able to refinance. As of the Petition Date, billions of dollars of project-level debt had also reached hyper-amortization, with several secured lenders having imposed cash traps. In March 2009, Citibank, a lender on one of the defaulted loans, had begun foreclosure proceedings against one property. In addition to the project-level debt, the Group had debt of more than $8.4 billion at the parent level. Much of this debt was in default and it, too, could not be refinanced. Beyond the unsecured debt of the parent companies were thousands of equityholders who depended, in large part, on the net cash flow of and the equity in the project-level Debtors as a principal source of protection for their investment.

Faced with the unprecedented collapse of the real estate markets, and serious uncertainty as to when or if they would be able to the refinance the project-level debt, the Debtors' management had to reorganize the Group's capital structure. Movants do not explain how the billions of dollars of unsecured debt at the parent levels could be restructured responsibly if the cash flow of the parent companies continued to be based on the earnings of subsidiaries that had debt coming due in a period of years without any known means of providing for repayment or refinance. That is not to conclude, as Movants imply, that the interests of the subsidiaries or their creditors should be sacrificed to the interests of the parents and their creditors. As further discussed below, there need be no sacrifice of fundamental rights. The point is that a judgment on an issue as sensitive and fact-specific as whether to file a Chapter 11 petition can be based in good faith on consideration of the interests of the group as well as the interests of the individual debtor.

Indeed, there is authority that under the circumstances at bar, the interests of the parent companies *must* be taken into account. The Operating Agreements of many of the project-level Debtors contained provisions that required the appointment of two "Independent Managers." The Operating Agreements do not enumerate the duties of the Independent Managers except in the following instance, which is obviously highly relevant to the instant Motions: "To the extent permitted by law … the Independent Managers shall consider only the interests of the Company, *including its respective creditors,* in acting or otherwise voting on the matters referred to in Article XIII (p)." (emphasis added). Article XIII (p) requires the "unanimous written consent of the Managers of the Company, including both of the Independent Managers" before the SPE can take any action to file or consent to the filing, as debtor, of any bankruptcy proceeding. The Operating Agreements further provide that, "in exercising their rights and performing their duties under this Agreement, any Independent Manager shall have a fiduciary duty of loyalty and care similar to that of a director of a business corporation organized under the General Corporation Law of the State of Delaware."

Independent Manager is defined in the ING Clarion Debtors' documents as a:

> natural person who is not … (i) a stockholder, director, manager … , trustee, officer, employee, partner, member, attorney or counsel of the Company or any Affiliate of the Company; (ii) a creditor, customer, supplier or other Person who derives any of its purchases or revenues from its activities with the Company or any Affiliate of the Company; (iii) a Person controlling or under common control with any such stockholder, partner, member, creditor, customer, supplier or other Person; or (iv) a member of the immediate family of any such stockholder, director, officer, employee, partner, member, creditor, customer, supplier or other Person.

The provision allows a "person who satisfies the foregoing definition other than subparagraph (ii)" to serve as Independent Manager if "such individual is an independent manager provided by a nationally-recognized company that provides professional independent directors, managers or trustees … or if such individual receives customary director, manager or trustee's fees for so serving … ." Similarly, an individual who "otherwise satisfies the foregoing definition except for serving as an independent director, manager or trustee of one or more Affiliates of the Company that are 'Special Purpose Entities' " may serve as Independent Manager if such individual is "provided by a nationally recognized company that provides professional independent directors, managers and trustees ... ." The Operating Agreements for the Helios Debtors define special purpose entity slightly differently, as "an entity whose organizational documents contain restrictions on its activities and impose requirements intended to preserve such entity's separateness in compliance with rating agency standards."

The drafters of these documents may have attempted to create impediments to a bankruptcy filing; in considering a filing, the Independent Managers are directed to consider only the interests of the Company, including its "creditors"-meaning the lender as the only substantial creditor of the entity. However, it is also provided, appropriately, that the Independent Managers can act only to the extent permitted by applicable law, which is deemed to be the corporate law of Delaware. Delaware law in turn provides that the directors of a solvent corporation are authorized-indeed, required-to consider the interests of the shareholders in exercising their fiduciary duties. In *North American Catholic Educational Programming Foundation, Inc. v. Gheewalla,* 930 A.2d 92 (Del.2007), the Delaware Supreme Court held for the first time that the directors of an insolvent corporation have duties to creditors that may be enforceable in a derivative action on behalf of the corporation. But it rejected the proposition of several earlier Chancery cases that directors of a Delaware corporation have duties to creditors when operating in the "zone of insolvency," stating

> [w]hen a solvent corporation is navigating in the zone of insolvency, the focus for Delaware directors does not change: directors must continue to discharge their fiduciary duties to the corporation and its shareholders by exercising their business judgment *in the best interests of the corporation for the benefit of its shareholder owners.*

930 A.2d at 101 (emphasis supplied).

This statement is a general formulation that leaves open many issues for later determination-for example, when and how a corporation should be determined to be insolvent. But there is no contention in these cases that the Subject Debtors were insolvent at any time-indeed, Movants' contention is that they were and are solvent. Movants therefore get no assistance from Delaware law in the contention that the Independent Managers should have considered only the interests of the secured creditor when they made their decisions to file Chapter 11 petitions, or that there was a breach of fiduciary duty on the part of any of the managers by voting to file based on the interests of the Group.

The record at bar does not explain exactly what the Independent Managers were supposed to do. It appears that the Movants may have thought the Independent Managers were obligated to protect only their interests. For example, an officer of ING Clarion testified that "the real reason" he was disturbed by the Chapter 11 filings was the inability of the Independent Managers to prevent one:

> Well, my understanding of the bankruptcy as it pertains to these borrowers is that there was an independent board member who was meant to, at least from the lender's point of view, meant to prevent a bankruptcy filing to make them a bankruptcy-remote, and that such filings were not anticipated to happen.

However, if Movants believed that an "independent" manager can serve on a board solely for the purpose of voting "no" to a bankruptcy filing because of the desires of a secured creditor, they were mistaken. As the Delaware cases stress, directors and managers owe their duties to the corporation and, ordinarily, to the shareholders. Seen from the perspective of the Group, the filings were unquestionably not premature.

B. *Inability to Confirm a Plan*

In addition to prematurity, Metlife contends that objective futility has been established and its cases should be dismissed because the Subject Debtors will never be able to confirm a plan over its opposition. [Metlife argues that as the only creditor it will be the only holder of an impaired claim and thus will be the able to block any reorganization plan by virtue of Bankruptcy Code §1129(a)(10), which creates as a prerequisite to confirmation that at least one class of impaired claims accepts the plan if there is at least one class of such claims.] In making this argument, it is Metlife that is acting prematurely. There is no requirement in the Bankruptcy Code that a debtor must prove that a plan is confirmable in order to file a petition. * * *

Metlife's argument that a plan cannot be confirmed over its objection reflects its view of the leverage it has in the subject cases. Its invocation of its asserted leverage is ironic, in view of the fact that Metlife also asserts that the Subject Debtors' filings were taken in subjective bad faith. In any event, we turn to the requirement that a Chapter 11 filing be made in subjective good faith.

C. *Subjective Faith*

The second element in analyzing whether a Chapter 11 petition has been filed in good faith is whether the debtor has exercised subjective good faith. The test in *C-TC 9th Ave. P'ship* is a two-fold test, requiring proof of subjective bad faith as well as objective futility.

Movants do not contend that the Boards of the respective debtors did not act deliberately, or that they did not have an intent to reorganize the companies. In addition to their contentions relating to prematurity and lack of financial distress, they assert that the Subject Debtors acted in subjective bad faith because (i) they failed to negotiate prior to filing, and (ii) the initial "Independent Managers" of several of the SPE's were fired and replaced shortly before the Petition Date.

(i) Failure to Negotiate

The Bankruptcy Code does not require that a borrower negotiate with its lender before filing a Chapter 11 petition. BAPCPA contains a requirement that a consumer debtor obtain credit counseling before filing, Bankruptcy Code §109(h), and an obscure provision of BAPCPA provides that an unsecured claim on a consumer debt can be reduced by up to 20% if the lender "unreasonably refused to negotiate a reasonable alternative repayment schedule," as defined. §502(k). Neither of these provisions has any relevance here, except to demonstrate that Congress knows how to impose a filing requirement when it wants to do so. There are often good reasons for a commercial borrower and its lender to talk before a bankruptcy case is filed. But that does not mean that a Chapter 11 case should be deemed filed in bad faith if there is no prepetition negotiation. [Moreover, on] on this record, there is no evidence that pre-filing talks would have been adequate to deal with the extent of the problem. * * *

(ii) The Discharge of the Independent Managers

The second principal bad faith charge against the Debtors is that they engineered the discharge of the original Independent Managers of some of the Subject Debtors and replaced them with other Independent Managers. The basic facts are not in dispute. As discussed above, the Operating Agreements of some of the SPE's required that there be two independent managers or directors. The organizational documents permitted these independent managers to be supplied by a "nationally recognized company that provides professional independent directors, managers and trustees." In the cases at bar, Corporation Service Company ("CSC") supplied at least two "independent managers" who served on the Boards of over 150 project-level debtors. It does not appear that these managers had any expertise in the real estate business and as mentioned above, some of the lenders thought the independent managers were obligated to protect their interests alone. As articulated by Debtors' counsel, "the assumption by the lenders was that the independent director was not really independent."

In any event, it is not disputed that the CSC-appointed independent managers were, prior to the Petition Date, terminated from the Boards of those of the Subject Debtors that maintained the independent-manager requirement. The terminations "came as a surprise" to the independent managers because there was "no prior indication such termination was being contemplated." Moreover, the managers did not learn of their termination until after the bankruptcy filings. It is also undisputed that the Debtors selected two "seasoned individuals," Charles Cremens and John Howard, to serve as successor independent managers or directors on the Boards. Cremens and Howard served on the Boards during the spring of 2009 when the Debtors reviewed their restructuring prospects and ultimately voted to file under Chapter 11. Nolan explained the decision to replace the independent managers as follows:

> Given the significance, complexity, and time-consuming nature of assessing potential bankruptcy filings involving numerous entities, the project entities' stockholders and members desired independent managers with known experience in restructuring environments and complex business decisions, who understood the capital markets, who could commit significant time to learning about the projects, and who would bring critical, independent thinking to the restructuring challenges these project entities were facing.

Nolan also asserted that the terminations were not disclosed to CSC or to the original managers themselves until after the bankruptcy filings due to concern that such information "could subject the company to publicity about potential restructuring strategies ..." and because the Debtors had no contractual obligation to inform the managers.

On this record it cannot be said that the admittedly surreptitious firing of the two "Independent Managers" constituted subjective bad faith on the part of the Debtors sufficient to require dismissal of these cases. The corporate documents did not prohibit this action or purport to interfere with the rights of a shareholder to appoint independent directors to the Board. The new Independent Managers satisfied the requirements of that position. As discussed above, the Independent Managers did *not* have a duty to keep any of the Debtors from filing a bankruptcy case. As managers of solvent companies charged to act in the same fashion as directors of a Delaware corporation, they had a *prima facie* fiduciary duty to act in the interests of "the corporation and its shareholders." *Gheewalla,* 930 A.2d at 101. It may be for that reason that the two CSC-nominated Independent Managers voted in favor of the Chapter 11 filings of those debtors on whose boards they still served.

In *In re Kingston Square Assoc.,* the Court declined to grant motions to dismiss on bad faith grounds where the debtors' management, precluded from filing voluntary cases, colluded with creditors to engineer involuntary filings. The Court found that this far more egregious action was "suggestive of bad faith," but that the cases should not be dismissed as the collusion was not rooted in a "fraudulent or deceitful purpose" but designed "to preserve value for the Debtors' estates and creditors." 214 B.R. at 734, 736.

The Debtors here have established that the filings were designed "to preserve value for the Debtors' estates and creditors," including the Movants. Movants are wrong in the implicit assumption of the Motions that their rights were materially impaired by the Debtors' Chapter 11 filings. Obviously, a principal purpose of bankruptcy law is to *protect* creditors' rights. Secured creditors' access to their collateral may be delayed by a filing, but secured creditors have a panoply of rights, including adequate protection and the right to post-petition interest and fees if they are oversecured. Bankruptcy Code §§361, 506(b). Movants complain that as a consequence of the filings they are receiving only interest on their loans and have been deprived of current amortization payments, and Metlife complains that it is not even receiving interest on its mezzanine loan, which is secured only by a stock interest in its borrower's subsidiary. However, Movants have not sought additional adequate protection, and they have not waived any of their rights to recover full principal and interest and post-petition interest on confirmation of a plan. Movants complain that Chapter 11 gives the Debtors excessive leverage, but Metlife asserts it has all the leverage it needs to make sure that its rights will be respected.

It is clear, on this record, that Movants have been inconvenienced by the Chapter 11 filings. For example, the cash flows of the Debtors have been partially interrupted and special servicers have had to be appointed for the CMBS obligations. However, inconvenience to a secured creditor is not a reason to dismiss a Chapter 11 case. The salient point for purposes of these Motions is that the fundamental protections that the Movants negotiated and that the SPE structure represents are still in place and will remain in place during the Chapter 11 cases. This includes protection against the substantive consolidation of the project-level Debtors with any other entities. There is no question that a principal goal of the SPE structure is to guard against substantive consolidation, but the question of substantive consolidation is entirely different from the issue whether the Board of a debtor that is part of a corporate group can consider the interests of the group along with the interests of the individual debtor when making a decision to file a bankruptcy case. Nothing in this Opinion implies that the assets and liabilities of any of the Subject Debtors could properly be substantively consolidated with those of any other entity.

These Motions are a diversion from the parties' real task, which is to get each of the Subject Debtors out of bankruptcy as soon as feasible. The Movants assert talks with them should have begun earlier. It is time that negotiations commence in earnest. * * *

[The material on "Dismissal and Abstention" in chapter 3C, which begins on *page 79* should be supplemented by the following.]

Unsurprisingly, there has been a surfeit of litigation in recent years over what the vaguely (and sometimes poorly) drafted Bankruptcy Reform Act of 2005 means to individual debtors and their fresh start under either Chapter 7 or Chapter 13 of the Bankruptcy Code. Now more than ever, a thorough treatment of the individual debtor in bankruptcy requires a specialized course (as has long been the case for a thorough treatment of the business debtor in bankruptcy). That said, some highlights of recent case law are summarized below.

The Supreme Court has settled the issue presented by *Ross-Tousey*. In Ransom v. FIA Card Services, N.A., 131 S.Ct. 716 (2011), the Court held that for the purposes of §707(b), a debtor who has no monthly vehicle loan or lease payment may not claim a vehicle ownership expense deduction when calculating her disposable income.

Also relevant to §707(b), Congress granted a special exemption from the abuse presumption under §707(b) for qualifying disabled veterans or members of a reserve component of the Armed Services or National Guard. See §707(b)(2)(D).

Important though it is, the needs test is not the only available tool used to police bankruptcy filings. Courts continue to dismiss cases under §707 based on the totality of the circumstances, i.e., even where the debtor does or may satisfy the needs test and thus avoid a presumption of abuse. See, e.g., In re Piazza, 719 F.3d 1253 (11th Cir. 2013) (dismissal "for cause," including consideration of ability to pay, under §707(a)); In re Witcher, 702 F.3d 619 (11th Cir. 2012) (dismissal for "abuse," including consideration of ability to pay, under §707(b)).

Beyond statutory construction, the Supreme Court has considered the question of whether the 2005 Reform Act's constraint on credit counseling withstands constitutional scrutiny. In Milavetz, Gallop & Milavetz, P.A. v. U.S., 559 U.S. 229 (2010), the Court first decided that a "debt relief agency" under the Act includes lawyers in their representation of clients. The Court nevertheless upheld the provisions in question. It narrowly read the language in Bankruptcy Code §526(a)(4) that prevents a debt relief agency from advising a client "to incur more debt in contemplation of such person filing" a bankruptcy petition. As narrowed—merely to prevent advice that would lead a person to load up on debt when the impelling reason is anticipation of bankruptcy—the provision is more likely to survive the First Amendment than if it were broader. But the Court does not reach that question because the constitutional challenge in the case was on vagueness alone. The Court also upholds the constitutionality of §528's disclosure requirements as applied to debt relief agencies, such as the requirement to execute a written contract that clearly and conspicuously explains its terms. The Court characterized these requirements as legitimately intended to combat the problem of inherently misleading commercial advertisement.

IV. THE AUTOMATIC STAY

[The material on "Scope of the Automatic Stay" in chapter 4B, which begins on ***page 113*** should be supplemented by the following.]

It is not always easy to determine when the automatic stay applies. Consider, for example, In re Panther Mountain Land Development, LLC, 686 F.3d 916 (8th Cir. 2012), which denied application of the stay to a mortgagee's attempt to challenge the validity of a debtor's improvement districts, which under Arkansas law, are pseudo-governmental entities with some control rights over the debtor's land. The court reasoned that although the mortgagee's action could conceivably affect the value of the estate "in some undetermined and indirect manner," the action "will neither divest the Debtor of its property nor is there any evidence suggesting the action is likely to so substantially diminish the property's value as to effectively divest the Debtor of its property."

Consider also the court's treatment of the industrial tools at issue in *Plastech*, the next case. These tools, or at least some of them, were in some sense owned by Chrysler, Plastech's customer, but Plastech's interest in them is harder to characterize. The court applies the automatic stay to prevent Chrysler from taking possession of the tools, though one might wonder whether this is sound law or policy.

IN RE PLASTECH ENGINEERED PRODUCTS, INC

United States Bankruptcy Court, E.D. Michigan, 2008
382 B.R. 90

SHEFFERLY, BANKRUPTCY JUDGE

Plastech Engineered Products, Inc. is a privately held entity engaged in business as a tier one automobile supplier and designer and maker of blow-molded and injected-molded plastic products primarily for use in the automotive industry. It has a number of subsidiary entities engaged in business in the same industry. (Plastech and its subsidiaries will be collectively referred to as the "Debtor.") The Debtor is the largest female owned company in Michigan and it is certified as a minority business enterprise by the State of Michigan. The Debtor has been in business since 1988. Its products include automotive interior trim, under-hood components, bumper and other exterior components and cock-pit modules. The Debtor's major customers are General Motors ("GM"), Ford Motor Company, Chrysler, and Johnson Controls, Inc. ("JCI") (collectively referred to as the "Major Customers"). The Debtor has 36 manufacturing facilities in North America and 2 corporate locations. The Debtor employs over 7,700 individuals. The Debtor's annual sales are approximately $1.2 billion to $1.3 billion. The Debtor has basically three levels of financing. There is a revolving credit facility with various lenders (collectively referred to as "Revolving Lenders"). There are first and second lien term loans involving various lenders (collectively referred to as "First Lien Term Lenders" and "Second Lien Term Lenders").

Recent developments in the domestic automotive market combined with the rising prices of certain commodities have put a strain on the Debtor's liquidity position in recent years. Further, the decline of overall sales in the domestic automotive industry has created certain over capacity in the automotive industry worldwide, resulting in increased competition among automotive suppliers such as the Debtor, intensifying the pressure upon them to remain competitive.

In February, 2007, the Debtor entered into a refinancing that created the revolving credit facility, the first lien term loan and the second lien term loan. Goldman served as the lead arranger, syndication agent and administrative agent for the refinancing. The revolving credit facility provided the Debtor with up to $200,000,000 of revolving credit subject to a formula and available collateral. The first lien term loan provided the Debtor with up to $265,000,000 of secured term debt. The second lien term loan provided the Debtor with up to $100,000,000 of additional secured term debt.

To assist it in obtaining the refinancing, the Debtor received commitments from the Major Customers to provide the Debtor with certain financial accommodations. On February 12, 2007, the Debtor entered into a Financial Accommodation Agreement ("First Accommodation Agreement") with the Major Customers. * * *

Specifically, in exchange for the financial accommodations made by the Major Customers, the Financial Accommodation Agreement grants them certain rights in the tooling used in the Debtor's manufacture of components parts for the Major Customers. Section 4.0 of the First Accommodation Agreement is titled "Tooling Acknowledgment." It states as follows:

> (1) Plastech acknowledges and agrees that exclusive of Unpaid Tooling (as defined below) all tooling, dies, test and assembly fixtures, jigs, gauges, patterns, casting patterns, cavities, molds, and documentation, including engineering specifications, PPAP books, and test reports together with any

accessions, attachments, parts, accessories, substitutions, replacements, and appurtenances thereto (collectively, "*Tooling*") used by Plastech in connection with its manufacture of component and service parts for each Major Customer (collectively, the "*Major Customer Owned Tooling*") are owned by the respective Major Customers (or a customer of the Major Customers in the case of JCI) and are being held by Plastech or, to the extent Plastech has transferred the Major Customer Owned Tooling to third parties, by such third parties, as bailees at will. * * *

(2) Neither Plastech, nor any other person or entity other than the Major Customers have any right, title or interest in the Major Customer Owned Tooling other than Plastech's obligation, subject to the Major Customers' respective unfettered discretion, to utilize the Major Customer Owned Tooling in the manufacture of the Major Customers' component and service parts. The Major Customers and their respective designee(s) shall have the right to take immediate possession of the Major Customer Owned Tooling at any time without payment of any kind from the Major Customers to Plastech should the Major Customers elect to exercise such right, and Plastech agrees to cooperate with each of the Major Customers in their taking possession of their respective Major Customer Owned Tooling, including allowing access to Plastech's facilities. The rights and obligations contained in this Section shall continue notwithstanding the expiration or termination of this Agreement.

(3) In the event of a dispute between Plastech and a Major Customer over whether any Tooling is Major Customer Owned Tooling or Unpaid Tooling, the Tooling subject to the dispute will be presumed to be Major Customer Owned Tooling pending resolution of the dispute, and the Major Customer will have the right to immediate possession of the Tooling pending resolution of the dispute (and Plastech may not withhold delivery of possession of the Unpaid Tooling to such Major Customer pending such resolution), but will remain subject to any claim or right to payment of Plastech for the disputed amounts (despite Plastech's relinquishment of possession). * * *

On Friday morning, February 1, 2008, Larry Walker, the director of exterior procurement for Chrysler, delivered a letter (J. Ex. 107) to the Debtor. The letter was addressed to Julie Brown, CEO and was hand delivered at the Debtor's office. Ms. Brown was not present and the letter was delivered to another employee. The February 1, 2008 letter read as follows:

Dear Ms. Brown:

Please be advised that effective immediately, Chrysler is terminating all purchase orders and supply agreements with Plastech, including, but not limited to, the Amended Long Term Productivity Agreement dated February 12, 2007 in accordance with the terms thereof and the letters previously sent by our counsel to Mr. Scott dated January 15, 2008 and January 15, 2008. As required by Chrysler's General Terms and Conditions and the Second Financial Accommodation Agreement dated January 22, 2008 and Financial Accommodated Agreement dated February 12, 2007, please make all tooling associated with Chrysler's production available to it for immediate pick-up and otherwise cooperate with Chrysler in its taking possession of the same.

Very truly yours,

Larry Walker Director-Exterior Procurement Chrysler LLC * * *

Chrysler perceived the Debtor to be in a "meltdown" and determined that it would be less costly to Chrysler to implement its own plan "B" by moving its tooling from the Debtor to other suppliers to resource the parts previously made by the Debtor for Chrysler. Chrysler understood in making this decision that there would be an initial interruption in its parts supply while it removed the tooling from the Debtor and resourced the parts to other suppliers. However, Chrysler had concluded that this initial interruption, although resulting in the shut down of certain of Chrysler's plants and the idling of substantial numbers of employees, would ultimately be less costly than continuing to provide financial accommodations to the Debtor and continuing its relationship with the Debtor.

Immediately after delivering the letter, Chrysler filed suit against the Debtor in Wayne County Circuit Court and obtained an ex parte temporary restraining order and order of possession that required the Debtor to immediately deliver possession of all of the tooling that it utilized in the production of Chrysler's parts, allow Chrysler immediate access to the Debtor's facilities to inspect, load, remove and transport the tooling, and to provide all reasonable and necessary assistance to Chrysler to take possession of the tooling. The restraining order was signed on Friday, February 1, 2008 at 3:35 p.m. Later that same day, the Debtor filed this Chapter 11 case.

On the next day, Saturday, February 2, 2008, Chrysler filed a motion for relief from the automatic stay so that it could be permitted to immediately enter onto the Debtor's premises and remove the tooling used by the Debtor in production of Chrysler's parts. * * *

Chrysler requests that the Court lift the automatic stay of §362 to permit it to enter onto the Debtor's premises and take all of the tooling necessary for production of its component parts. Chrysler has paid over $167,000,000 for tooling used by the Debtor to make parts for Chrysler and asserts that it owns the tooling that it has paid for. Chrysler acknowledges that there is approximately $13,400,000 of unpaid tooling that the Debtor uses in making component parts for Chrysler but says that it will immediately pay the $13,400,000 into an escrow account so that it may also take possession of the unpaid tooling as well as the paid tooling. Chrysler relies upon the tooling acknowledgments contained in the First and Second Accommodation Agreements as providing it with ownership of the tooling it has paid for and the right to immediate possession of both the paid and unpaid tooling, in accordance with the plain terms of those agreements. According to Chrysler, the Debtor has no rights in the paid tooling and any rights in the unpaid tooling will be extinguished upon payment by Chrysler of the remaining $13,400,000 owing. In the adversary proceeding, Chrysler requests turnover of all of the tooling by entry of an order compelling the Debtor to immediately return the tooling and, until such time as the tooling is returned, an order compelling the Debtor to continue shipping existing inventory and component parts according to the price and terms established by previously submitted Chrysler purchase orders. Without the relief from the automatic stay and without the entry of a preliminary injunction, Chrysler alleges that it will suffer an interruption of supply, immediately idling many of its plants and employees and causing it catastrophic losses. Chrysler also contends that it properly terminated all of its contractual relationships with the Debtor in accordance with the terms of the governing documents. However, Chrysler further states that the Court need not adjudicate the propriety and effectiveness of its termination of the contractual relationships between Chrysler and the Debtor because, in any event, Chrysler is entitled to immediate possession of the Chrysler owned tooling and the unpaid tooling pursuant to the tooling acknowledgments contained in the First and Second Accommodation Agreements.

The Debtor ... asserts that it is premature in such an early stage of this Chapter 11 case to grant any relief from the automatic stay to Chrysler. Even though the First and Second Accommodation Agreements contain tooling acknowledgments, the Debtor maintains that it still has an interest in both the paid and unpaid tooling, and that all of this tooling is necessary to an effective reorganization of the Debtor. The Debtor contends it would be inconsistent with the policies of Chapter 11 to permit Chrysler in the infancy of this case to take possession of the tooling. The Debtor alleges that if the Court were to grant such relief to Chrysler, the Debtor would immediately be forced to close many of its plants and would be unable to continue to provide its other Major Customers with their component parts, thereby effectively ending the Debtor's business. The Debtor also argues that even if Chrysler is able to show that it is likely to be successful in ultimately obtaining possession of the tooling in the adversary proceeding, the Court should not grant preliminary injunctive relief in the adversary proceeding because any harm suffered by Chrysler is somehow "self inflicted," and that Chrysler could avoid any such harm by continuing to leave its tools with the Debtor and continuing to purchase product from the Debtor. Further, even if Chrysler does experience harm in the absence of an injunction, the Debtor argues that such harm is not irreparable and, in any event, is greatly outweighed by the harm that the Debtor would suffer if the injunction is granted. * * *

The term "tooling" as used in the automobile industry generally refers to certain tangible personal property that it is used to make metal or plastic parts for an automobile. Donald Coates, the Debtor's vice president of manufacturing, planning and strategy, explained that there are generally three types of tooling. Arthur Nelson, the senior director of the operations group at BBK also testified regarding the three types of tooling. Basically, the two witnesses agreed that there are "primary tools," consisting of a mold, stamp or die; "secondary tools" such as a sensor for quality requirements or the end of an arm tool on a robot; and "secondary equipment" consisting of stand alone pieces of equipment. Generally, Chrysler issues purchase orders for the required tooling to its parts supplier, in this case the Debtor, and then pays the supplier for the tooling after the tool has been manufactured, tested and approved. The tool manufacturer is then paid by the supplier. The tooling is used by the supplier at its premises and is stamped with an identification as Chrysler's tool. In this case, Chrysler maintains a list of the tooling (J. Ex. 103) that includes both paid and unpaid tooling. Chrysler relies on the tooling acknowledgments contained in the First and Second Accommodation Agreements to support its assertion that the Debtor does not have an interest in any of the tooling paid for by Chrysler and therefore it is not protected by the automatic stay of §362. The Court disagrees. Even with respect to the tooling paid for by Chrysler, it is undisputed that the Debtor presently holds a possessory interest in that tooling. That interest alone is sufficient to constitute an interest under §541 and sufficient to invoke the provisions of the automatic stay of §362(a)(3). * * *

Even assuming that the Debtor has only a possessory interest in the tooling paid for by Chrysler, that is a sufficient interest by itself to cause the application of the automatic stay. … The tooling need not be "owned" by the Debtor in order for the stay to apply. The stay protects *interests in property* whether an ownership interest, possessory interest or some other interest. Thus, without deciding the nature or extent of the Debtor's interest in both the paid and unpaid tooling, and without diminishing any of Chrysler's rights in both the tooling that it has paid for as well as the unpaid tooling under the tooling acknowledgments, it is clear to the Court that the automatic stay applies to both categories of tooling. * * *

Section 362(d)(1) provides that on request of a party in interest and after notice and a hearing, the Court shall grant relief from the automatic stay, such as by terminating, annulling, modifying, or conditioning such stay "(1) for cause, including the lack of adequate protection of an interest in property of such party in interest." * * *

In this case Chrysler asserts that the cause to lift the automatic stay consists of the following:

1. Chrysler properly terminated its pre-petition contractual relationship with the Debtor and may now resource its business with other suppliers;

2. Even if it has not properly terminated its contractual relationship with the Debtor, Chrysler is still entitled to immediate possession of the tooling that it has paid for under the tooling acknowledgments in the First and Second Accommodation Agreements;

3. Even if there remains some unpaid tooling, if there is a dispute over payment, Chrysler is still entitled to immediate possession of such unpaid tooling under the tooling

acknowledgments in the First and Second Accommodation Agreements;

4. The Debtor cannot continue to produce component parts for Chrysler in accordance with the pricing and terms and conditions of Chrysler's existing purchase orders without requesting additional monetary accommodations from Chrysler;

5. If Chrysler does not obtain possession of the tooling used by the Debtor to produce parts for it, Chrysler will have an interruption in the supply of parts causing it to shut down certain of its plants and idling many of its employees resulting in substantial damages to it; and

6. The interruption of production and the consequent losses will harm Chrysler's goodwill.

The evidence shows that Chrysler bargained for the tooling acknowledgments in the First and Second Accommodation Agreements. In exchange for those rights, Chrysler provided the Debtor with substantial financial accommodations consisting of funds that it was not contractually obligated to pay and advanced payment of other funds that it was contractually obligated to pay. The evidence also shows that the Debtor was requesting even more financial accommodations in the draft of the Third Accommodation Agreement and requiring even more from Chrysler going forward. The evidence also shows that if Chrysler does not receive possession of its tooling, it will be forced to either continue to purchase parts from the Debtor on some basis that may require it to make additional accommodations going forward or, alternatively, close many of its plants and idle many of its employees while it begins the process of resourcing with new suppliers without being able to transfer possession of the tools used by the Debtor in making parts for Chrysler. Richard Schmidt, the senior manager of material supply operations at Chrysler, testified that if possession of the tools is not received at the end of the current interim agreement with the Debtor, it could be as little as five hours before Chrysler would see disruptions in its assembly lines, which would be followed by lay offs and, ultimately, substantial damages to Chrysler. [Chrysler and the Debtor entered into an interim post-petition agreement for the Debtor to produce parts for Chrysler pending the outcome of this hearing. This interim agreement would cost Chrysler $3,000,000 above the price for its parts during this period to help cover the Debtor's "cash burn."] There is evidence establishing that Chrysler will suffer economic harm either by having to contribute additional financial accommodations to the Debtor, or by having to shut down certain of its assembly lines and idle certain of its workers if it does not obtain the tooling.

On the other hand, if the stay is lifted and Chrysler is permitted to take possession of the tooling used to make parts for it, the evidence shows that many of the Debtor's plants will have to be immediately shut down. Mathew Demars, the Debtor's president of interior and exterior business units, testified that of the Debtor's 36 manufacturing facilities, 21 produce parts for Chrysler. Of the 21, two of them are virtually entirely engaged in making parts for Chrysler and another 9 of them have 25% or more of Chrysler revenue as part of their operating structure. The cost to close these plants is $8,000,000 to $9,000,000 per facility according to Demars. Ordinarily, if the Debtor had to shut down a plant, it would do so in coordination with its customers. To protect the Debtor's Major Customers before a plant closure in order minimize impact on their production, Demars explained that the Debtor would build a parts bank and ensure an uninterrupted flow of parts to that customer, then transfer the tooling to a new facility. The time to accomplish that can be three to four weeks because of the need to implement the "PPAP" process to ready the new production line for the making of parts. If Chrysler is permitted to take immediate possession of all of its tooling at this time, Demars explained that 11 of the Debtor's plants would immediately turn to negative margin plants and 8 of them would immediately have to close. The testimony was conflicting between Chrysler's witnesses, who believe that the removal of the tooling from the Debtor could be accomplished promptly and without extended disruption to the Debtor's other business operations, and the Debtor's witnesses, who believe that Chrysler's removal of the tooling would cause an immediate, extended and disastrous impact on the Debtor's ability to provide parts for its customers. However, the evidence in the record persuades the Court that regardless of which estimate of timing is closer to reality, it is a fact that removal of Chrysler's tooling will cause a substantial disruption to the Debtor's operations and significantly impair its ability to continue to produce parts for its other Major Customers.

The record demonstrates that Chrysler will suffer economic harm if the Court concludes there is not cause to lift the stay at this time. The record also demonstrates that the Debtor will suffer economic harm if the Court concludes that there is cause to lift the stay. But in the process of balancing the competing policies to determine whether sufficient cause has been shown, there are other facts in the record that are important to the Court. First, it is very early in this Chapter 11 case. The motion to lift stay was filed literally the day after the Debtor filed its Chapter 11 petition. This case is in its infancy. This is not a small case. It is a large case with 36 manufacturing facilities, 7,700 employees and many business entities who are suppliers to the Debtor and depend themselves upon the Debtor's business. The Debtor has approximately $500,000,000 of secured debt. It has projected annual sales of over $1 billion to its other Major Customers, without even considering the Chrysler sales volume. It is an important supplier to GM, Ford and JCI, that has been in business for over 20 years. There are other creditors in this case who claim an interest in the tooling Chrysler seeks to take. In short, there are many parties who have legitimate and substantial interests in this case that will be greatly affected if not destroyed by a lift of the automatic stay at this point in the case. Chrysler's rights and interests are valid and important, but so are those of the Debtor and the other constituents in this case. Determining cause is not a litmus test or a checklist of factors. It requires consideration of many factors and a balancing of competing interests. After carefully considering the evidence in this record, including the impact upon Chrysler, the Debtor, the Debtor's employees, other Major Customers, and secured and unsecured creditors, the Court concludes that Chrysler has not met its burden of proof to demonstrate "cause" to lift the automatic stay under §362(d)(1). * * *

During the course of this hearing, some parties have ramped up the rhetoric calling Chrysler's conduct "over reaching," and "precipitous," and that its damages, if any, are "self inflicted." The Court does not share those views. Chrysler has legitimate and substantial interests at stake in seeking to enforce the rights that it bargained for in the tooling acknowledgments contained in the First and Second Accommodation Agreements. Chrysler correctly points out that it had no contractual obligation to provide any financial accommodations to the Debtor once the Second Accommodation Agreement expired on January 31, 2008. The Court disregards entirely and considers inappropriate the pejorative labels for Chrysler and Chrysler's conduct. Chrysler took the actions that it believed were in its best interest and consistent with its contractual provisions when it sent the February 1, 2008 letter and filed suit in Wayne County Circuit Court. Had the Debtor not filed Chapter 11, Chrysler's exercise of those rights might now be concluded. But the larger point here is that the Debtor did file a Chapter 11 case and exercised a legitimate right that it has under the law in doing so. The Court appreciates the fact that Chrysler has legitimate and substantial interests at stake in this Chapter 11. So too do the Debtor, the other customers and the lenders. While it is hard to understand how the Debtor could ever forge a long term relationship with its customers by litigating with them, the Court is persuaded that the filing of Chapter 11 gives the Debtor an opportunity, a temporary window, to negotiate with its customers, lenders and other constituents. The law affords that breathing space to the Debtor when it filed its Chapter 11 petition for relief. But it is not unlimited, and the Debtor should use it wisely. For all of these reasons, the Court has determined to deny the relief requested.

[The material on "Exceptions to the Automatic Stay" in chapter 4C, which begins on **page 124** should be supplemented by the following. The second principal case below, *National Gas*, as well as the related discussion, can also be covered in connection with the material on "Fraudulent Conveyances" in chapter 8C, which begins on **page 309**, and in connection with the material on "Scope of Preference Law" in chapter 8D(1), which begins on **page 353**.]

Section 362(b)(4) of the Bankruptcy Code exempts from the automatic stay a governmental exercise of its police or regulatory power over a debtor. That said, it is sometimes difficult to distinguish between such exercise on the one hand and the government's attempt to have the debtor satisfy a debt on the other. The first case below, *Solis*, addresses this distinction.

Beyond police and regulatory powers, broadly speaking, sections 362(b)(6), (7), (17), and (27) of the Bankruptcy Code exempt from the automatic stay the exercise of rights under securities agreements. Sections 546(e), (f), (g), (j) and 548(d) provide corresponding exemptions from the trustee's avoiding powers. (Avoiding powers are discussed in Chapter 8 of the casebook). As described in the second case below, *National Gas Distributors*, these exemptions, expanded by Congress with the Reform Act of 2005, were designed to prevent systemic collapse of the securities and derivatives markets, which rely on counterparties' rights to immediate satisfaction. The fear was that, but for these exemptions, the bankruptcy of a large, interdependent financial institution would create a contagion effect as each firm failed in turn from its inability to access the assets of another.

As the financial meltdown of 2008-09 taught us, the exemptions, sometimes called safe harbors, are no sure barrier to contagion. Lehman Brothers failed, AIG was on the verge of collapse, and other large institutions would have followed but for government intervention. In essence, the safe harbors make it relatively easy for firms to raise capital prior to financial distress but relatively difficult to retain it after such distress.

With this tradeoff, among other factors, in mind, consider whether *National Gas*—which treated a seemingly ordinary supply contract as an exempt swap agreement—was correct to take such an expansive view of the safe harbors. Contemplate whether a narrower approach based on congressional objective, might make more sense either as a matter of interpretation of the current code or perhaps through statutory reform.

Additionally, whatever the merits, you should be aware that *National Gas* is no aberrant decision. A number of courts have given sweeping scope to the securities transaction safe harbors. For example, in the case of In re MBS Management Services, Inc., 690 F.3d 352 (5th Cir. 2012), the court exempted from voidable preference treatment a debtor's payment, pursuant to a requirements contract, of an electricity bill, and in Enron Creditors Recovery Corp. v. Alfa, S.A.B. de C.V., 651 F.3d 329 (2nd Cir. 2011), the court exempted from avoidance a debtor's redemption of its own debt obligations. See also In re Quebecor World (USA) Inc., 719 F.3d 94 (2nd Cir. 2013), where the court found that a debtor's repurchase of its own notes through a financial intermediary was deemed a "transfer made by or to (or for the benefit of) a financial institution in connection with a securities contract."

This said, there are courts that set limits. For example, *Quebecor World* conflicts with In re Munford Inc., 98 F.3d 604 (11th Cir. 1996). And, for another example, in the case of In re Lehman Bros. Holding, Inc. 439 B.R. 811 (Bankr. S.D.N.Y. 2010), the court held that the setoff of collateral against an "unrelated swap exposure" did not qualify for a safe harbor exemption merely because the transaction related to a swap agreement.

Moreover, some (though not all) courts have held that despite a safe harbor from actions by the debtor, individual creditors can bring state law fraudulent conveyance actions against transferees where financial market stability is not implicated. Believing themselves, in this context, to be unbound by the specific language of the safe harbor provisions, these courts focused on the congressional motivation for the provisions and concluded that "[p]rotecting the financial markets is not necessarily the same thing as protecting investors in the public markets." In re Lyondell Chemical Co., 503 B.R. 348, 373 (Bankr. S.D.N.Y. 2014). See also In re Tribune Company Fraudulent Transfer

Litigation, 499 B.R. 310 (S.D.N.Y. 2013). Cf. Whyte v. Barclays Bank PLC, 494 B.R. 196 (S.D.N.Y. 2014) (purpose of safe harbor would be undercut if, while bankruptcy trustee is prohibited from avoiding swap transactions, a litigation trustee as assignee of creditors' claims could proceed).

Finally, note that while the specific issue before the court in *National Gas* is application of the trustee's avoiding powers, the case turns more generally on whether the statutory safe harbors are appropriately applied to transactions beyond Congress' core concerns in the adoption of the securities exemptions. Such application can afford a safe harbor not only from avoidance of fraudulent or preferential transfers but, if a transfer occurs after a bankruptcy petition, from the automatic stay as well.

SOLIS V. SCA RESTAURANT CORP.

United States District Court, E.D.N.Y., 2011
463 B.R. 248

BIANCO, DISTRICT JUDGE

This action was commenced by plaintiff Hilda L. Solis, Secretary of the United States Department of Labor ("DOL"), pursuant to … the Fair Labor Standards Act ("FLSA"). … In a complaint filed against Quarta and SCA Restaurant Corp. on May 21, 2009, the DOL alleges that defendants violated Sections 7 and 15(a)(2) of the FLSA by failing to pay minimum wage and overtime compensation to the employees of SCA Restaurant Corp., and that defendants violated Sections 11(c) and 15(a)(5) of the FLSA by failing to keep full and accurate records concerning their employees' wages, hours, and conditions of employment. The DOL sought an injunction … permanently restraining defendants from violating … the FLSA, and an order … finding defendant liable for unpaid overtime compensation and an equal amount of liquidated damages.

After the DOL filed the instant suit, Quarta filed for voluntary bankruptcy under Chapter 7 of the Bankruptcy Code in the Eastern District of New York. In the instant motion, Quarta urges the Court to find that the DOL's action is stayed under the automatic stay provision pursuant to Section 362 of the Bankruptcy Code. * * *

The automatic stay is a fundamental component of a bankruptcy petition, as it "provides the debtor with a breathing spell from his creditors" and "allows the bankruptcy court to centralize all disputes concerning property of the debtor's estate in the bankruptcy court so that reorganization can proceed efficiently, unimpeded by uncoordinated proceedings in other arenas." *Shugrue v. Air Lines Pilots Ass'n, Int'l (In re Ionosphere Clubs, Inc.),* 922 F.2d 984, 989 (2d Cir. 1990) (internal citations and quotation marks omitted).

Section 362(b)(4) of the Bankruptcy Code provides an exception to the automatic stay for actions by a governmental unit to enforce its police or regulatory power ... .

As the Second Circuit explained, "the purpose of this exception is to prevent a debtor from frustrating necessary governmental functions by seeking refuge in bankruptcy court." *SEC v. Brennan,* 230 F.3d 65, 71 (2d Cir. 2000) (internal quotation and citations omitted). "Thus, 'where a governmental unit is suing a debtor to prevent or stop violation of fraud, environmental protection, consumer protection, safety, or similar police or regulatory laws, or attempting to fix damages for violation of such a law, the action or proceeding is not stayed under the automatic stay.' " *Id.* (quoting H.R. Rep. No. 95-595 at 343).

In attempting to apply the § 362(b)(4) exception, courts look to the purposes of the law that the government seeks to enforce to distinguish between situations in which a "state acts pursuant to its 'police and regulatory power,' and where the state acts merely to protect its status as a creditor." *Safety-Kleen, Inc. v. Wyche (In re Pinewood),* 274 F.3d 846, 865 (4th Cir. 2001) (quoting *Universal Life Church, Inc. v. United States (In re Universal Life Church, Inc.).* Two tests have been historically applied to resolve this question: (1) the "pecuniary purpose" test (also known as the "pecuniary interest" test), and (2) the "public policy" test. Under the pecuniary purpose test, a court looks to whether a governmental proceeding relates to public safety and welfare, which favors application of the stay exception, or to the government's interest in the debtor's property, which does not. "If it is evident that a governmental action is primarily for the purpose of protecting a pecuniary interest, then the action should not be excepted from the stay." *Eddleman v. U.S. Dep't of Labor,* 923 F.2d 782, 791 (10th Cir. 1991), *overruled in part on other grounds by Temex Energy, Inc. v. Underwood,* 968 F.2d 1003 (10th Cir. 1992).

Other courts have backed away from the "pecuniary purpose" test, and apply a broader "pecuniary advantage" test. *United States v. Commonwealth Cos. (In re Commonwealth Cos.),* 913 F.2d 518, 523-25

(8th Cir. 1990). Under the "pecuniary advantage" test, the relevant inquiry is not whether the governmental unit seeks property of the debtor's estate, but rather whether the specific acts that the government wishes to carry out would create a pecuniary advantage for the government vis-a-vis other creditors. Thus, the "pecuniary advantage" analysis has been used as an alternative formulation of the first test.

The second test—namely, the public policy test—distinguishes "'between proceedings that adjudicate private rights and those that effectuate public policy.' " *Chao v. Hosp. Staffing Servs., Inc.,* 270 F.3d 374, 385-86 (6th Cir. 2001) (quoting *In re Commerce Oil Co.,* 847 F.2d 291, 295 (6th Cir. 1988)). An action may further both public and private interests. Where "an action furthers both public and private interests," reviewing courts should exempt the action from the automatic stay if "the private interests do not significantly outweigh the public benefit from enforcement." *Chao,* 270 F.3d at 390.

The tests are overlapping to some extent, and there also appears to be some confusion in the case authority as to whether both the pecuniary test and the public purpose test must be satisfied for an action to be exempted, or whether one is sufficient. * * *

The Second Circuit has not yet ruled on which test to apply. In a prior opinion, this Court held that the pecuniary advantage test, rather than the pecuniary interest test, should be utilized.

However, in an abundance of caution, the Court has examined the facts of this case under each of the above-referenced tests and concludes, for the reasons set forth below, that the § 362(b)(4) exception applies in the instant case regardless of which test is utilized. In other words, the instant lawsuit is exempt from the automatic stay under both the first test—whether the "pecuniary purpose" test or the "pecuniary advantage" test is utilized—as well as the "public policy" test. * * *

First, the instant case is exempt from the stay under the pecuniary purpose or interest test, as well as the pecuniary advantage test.

With respect to the pecuniary purpose or interest test, the government has no pecuniary interest in defendants' estate. The government seeks an injunction to prevent further violations of the FLSA, as well as liquidated damages equal to the amount of the employees' unpaid overtime compensation. If the government succeeds, the DOL will not obtain title to any goods, nor be able to enforce a monetary judgment against defendants.

For the same reasons, the action at issue passes the broader pecuniary advantage test. Should the government succeed in winning a monetary judgment against defendants, enforcement of the money judgment will take place in bankruptcy court. Consequently, the suit's monetary claims would be subject to bankruptcy procedures just like any other claim against the debtor, and would not, therefore, confer any advantage on the government vis-a-vis other creditors. * * *

The DOL's action also satisfies the public policy test. The action enforces the DOL's regulatory powers under the FLSA—specifically, ensuring that covered employees receive minimum wage and overtime compensation, and that employers maintain proper wage and hour records. The injunction sought by DOL would serve to prevent further violations, protect labor conditions, and prevent "unfair labor competition in the market from companies who pay substandard wages." *Chao v. BDK Indus., LLC,* 296 B.R. 165, 168 (C.D. Ill. 2003). Moreover, should the DOL succeed in obtaining a money judgment against the defendant, such a judgment could deter unlawful behavior by others. Thus, this Court holds that actions undertaken by the DOL to enforce wage and hour protections fall squarely within the §362(b)(4) exemption.

Although never addressed by the Second Circuit, numerous courts have reached a similar conclusion in analogous cases. For example, in *Eddleman v. U.S. Dep't of Labor,* the DOL filed an administrative action against a mail-hauling business that worked under a contract with the United States Postal Service. The DOL alleged violations of the Service Contract Act ("SCA"), which requires federal government contractors to pay certain minimum wages and benefits, and to keep adequate records of hours worked and wages paid. The DOL sought to liquidate claims for back wages owed to the Eddlemans' employees, and to put the Eddlemans on a list of SCA violators, which would debar them from contracting with the government for three years.

In the *Eddleman* case, the Tenth Circuit held that the DOL action was exempt from the automatic stay under §362(b)(4). The "public policy" test presented "no barrier" to the DOL action because seeking back pay on behalf of specific individuals was not "an assertion of private rights." Instead, it was a method of "enforcing the policies underlying the SCA. This was especially true because back-pay claimants would not receive any extra priority as a result of the DOL action, since collection of the claims would proceed in bankruptcy court.

Although the violations at issue in *Eddleman* concerned the SCA and not the FLSA, both acts seek to ensure that employers pay their employees in accordance with overtime and minimum wage laws, and that they keep adequate and accurate records reflecting those payments. Accordingly, the same analysis would apply in determining whether an action concerning unpaid minimum wages or overtime compensation satisfies the relevant tests, regardless of whether the action is brought pursuant to the SCA or the FLSA.

Defendant seeks to distinguish *Eddleman,* arguing that while the DOL's pursuit of liquidated damages was an assertion of private rights that would not, accordingly, pass the public policy test, the *Eddleman* court exempted the action from the automatic stay because DOL also sought an injunction debarring the defendants from contracting with the government. Yet the *Eddleman* court made clear that the public policy test "present[ed] no barrier to DOL's actions," because the liquidation of back-pay claims was not an assertion of private rights, but was "another method of enforcing the policies underlying the SCA." Moreover, in the action at bar, the DOL does not seek only liquidated damages, but also an injunction preventing further violations of the FLSA. Thus, the *Eddleman* case is directly on point and this Court finds the analysis persuasive. * * *

Defendants' heavy reliance upon the Sixth Circuit decision in *Chao v. Hospital Staffing Services* is entirely misplaced. The *Chao* case addressed the narrow issue of whether an action seeking an injunction under Section 17 of the FLSA to prevent "hot goods" from entering the market is exempt from the automatic stay. "Hot goods" are goods produced by employees who were paid below the minimum wage. In the *Chao* case, the Secretary of the Department of Labor brought a "hot goods" action under the FLSA to prevent the dissemination of business records that the debtor employer had allegedly produced at a competitive disadvantage by paying employees a substandard wage. The Secretary sought an injunction to prevent the records from moving in interstate commerce.

The Sixth Circuit held that the suit was not exempt from the automatic stay. In particular, the court concluded that the suit did not pass the public policy test because it was brought primarily to assert and protect the private rights of certain individuals. The court explained that, although some "hot goods" cases would qualify for an exemption, this particular suit concerned medical records relating to services already rendered by employees, so the suit would not prevent unfair competition in the marketplace. Moreover, a successful suit by the

Secretary would result in an injunction that would require the debtor to pay the employees' wages in order to "free" the goods. In the court's view, this requirement created "a significant property interest" in the debtor, and enforcing an injunction to obtain that property interest would function as a "vehicle to enforce the private rights of the employees" to their wages."

The *Chao* case is clearly distinguishable from the instant case. First, the Sixth Circuit's holding in *Chao* (as noted above) was based upon the "peculiar circumstances" of that case where the "hot goods" relief sought did not (in the court's view) trigger the FLSA's concern about preventing unfair competition in the marketplace. In contrast, the instant case is not a "hot goods" case; rather, the DOL seeks an injunction pursuant to Section 17 against further violations of the FLSA, as well as liquidated damages under Section 16(c). Those types of relief undoubtedly implicate a "public policy" interest. In fact, the Sixth Circuit recognized the "important continuing public interest in restraining future violations of the FLSA's minimum wage and overtime provisions" and the "significant public interest in protecting other businesses from unfair competition" in distinguishing the peculiar "hot goods" situation from other situations. *Id.* at 392. ("In this particular case, however, that significant public interest in protecting other businesses from unfair competition is not present because the 'goods' are merely records relating to services already rendered by employees."). Moreover, to the extent that the Sixth Circuit in *Chao* may have been concerned that the "hot goods" relief sought could under the circumstances of that case force actual payment of back wages outside of the bankruptcy process, no such concern exists in the instant case, since any judgment for damages entered against the defendant would be resolved in Bankruptcy Court.

In sum, the DOL brings this action under Sections 16(c) and 17 of the FLSA to serve the valid public policy purposes of enjoining further violations of the FLSA, protecting labor conditions, preventing unfair competition in the labor market, and deterring unlawful behavior by others. Successful prosecution of this action will not create a pecuniary interest for the government in the debtor's property, nor will it result in a pecuniary advantage to the government over other creditors. Accordingly, this action is exempt from the automatic stay under § 362(b)(4), the police and regulatory power exemption.

IN RE NATIONAL GAS DISTRIBUTORS

United States Court of Appeals, Fourth Circuit, 2009
556 F.3d 247

NIEMEYER, CIRCUIT JUDGE

On December 14, 2006, the Trustee in this Chapter 11 bankruptcy of National Gas Distributors, LLC, a distributor of natural gas to industrial, governmental, and other customers, commenced these adversary proceedings under Bankruptcy Code §§548(a) and 550(a) against three of National Gas' customers by filing complaints to avoid numerous natural gas supply contracts entered into with these customers during the year before the bankruptcy petition was filed. The Trustee alleged that the contracts and transfers of natural gas were fraudulent conveyances because they were made for less than market value and when the debtor was insolvent.

The customers, E.I. du Pont de Nemours and Company, the Smithfield Packing Company, Inc., and Stadler's Country Hams, Inc., filed motions to dismiss the Trustee's complaints or alternatively for summary judgment, claiming that the contracts were "swap agreements," which would provide them with a complete defense to the Trustee's complaints under the Bankruptcy Code §§546(g), 548(c), and 548(d)(2)(D). Specifically, they claimed that the contracts were "commodity forward agreements," which are included in the definition of "swap agreements." *See* §101(53B)(A)(i)(VII). They also claimed that they had taken the transfers in good faith, an assertion that the Trustee does not dispute.

The bankruptcy court denied the motions by orders dated May 24, 2007, finding that the contracts in question were not "swap agreements" as defined in Bankruptcy Code §101(53B) but simply "agreement[s] by a single end-user to purchase a commodity" and therefore were not exempt from avoidance. Relying mostly on legislative history, the court concluded that in exempting "swap agreements," Congress intended to protect financial markets from the destabilizing effects of bankruptcy and that because the natural gas supply contracts in this case were physically settled and not traded in financial markets, exempting them from avoidance proceedings would not serve Congress' purposes.

The customers thereafter filed motions requesting the bankruptcy court to amend its orders insofar as the court made conclusions about the supply contracts that appeared to be factual in nature. The bankruptcy court denied the motions by orders dated June 20, 2007, noting that it had not decided the boundaries of what a swap agreement was under § 101(53B) but rather concluded, as a matter of law, that each contract at issue in this case was "simply an agreement by a single end-user to purchase a commodity" and therefore was not a swap agreement.

In this direct interlocutory appeal from the bankruptcy court's orders, we conclude that the grounds given by the bankruptcy court in finding that the contracts in this case were not swap agreements are not supported by the definition of "swap agreement" in §101(53B). Accordingly, we reverse and remand for further proceedings, allowing the customers to attempt to demonstrate factually and legally that their natural gas supply contracts were swap agreements based on any classification included in §101(53B).

I

During the year before National Gas filed its petition, du Pont, Smithfield Packing, and Stadler's Country Hams purchased natural gas for specific facilities under a series of contracts with National Gas. The contracts consisted of a "Base Contract for Sale and Purchase of Natural Gas," using Standard Form 6.3.1 of the North American Energy Standards Board, Inc., and a series of e-mails confirming telephone conversations between representatives of the parties in which they fixed the price of future deliveries of natural gas during specified time periods. Performance of the contracts formed in this way always commenced more than two days after the contract's formation and fixed the price of gas for a period of months for each designated facility. The contracts required National Gas to sell and deliver the gas and the customer to receive and purchase the gas at the specified price, regardless of the market price of natural gas, or to pay the difference between the agreed-upon price and the market price.

In this manner, these natural gas supply contracts provided a hedge against fluctuations in the market price of natural gas and the adverse effects such fluctuations might have on the customers' operations. Although the contracts were not transferred on exchanges, nor did they even involve the use of brokers or middlemen, the customers did use them, along with other forwards and derivatives, to manage their commodity risks.

There is no suggestion in this case that any party breached any one of the contracts, and the Trustee agrees that the customers in this case acted in good faith both in entering into the contracts and in receiving transfers under them.

On January 20, 2006, National Gas filed a voluntary petition for relief under Chapter 11 of the Bankruptcy Code, and shortly thereafter, the bankruptcy court appointed Richard M. Hutson, II, as Trustee. The Trustee thereafter filed complaints against more than 20 former customers of National Gas, including du Pont and Smithfield Packing, seeking to avoid the contracts under Bankruptcy Code §548(a) and to recover the transfers from the customers pursuant to Bankruptcy Code §550(a) on the ground that the contracts and transfers were fraudulent. The Trustee alleged that National Gas entered into contracts to sell natural gas to the customers at below market prices and that at the time of the transfers, National Gas was insolvent, thereby resulting in a constructively fraudulent conveyance. *See* §548(a)(1)(B) In the alternative, the Trustee alleged that the former management of National Gas intentionally used the contracts to "hinder, delay, or defraud" National Gas' creditors, thereby engaging in an actually fraudulent conveyance. *See* §548(a)(1)(A). The Trustee sought to recover the cash value of the difference between the market prices when the customers took delivery and the prices they paid under the contracts, which the Trustee alleged is over $4 million.

The customers, du Pont and Smithfield Packing, filed motions to dismiss the complaints or for summary judgment, contending that the Trustee cannot avoid the contracts and transfers because "each Transfer was made by or to a swap participant under or in connection with a swap agreement" and was thus not avoidable under Bankruptcy Code §§546(g) and 548(d)(2)(D). As they asserted, a "swap agreement" is defined in §101(53B) to include a "commodity forward agreement," which they allege covers the natural gas supply contracts in this case. The customers also contended that they received the transfers for value and that, as conceded by the Trustee, they received such transfers "in good faith."

The bankruptcy court denied the customers' motions by orders dated May 24, 2007, concluding that the natural gas supply contracts in this case were not "commodity forward agreements." Based on legislative history, as well as its construction of § 101(53B), the court ruled that the natural gas supply contracts in this case were insufficiently tied to financial markets to be commodity forward agreements. *In re Nat'l Gas Distributors, LLC,* 369 B.R. 884 (Bankr. E.D.N.C. 2007). More particularly, the court found that "commodity forward agreements" must be "regularly the subject of trading" in financial markets and must be settled by financial exchanges of differences in commodity prices, whereas the contracts in this case were directly negotiated between the seller and purchaser and contemplated physical delivery of the commodity to the purchasers. *Id.* at 898-99.

The customers filed motions to amend the May 24 orders, requesting the court to eliminate or clarify certain statements in its opinion that could be construed as factual findings and to leave open factual issues for later development. By orders dated June 20, 2007, the bankruptcy court denied the motions to amend, stating that it had "not endeavor[ed] to determine the defining boundaries of 'swap agreements' under the Bankruptcy Abuse Prevention and Consumer Protection Act of 2005, or anything approaching an issue that broad." The court noted that it had only decided "whether, as a matter of law, the contract between the parties came within the newly expanded definition of swap agreement," *i.e.,* "within the parameters of a swap agreement as defined by § 101(53B)." After pointing out that it did not purport to construe the various types of agreements that qualified as swap agreements, it said that it "determined, after review of the pleadings, the contract and related documents submitted by [the customers], the relevant statutes, and the legislative history, that the contract[s] *at issue here* [are] simple supply contract[s]" and that the contracts were "not in that league" of agreements defined as "swap agreements." * * *

II

Since enactment of the 1978 Bankruptcy Code, Congress has provided safe harbors from the destabilizing effects of bankruptcy proceedings for parties to specified commodities and financial contracts in order to protect financial markets. To do this, Congress limited the application to these parties of Bankruptcy Code provisions such as the automatic stay and trustee avoidances of preferences and fraudulent conveyances. It was thought that financial market stabilization would be achieved under the following rationale:

> These exceptions or "safe harbors" are necessary, it is thought, for the protection of financial markets, including over-the-counter ("OTC") markets on which most derivatives contracts are executed. Without these safe harbors, markets might suffer serious shocks-perhaps even a systemic liquidity crisis, causing markets to collapse-when debtors enter bankruptcy. Counterparties to financial contracts would find themselves subject to the automatic stay for extended periods. They would be unable to liquidate volatile contracts and thereby limit their exposure to market movements. Additionally, a debtor in bankruptcy would be free to "cherrypick" multiple contracts

with the same party. Instead of netting the contracts—*i.e.,* set-ting-off losses under some contracts against gains under oth-ers *with the same counterparty*—the debtor could dispose of the contracts independently. "In-the-money" contracts could be assumed; "out-of-the-money" contracts could be rejected. In this way, the debtor could lock-in gains on profitable con-tracts and (due to its insolvency) limit liability for losses under unprofitable ones. The counterparty to these contracts would find itself paying in full on the assumed contracts and receiv-ing only a fraction of its claim on the rejected. Losses from indefinite exposure to market movements and from cherry picking could produce financial distress in the counterparty itself, forcing it to default on its own contracts with other par-ties. As one distressed party infects another, a domino effect could ensue, undermining the entire financial market.

Edward R. Morrison & Joerg Riegel, *Financial Contracts and the New Bankruptcy Code: Insulating Markets From Bankrupt Debtors and Bankruptcy Judges,* 13 Am. Bankr. Inst. L.Rev. 641, 642 (2005).

This explanation appears to be an accurate description of the basis on which Congress relied to justify providing safe harbors to partici-pants in financial derivatives markets. As the House Report in connec-tion with the 1982 Amendments to the Bankruptcy Code stated:

Due to the structure of the clearing system in the commodities industry and the sometimes volatile nature of the commodities market, the Bankruptcy Code, as enacted in 1978, expressly provides certain protections to the commodities market to in-sure the stability of the market. These protections are intended to prevent the insolvency of one commodity firm from spread-ing to other brokers or clearing agencies and possibly threat-ening the collapse of the market.

H.R.Rep. No. 97-420, at 2 (1982) *reprinted in* 1982 U.S.C.C.A.N. 583, 584 (citation omitted). And similarly, in connection with the 1990 Amendments to the Bankruptcy Code, the House Report stated:

U.S. bankruptcy law has long accorded special treatment to transactions involving financial markets, to minimize volatil-ity. Because financial markets can change significantly in a matter of days, or even hours, a non-bankrupt party to ongoing securities and other financial transactions could face heavy losses unless the transactions are resolved promptly and with finality.

H.R.Rep. No. 101-484, at 2 (1990), *reprinted in* 1990 U.S.C.C.A.N. 223, 224.

With the 2005 Amendments to the Bankruptcy Code, adopted in the Bankruptcy Abuse Prevention and Consumer Protection Act of 2005 ("BAPCPA"), Congress substantially expanded the protections it had given to financial derivatives participants and transactions by expanding the definition of "swap participants" and "swap agreements" that are exempted from the automatic stay and from trustees' avoidance powers. As the House Report attached to the 2005 bill explained:

> As amended, the definition of "swap agreement" will update the statutory definition and achieve contractual netting across economically similar transactions that are the subject of recurring dealings in the swap agreements.
>
> The definition of "swap agreement" originally was intended to provide sufficient flexibility to avoid the need to amend the definition as the nature and uses of swap transactions matured. To that end, the phrase "or any other similar agreement" was included in the definition.

H.R.Rep. No. 109-31, pt. 1, at 121 (2005), *reprinted in* 2005 U.S.C.C.A.N. 88, 183. The current definition of "swap agreement" is now extremely broad, covering several dozen enumerated contracts and transactions, as well as combinations of them, options on them, and similar contracts or transactions. *See* Bankruptcy Code §101(53B)(A). And the Code now protects *all* counterparties to these agreements, whereas before 2005, the Code's safe harbors protected only certain counterparties. … The resulting statutory scheme may be summarized readily, although its application proves more difficult. Under the Bankruptcy Code, trustees are authorized to avoid contracts and transfers of debtors' property "made or incurred on or within 2 years before the date of the filing of the petition" when the contract or transfer amounts to a fraudulent contract or transfer, as fraudulent is defined in the Code. Bankruptcy Code §548(a). The Code, however, exempts from this avoidance authority transfers "made by or to a swap participant or financial participant, under or in connection with any swap agreement." Bankruptcy Code §546(g); *see also* §548(d)(2)(D). The term "swap participant" is defined to mean "an entity that … has an outstanding swap agreement with the debtor." Bankruptcy Code §101(53C). And "swap agreement," in turn, is defined to mean, as relevant here:

> (i) any agreement, including the terms and conditions incorporated by reference in such agreement, which is— …

(II) a spot, same day-tomorrow, tomorrow-next, forward, or other foreign exchange or precious metals agreement; [or]

(VII) a commodity index or a commodity swap, option, future, or forward agreement;

(ii) any agreement or transaction that is similar to any other agreement or transaction referred to in this paragraph and that—

(I) is of a type that has been, is presently, or in the future becomes, the subject of recurrent dealings in the swap markets (including terms and conditions incorporated by reference therein); and

(II) is a forward, swap, future, or option on one or more rates, currencies, commodities, equity securities, or other equity instruments, debt securities or other debt instruments, quantitative measures associated with an occurrence, extent of an occurrence, or contingency associated with a financial, commercial, or economic consequence, or economic or financial indices or measures of economic or financial risk or value; or

(iii) any combination of agreements or transactions referred to in this subparagraph.

Bankruptcy Code §101(53B)(A). Most of the transactions listed in the definition, however, are not defined in the Bankruptcy Code. As a result, courts must rely on normal principles of statutory interpretation, including dictionary definitions and legislative history.

In this case, National Gas' customers, du Pont and Smithfield Packing, [allege] that their natural gas supply contracts with National Gas were "swap agreements" as defined in §101(53B) in that they were "commodity forward agreements," a class of transactions listed in the definition of "swap agreement." §101(53B)(A)(i)(VII). "Commodity forward agreement," however, is not itself defined in the Bankruptcy Code, and no case to date has provided a definition.

The bankruptcy court, in a staunch effort, conducted an analysis of §101(53B) and drew on legislative history to conclude that a "commodity forward agreement" has to be traded in a financial market and cannot involve physical delivery of the commodity to an end user. 369 B.R. at 898-99. Concluding that the contracts in this case were not traded in financial markets but were simply natural gas supply contracts, the bankruptcy court held that they were not "commodity forward agreements" exempt from the Trustee's avoidance authority. *Id.* at 900.

In this case of first impression, we are therefore left to define "commodity forward agreement" without being given any definition by the Bankruptcy Code.

III

At the outset, we note that the Bankruptcy Code and the financial marketplace recognize differences in the definitions of terms that common parlance might not recognize. Thus, the Bankruptcy Code uses both "forward *contract*" and "forward *agreement*" but defines only "forward *contract*," and not "forward *agreement*," apparently making a a distinction between the terms. The House Report that accompanied the 2005 Amendments enacted as part of BAPCPA appears to confirm this:

> The use of the term "forward" in the definition of "swap agreement" is not intended to refer only to transactions that fall within the definition of "forward contract." Instead, a "forward" transaction could be a "swap agreement" even if not a "forward contract."

H.R. Rep. 109-31, pt. 1, at 122, *reprinted in* 2005 U.S.C.C.A.N. at 184. And this legislative history comports with the distinction made between "contracts" and "agreements" in *Black's Law Dictionary.* As *Black's* states, "[t]he term 'agreement,' although frequently used as synonymous with the word 'contract,' is really an expression of greater breadth of meaning and less technicality. Every contract is an agreement; but not every agreement is a contract." *Black's Law Dictionary* 74 (8th ed.2004).

A distinction also exists in the meanings of a "*future* agreement" and a "*forward* agreement." Even though both are included in the definition of a "swap agreement," Bankruptcy Code §101(53B)(A), the marketplace makes a distinction, at least where the terms "future" and "forward" are used in conjunction with "contract." The Chicago Mercantile Exchange's online glossary's definition states that "[i]n contrast to *futures* contracts, *forward* contracts are not standardized and not transferable." *CME Glossary of Terms,* http:// www. cme. com/ glossary/ F. html (last visited Jan. 16, 2009).

In holding in this case that the natural gas supply contracts are not "commodity forward agreements" exempt from the Trustee's avoidance efforts, the bankruptcy court concluded that all of the agreements or transactions listed in §101(53B)(A)(i) were "financial instruments traded in the swap markets," and therefore, if any agreement was not traded on an exchange or in a financial market, it could not be a "swap agreement." 369 B.R. at 898-99. To support its conclusion, the court referred to repeated references in the legislative history to "swap markets" and relied on its construction of the language of §101(53B):

> It is true enough that §101(53B)(A)(i) lists numerous agreements that fall within the definition of "swap agreement." Section 101(53B)(A)(ii) provides for additional agreements or transactions that are "similar" to those referred to in §101(53B)(A)(i) *and* are the subject of recurrent dealings in the swap market *and* are forwards, swaps, futures, or options "on one or more rates, currencies, commodities, equity securities, or other equity instruments … ." The word "similar," rather than expanding the universe of agreements that come within the umbrella of swap agreements, actually limits the agreements to those that "bear[ ] a family resemblance" to the other agreements and transactions that enjoy the protections of the Bankruptcy Code. The other agreements described in §101(53B)(A)(i) are found in financial markets. They do not include contracts between a seller and an end-user for delivery of a product that happens to be a recognized commodity.

Id. at 899. After concluding that each contract in this case was "simply an agreement by a single end-user to purchase a commodity," which was physically delivered to the purchaser, *id.,* the court explained that a traditional supply contract is not "swept into the realm of swap agreements":

> There is nothing to suggest that the contract between Smithfield and the debtor was traded on a financial market, so in this case only the debtor's estate and Smithfield would be affected by a recovery. *Id.*

If one were to assume, as the bankruptcy court did, that all swap agreements, including "commodity forward agreements," must be traded on exchanges or in financial markets and that the contracts in this case were simple supply contracts, the court's position is logically sound. The assumptions, however, do not withstand closer scrutiny.

Because the term "agreement" is broader than the term "contract," as discussed above, a forward *contract* must also be a forward *agreement* (although it does not follow that every forward agreement is a forward contract). We can therefore look to the Bankruptcy Code's definition of "forward contract," *see* §101(25), to determine whether the bankruptcy court gave too restrictive a definition for "forward agreement." If a forward contract need not be traded on an exchange or in a financial market, it follows that neither does a forward agreement need to be traded on an exchange or in a financial market.

The Bankruptcy Code does not require that a "forward contract" be traded on an exchange or in a market. Section 101(25)(A) defines "forward contract" to mean "a contract (other than a commodity contract)," distinguishing a "forward contract" from a "commodity contract." The term "commodity contract" specifically includes contracts "on, or subject to the rules of, a contract market or board of trade." Bankruptcy Code §761(4). By explicitly excluding "commodity contracts" from the definition of "forward contracts," Congress apparently intended that "forward contracts" need not be traded on any exchange or in any financial market. Congress reinforced this reading in 2006, when it amended §101(25)(A) to include "as defined in section 761" in the parenthetical after "commodity contract." Pub.L. No. 109-390, § 5(a)(1), 120 Stat. 2692, 2695 (2006). The legislative history stated that this was a "technical and clarifying change ... .." H.R.Rep. No. 109-648, pt. 1, at 6-7 (2006), *reprinted in* 2006 U.S.C.C.A.N. 1585, 1591-92.

Courts have accordingly found no requirement that "forward contracts" be traded on an exchange or in a market, noting that they may be directly negotiated, in much the same manner as the contracts in this case. *See, e.g., In re Olympic Natural Gas Co.,* 294 F.3d 737, 741 (5th Cir.2002). And, various non-bankruptcy cases have used "forward agreement" to refer to non-market traded, private agreements. *See Donoghue v. Centillium Communications, Inc.,* No. 05 Civ. 4082(WHP), 2006 WL 775122, at 2 (S.D.N.Y. Mar.28, 2006); *Breyer v. First Nat'l Monetary Corp.,* 548 F.Supp. 955, 962 (D.C.N.J.1982).

Finally, *Black's Law Dictionary* distinguishes a "forward contract" from a "futures contract" on the basis that a futures contract is traded on a formal exchange. "Unlike a futures contract, a forward contract is not traded on a formal exchange." *Black's Law Dictionary* 345 (8th ed.2004).

The weight of authority thus indicates that "forward *contracts*" are not found only in the financial markets. Rather, they may be directly negotiated, as were the contracts in this case. Because we conclude that every "forward *contract*" is also a "forward *agreement,*" it follows that we must reject the district court's assumption that all of the agreements in §101(53B)(A)(i) must be "found in the financial markets." *See In re Enron Corp.,* 306 B.R. 465, 469 (Bankr. S.D.N.Y. 2004) (characterizing directly negotiated natural gas hedging agreements as "swap agreements"); *see also In re Interbulk, Ltd.,* 240 B.R. 195, 197 (Bankr. S.D.N.Y. 1999) (agreements negotiated by telephone were "swap agreements").

The bankruptcy court also assumed that the contracts in this case were "simple supply contract[s]," which are not within the definition of a swap agreement. 369 B.R. at 893, 900. But this assumption is an oversimplification. Although the contracts in this case did provide a supply of gas to the customers' facilities, they also were part of a series of contracts by which the customers hedged their risk of future fluctuations in the price of natural gas. Although it is true that these particular contracts were not traded in financial markets-and perhaps were not even assignable-they nonetheless could have an influence on markets in which participants enter into hedging agreements. A business can enter into a forward agreement with a party who then, in reliance on that forward agreement, enters into another contract with yet another market participant, who in turn may enter into even other contracts. And so a simple forward agreement may readily become tied into the broader markets that Congress aimed to protect in BAPCPA. The Seventh Circuit described this same type of situation in *Nagel v. ADM Investor Servs., Inc.,* 217 F.3d 436, 438-39 (7th Cir.2000), where farmers entered into forward contracts with grain merchants who, in reliance upon their contracts with the farmer, proceeded to turn around and enter into futures contracts on established commodities markets. In this case, the customers claim a similar relationship with markets, alleging that their contracts with National Gas were hedging contracts that were only a part of a larger risk management program in which the customers "regularly use[d] forwards and other derivatives."

The bankruptcy court's conclusion that these contracts were simple supply contracts also rested on the fact that the contracts involved the physical delivery of gas, thus distinguishing them from contracts settled financially. The court concluded that a "commodity forward agreement" must have a financial settlement, such as when settlement occurs by the "losing" party transferring cash or financial assets to the "winning" party at the specified time. Thus, supply contracts, contemplating physical delivery of the commodity to purchasers, could not qualify as "commodity forward agreements."

Although the legislative history of BAPCPA does provide support for the notion that traditional supply agreements are not "swap agreements," *see* H.R.Rep. No. 109-31, pt. 1, at 122, *reprinted in* 2005 U.S.C.C.A.N. at 183 (noting that "[t]raditional commercial arrangements, such as supply agreements" cannot be treated as swap agreements under the Bankruptcy Code), the conclusion that the contracts in this case are traditional supply contracts overlooks the fact that the contracts in this case contained real hedging elements. The contracts obliged the customers to buy, and National Gas to sell, gas on a future date at a price fixed at the time of contracting, regardless of fluctuations in the market price. And if either party did not perform, that party was required to pay the difference between the contract price and the market price.

Nothing in the Bankruptcy Code or in its legislative history suggests a requirement that a forward agreement cannot involve the actual delivery of the commodity. Numerous courts have found that "forward *contracts*" may be physically settled, and it follows that "forward *agreements* "may likewise be physically settled. *See In re Olympic Natural Gas Co.,* 294 F.3d at 742 (observing that there was "no reason to adopt the interpretation the Trustee advocates, and distinguish between 'financial' forward contracts, and 'ordinary purchase and sale' forward contracts, when the statutory language makes no such distinction").

Congress' inclusion of "spot" commodity transactions in the definitions contained in §101(53B) further refutes the bankruptcy court's position that "swap agreements" cannot involve physical delivery. The definition of a spot agreement is one in which the commodity is "available for immediate *delivery* after sale." *Merriam-Webster's Collegiate Dictionary* 1208 (11th ed.2007) (emphasis added). The definition of "swap agreement" in the BAPCPA includes "*spot,* same day-tomorrow, tomorrow-next, *forward,* or other foreign exchange or *precious metals agreement.*" Bankruptcy Code §101(53B)(A)(i)(II) (emphasis added). Similarly, in 2006, as part of the "technical and clarifying changes," Congress added "spot transaction" in the catchall clause in § 101(53B)(A)(ii).

We thus conclude that Congress did not preclude physical delivery in connection with a "commodity forward agreement," as defined in §101(53B)(A).

Because the bankruptcy court gave the definition of "commodity forward agreement" a more narrow reading than the statute bears, we reverse its orders of May 24, 2007, and June 20, 2007, and remand for further proceedings consistent with this opinion.

IV

In remanding, we do not direct the bankruptcy court to find that the contracts in this case are "commodity forward agreements" or "swap agreements." Rather, we return this case for further consideration of the issue in light of the law and the facts. In determining whether the contracts in this case are "commodity forward agreements," the bankruptcy court will not, unfortunately, have the benefit of developed case law, nor even the benefit of clear market-place definitions. The marketplace is creative, designing instruments to fit the needs of the moment, and Congress sought to anticipate this in BAPCPA. In doing so, however, Congress forwent describing the elements of transactions it sought to exempt from the effects of bankruptcy. Indeed, its repetitive generalized comments about protecting financial markets from the instability that bankruptcy proceedings might cause and the potpourri of agreements included in the term "swap agreement" barely distinguish any major commercial contract from a swap agreement.

Moreover, the policies informing these provisions of the Bankruptcy Code are often in tension. Even though an overarching policy of the Bankruptcy Code is to provide equal distribution among creditors, in enacting [the safe harbors for derivative contracts], Congress intended to serve a countervailing policy of protecting financial markets and therefore favoring an entire class of instruments and participants. * * *

Although we do not attempt to provide a definition ourselves, we can point to certain nonexclusive elements that the statutory language appears to require.

First, the subject of a commodity forward agreement must be a commodity. That is, substantially all of the expected costs of performance must be attributable to the expected costs of the underlying commodity, determined at the time of contracting. This element, which is inherent in the word "commodity," distinguishes a commodity forward agreement, in which the benefits or detriments depend on future fluctuations in commodity prices, from many supply contracts, in which costs attributable to other factors, such as packaging, marketing, transportation, service, and similar matters contribute to a greater portion of the costs.

Second, a forward commodity contract, in being "forward," must require a payment for the commodity at a price fixed at the time of contracting for delivery more than two days after the date the contract is entered into. Bankruptcy Code §101(25)(A) (requiring the same of "forward contracts"). A maturity date in the future means that the benefit or detriment from the contract depends on future fluctuations in the market price of the commodity.

Third, as a forward agreement in relation to a commodity, in addition to the price element, the quantity and time elements must be fixed at the time of contracting. Where *The Wall Street Journal* has used the term "forward agreement" and provided details of the transaction, it has always described fixed quantities and prices: "35 million shares," "$250,000 of marks," and "$1 million of bonds." Non-bankruptcy case law also accords the same meaning to "forward agreement." These requirements are confirmed by the common meaning given to a "forward contract" as "a privately negotiated investment contract in which a buyer commits to purchase something (as a quantity of a commodity, security, or currency) at a predetermined price on a set future date." *Merriam-Webster's Dictionary of Law* (contract), *available at* http:// dictionary. reference. com/ browse/ contract (last visited Jan. 16, 2009).

Finally, while the broad class of "swap agreements" includes contracts that are readily assignable and therefore tradable, "swap agreements" also include forward contracts, which are not necessarily assignable. The Chicago Mercantile Exchange's online glossary's definition states that "[i]n contrast to *futures* contracts, *forward* contracts are not standardized and not transferable." *CME Glossary of Terms,* http:// www. cme. com/ glossary/ F. html (last visited Jan. 16, 2009) (emphasis added). * * *

Thus, insofar as our holding precludes the bankruptcy court from requiring, in defining a "commodity forward agreement," that the contract be traded in a market or on an exchange or that it not involve physical delivery of the commodity, our holding does not define that instrument or hold that the contracts in this case are commodity forward agreements. We leave that to further legal and factual development on remand.

V. CLAIMS AGAINST THE ESTATE

[The material on "A Claim and When it Arises" in Chapter 5A, which begins on ***page 141***, should be supplemented as follows.]

In the recent case of U.S. v. Apex Oil Co. Inc., 579 F.3d 734 (7th Cir. 2009), the Seventh Circuit held that the obligation to comply with an environmental cleanup order did not constitute a dischargeable claim. The *Apex* court distinguished *Kovacs* on the ground that "the plaintiff in our case (the government) is not seeking a payment of money and the injunction that it has obtained does not entitle it to payment."

Turning now to *Epstein*, a footnote observed that the Court of Appeals for the Third Circuit was an outlier in its application of the accrued-under-state-law test to determine when a claim arises. The Third Circuit is an outlier no more. See In re Grossman's, Inc., 607 F.3d 114 (3rd Cir. 2010) (holding that a claim arises when an individual is exposed prepetition to a product or other conduct giving rise to an injury).

Also, in Travelers Indemnity Co. v. Bailey, 557 U.S. 137 (2009), the Supreme Court held that a 1986 injunction in support of an asbestos claims procedure for the Johns-Manville company applied not only to claims against the debtor Johns-Manville but also to any direct claims against Johns-Manville's insurer as a result of the insurer's own wrongdoing. This holding, however, was narrow in that it rested largely on the finality of the bankruptcy court's order rather than on the substance of that order.

[The material on "Allowing and Estimating Claims" in chapter 5B, which begins on ***page 154***, should be supplemented by the following.]

In an attempt to resolve financial distress without bankruptcy, a debtor and some of its creditors may agree to have the creditors exchange old debt for new debt with different terms such as a longer maturity or a lower principal amount. The value of the new debt may be below the stated principal amount of such debt and if the debtor soon enters bankruptcy despite the exchange the question arises whether the difference between value at the time of the exchange and the face amount of the new debt should be treated as an original issue discount. If so, the unaccrued portion of the discount would be disallowed as unmatured interest under Bankruptcy Code §502(b). In re Residential Capital, LLC, 501 B.R. 549 (Bankr. S.D.N.Y. 2013), held that discount created in such an exchange should not be characterized as unmatured interest, lest a debtor's attempts to work out financial distress be unduly burdened.

Claim disallowance was at issue in another recent case. Bankruptcy Code §502(d) disallows any claim of an entity against whom there is an outstanding obligation to the debtor based on an avoided transfer. As illustrated by In re KB Toys, Inc., 736 F.3d 247 (5th Cir. 2013), this provision has been interpreted to apply even where the holder of the claim has purchased it from the creditor who owes the obligation.

[The material on "Secured Claims" in chapter 5C, which begins on ***page 177***, should be supplemented by the following. The first paragraph below also supplements the material on "Treatment of Secured Claims" in chapter 12B, which begins on ***page 644***.]

Although *Rash* makes a distinction between a case in which the debtor retains collateral and one in which the debtor surrenders collateral, In re Brown, 746 F.3d 1236 (11th Cir. 2014) literally interprets Bankruptcy Code §506(a)(2), enacted after *Rash*, and ignores this distinction for the purposes of that provision. The court thus applies a replacement valuation even though the debtor surrendered the collateral.

Still on the question of how to value collateral, In re Residential Capital, LLC, 501 B.R. 549 (Bankr. S.D.N.Y. 2013) held that a prepetition security interest does not attach to goodwill generated in part by the effort and expense of a debtor in orchestrating a sale of its assets in bankruptcy. This decision could have significant implications for a holder of a blanket lien, which, on this rationale, may not encompass a debtor's entire going-concern value.

Turning to the protection of a security interest, once established, the Supreme Court's plurality opinion in *Till*, summarized in Note 5C.3, beginning on page 187 of the casebook, suggests that the "formula rate" to be applied in a Chapter 13 cramdown against a secured claim should also be applied in Chapter 11 cases. As illustrated by In re Texas Grand Prairie Hotel Realty, LLC, 710 F.3d 324 (5th Cir. 2013), however, not all courts are persuaded to follow this dictum, which is, in any case, of limited guidance given the vagaries inherent in a determination of the formula rate whether applied in Chapter 13 or Chapter 11.

VI. THE BANKRUPTCY ESTATE

[The material on "The Debtor's Interest in Property" in chapter 6A, which begins on *page 191*, should be supplemented by the following. This material can also be considered in connection with the material on "Fraudulent Conveyances" in chapter 8C, which begins on *page 309*.]

The recent financial crisis uncovered a number of Ponzi schemes, where the proprietor uses new investors' funds to repay old investors, stealing what he can until the demands for withdrawal overwhelm the cash on hand and cause the scheme to collapse. After the fall, it is typical for investors to fight over whatever assets remain or may be recovered and it is unsurprising that this process generates considerable litigation.

Questions of statutory or constructive trust arise, where some Ponzi scheme victims assert a right superior to other creditors, including other victims. One such claim of superiority was recently rejected, for example, in Grede v. FCStone, LLC, 746 F.3d 244 (7th Cir. 2014). Another question is whether a court can enjoin private tort suits by Ponzi scheme victims who seek to collect from a perpetrator's accomplice based on claims derivative of fraudulent conveyance actions that belong to the debtor's bankruptcy estate. This question was answered in the affirmative by In re Bernie L. Madoff Investment Securities LLC, 740 F.3d 81 (2nd Cir. 2014); compare In re Bernie L. Madoff Investment Securities LLC. 721 F.3d 54 (2nd Cir. 2013), which held that the doctrine of in pari delicto can bar a trustee from bringing common law claims against an accomplice. A related issue is whether an investor who collected from the debtor before bankruptcy can be made to return the collection as a fraudulent conveyance. In Perkins v. Haines, 661 F.3d 623 (11th Cir. 2011), for example, the court held that a collection of the amount invested in a Ponzi scheme, but not interest or profits earned, can be characterized as in exchange for value, based on the victim's right of restitution, even if the nature of the investment was the purchase of an equity interest in the fund. These and other Ponzi scheme issues, including what constitutes a good faith collection, will play out in the courts as the contests over limited assets continue.

VII. EXECUTORY CONTRACTS

[The material on "Rejection" in Chapter 7C, which begins on ***page 255***, should be supplemented as follows.]

On the question raised by the comparison between *Leasing Services* and *Register*, consider the following concise analysis provided by In re Ortiz, 400 B.R. 755, 769 (C.D. Calif. 2010):

> The court concludes that the bankruptcy court's decision that rejection of the promotional agreement, by itself, "terminated" the contract and extinguished [the nondebtor party's] ability to seek equitable relief for breach of contract was error. While there are many reasons why equitable relief enforcing a personal services contract may be unavailable, section 365 does not invite a court to invoke those reasons as a basis for treating rejection as a termination of the contract. Because section 365 adopts no specialized rule governing personal services contracts, the effect of rejection of a personal services contract is determined by section 365(g). This statute provides that rejection of an executory contract constitutes a breach of the contract and no more. To determine whether any provisions of the contract remain enforceable against the debtor, rather than as claims against the estate, courts must assess whether the right to an equitable remedy is a "claim" dischargeable in bankruptcy. This in turn requires an inquiry as to whether an equitable remedy is available under state law. Section 365 simply does not speak to which obligations may and may not be enforced post-bankruptcy against the debtor.

Consider also, recent court of appeals trademark opinions. In the case of In re Exide Technologies, 607 F.3d 957 (3rd Cir. 2010), a trademark licensor and debtor in bankruptcy attempted to rid itself of its licensee by rejecting the license agreement. The court held that the license agreement was not executory and thus could not be rejected, but Judge Ambro, in concurrence, reasoned that the licensee would have been protected in any case because under applicable nonbankruptcy law a trademark licensor's breach of the license agreement does not revoke the license. In Sunbeam Products, Inc. v. Chicago American Manufacturing, LLC, 686 F.3d 372 (7th Cir. 2012), the Seventh Circuit, speaking through Judge Easterbrook, agreed with Judge Ambro, holding in favor of a nondebtor licensee; the court expressly rejected the argument that Congress' adoption of Bankruptcy Code §365(n), to protect other sorts of licenses, implicitly permitted a debtor to revoke a trademark license through rejection of the license agreement.

Related to Bankruptcy Code §1113 discussed in *Northwest Airlines*, is §1114, which limits a debtor's ability to alter retiree benefits obligations. In the case of In re AMR Corp., 508 B.R. 296 (Bankr. S.D.N.Y. 2013), the court held that absent a corresponding determination under §1114, the rejection of a collective bargaining agreement under §1113 does not permit a debtor to modify its payment of benefits to retirees even if the rejected agreement was the source of those benefits. And in the case of In re Visteon, 612 F.3d 210 (3rd Cir. 2011), the court ruled that the restrictions of §1114 apply even under circumstances where, under applicable nonbankruptcy law, the debtor could have freely terminated its obligations. Other courts have held to the contrary. See, e.g., In re Chateaugay Corp., 945 F.2d 1205 (2d Cir. 1991).

Also related to the issues raised by *Northwest Airlines*, in the case of In re Journal Register Co., 488 B.R. 835 (Bankr. S.D.N.Y. 2013), the court held that a debtor could not circumvent the requirements of §1113 through a sale to a purchaser who would then terminate a labor contract. By contrast, in the case of In re City of Vallejo, 432 B.R. 262 (E.D. Cal. 2010), the court held that a Chapter 9 debtor could reject a collective bargaining agreement if it complied with the general rules of §365, as interpreted by *Bildisco*, regardless of whether such rejection would comply with the stricter requirements of §1113. The court so held because Congress did not expressly incorporate §1113 into Chapter 9 cases. If followed by other courts, this decision could prove significant as more and more municipalities are expected to face financial crisis, and may consider Chapter 9 filings, in the coming years.

VIII. THE AVOIDING POWERS

[The material on "Fraudulent Conveyances" in chapter 8C, which begins on ***page 309***, should be supplemented by the following.]

A corporation subject to significant environmental and tort liability spins off its assets in an attempt to leave the debt behind. Perhaps unsurprisingly, but as a matter of first impression in the jurisdiction, In re Tronox, Inc. 503 B.R. 239 (Bankr. S.D.N.Y. 2013), held that such transactions are both intentionally and constructively fraudulent.

[The material on "Reasonably Equivalent Value" in chapter 8C(1), which begins on *page 316*, should be supplemented by the following. The part of this supplemental material that addresses Bankruptcy Code §550(a) can also be considered in connection with the material on "Scope of Preference Law" in chapter 8D(1), which begins on *page 353*.]

Payment of an antecedent debt, even by an insolvent debtor, is deemed in exchange for reasonably equivalent value and thus not a fraudulent conveyance, but where a transfer is to a shareholder it is not always clear whether a transfer is in fact the payment of a debt as opposed to a return on equity. This issue is addressed in In re Fitness Holding International, Inc., 714 F.3d 1141 (9th Cir. 2013), which held that state law should determine whether a transfer is a debt payment, but observes that other courts have adopted a different approach.

Another, particularly interesting, take on the question of reasonably equivalent value, as part of fraudulent conveyance analysis, can be found in the next case, *TOUSA*. In this case, subsidiaries in a corporate affiliate issued secured guarantees of its parent's new loan obligations, the proceeds of which the parent used to repay the parent's earlier debt. In the lower courts, the district court found that an indirect benefit to such an issuing subsidiary as part of a corporate affiliate can qualify as at least part of reasonably equivalent value for the guarantee. In the opinion excerpted here, the Eleventh Circuit Court of Appeals does not entirely disagree, but expresses skepticism and relies on the bankruptcy court's factual determination that in this case, at least, any indirect benefit does not constitute reasonably equivalent value. Consider the court's reasoning on this point and how one might measure indirect value.

TOUSA addresses as well what Bankruptcy Code §550(a)(1) means by an "entity for whose benefit" a transfer is made. After it affirms the bankruptcy court's determination that the guarantees in question constituted fraudulent conveyances, the Eleventh Circuit holds that the subsidiary debtors could recover from the repaid creditors as beneficiaries of the fraudulent conveyances. Consider the consequences of the court's holding on this point.

Also consider the issue of beneficiary liability again in connection with the way voidable preference law treats guarantors of repaid loans. Voidable preference law is the next topic in the casebook.

IN RE TOUSA, INC.

United States Court of Appeals, Eleventh Circuit, 2011
680 F.3d 1298

Pryor, Circuit Judge

This bankruptcy appeal involves a transfer of liens by subsidiaries of TOUSA, Inc., to secure the payment of a debt owed only by their parent, TOUSA. On July 31, 2007, TOUSA paid a settlement of $421 million to the Senior Transeastern Lenders with loan proceeds from the New Lenders secured primarily by the assets of several subsidiaries of TOUSA. Six months later, TOUSA and the Conveying Subsidiaries filed for bankruptcy. In an adversary proceeding filed by the Committee of Unsecured Creditors of TOUSA, the bankruptcy court avoided the liens as a fraudulent transfer because the Conveying Subsidiaries did not receive reasonably equivalent value; ordered the Transeastern Lenders to disgorge $403 million of the loan proceeds because the transfer of the liens was for the benefit of the Transeastern Lenders; and awarded damages to the Conveying Subsidiaries. The Transeastern Lenders and the New Lenders, as intervenors, appealed. The district court quashed the judgment as to the Transeastern Lenders and stayed the appeal of the New Lenders. This appeal by the Committee of Unsecured Creditors presents two issues: (1) whether the bankruptcy court clearly erred when it found that the Conveying Subsidiaries did not receive reasonably equivalent value in exchange for the liens to secure loans used to pay a debt owed only by TOUSA, Bankruptcy Code §548; and (2) whether the Transeastern Lenders were entities "for whose benefit" the Conveying Subsidiaries transferred the liens, §550(a)(1). ***

As the second court to review the judgment of the bankruptcy court, we review the order of the bankruptcy court independently of the district court. We review determinations of law made by either court *de novo*. We review the findings of fact of the bankruptcy court for clear error. The factual findings of the bankruptcy court are not clearly erroneous unless, in the light of all the evidence, "we are left with the definite and firm conviction that a mistake has been made." * * *

The Bankruptcy Court Did Not Clearly Err When It Found That the Conveying Subsidiaries Did Not Receive Reasonably Equivalent Value in Exchange for the Liens They Transferred to the New Lenders.

The Committee argues that the bankruptcy court did not clearly err when it found that the conveyance of the liens by the Conveying Subsidiaries to the New Lenders was a fraudulent transfer. Section 548(a)(1)(B) of the Bankruptcy Code provides for the avoidance of "any transfer ... of an interest of the debtor in property, or any obligation ... incurred by the debtor, that was made or incurred ... within two years before the date of the filing" of the bankruptcy petition, if the debtor "received less than reasonably equivalent value in exchange for" the transfer or obligation, and the debtor (1) "was insolvent on the date such transfer was made or such obligation was incurred, or became insolvent as a result of such transfer or obligation;" (2) "was engaged in business or a transaction, or was about to engage in business or a transaction, for which any property remaining with the debtor was an unreasonably small capital;" or (3) "intended to incur, or believed that the debtor would incur, debts that would be beyond the debtor's ability to pay as such debts matured." Bankruptcy Code §548(a)(1)(B). The parties do not dispute, in this appeal, that the Conveying Subsidiaries were either insolvent, had unreasonably small capital, or were unable to pay their debts when the liens were conveyed. Their dispute concerns whether the Conveying Subsidiaries received less than reasonably equivalent value. * * *

The bankruptcy court endorsed a definition of "value" that the district court rejected as too narrow and potentially "inhibitory of contemporary financing practices," but we need not adopt the definition of either court. We decline to decide whether the possible avoidance of bankruptcy can confer "value" because the bankruptcy court found that, even if all the purported benefits of the transaction were legally cognizable, they did not confer reasonably equivalent value. Because these findings are not clearly erroneous, they settle this matter.

The bankruptcy court was entitled to find that the benefits of the transaction were not reasonably equivalent in value to what the Conveying Subsidiaries surrendered. "It has long been established that '[w]hether fair consideration has been given for a transfer is 'largely a question of fact, as to which considerable latitude must be allowed to the trier of the facts.' " *Nordberg v. Arab Banking Corp. (In re Chase & Sanborn Corp.)*, 904 F.2d 588, 593 (11th Cir.1990) (quoting *Mayo v. Pioneer Bank & Trust Co.*, 270 F.2d 823, 829–30 (5th Cir.1959) (Wisdom, J.)). The record supports the finding by the bankruptcy court that, for the Conveying Subsidiaries, the almost certain costs of the transaction of July 31 far outweighed any perceived benefits.

The Transeastern Lenders and New Lenders argue that the transaction of July 31 allowed the Conveying Subsidiaries to escape the "existential threat" of the likely bankruptcy that would ensue and that this chance to avoid bankruptcy was a benefit reasonably equivalent in value to the obligations the Conveying Subsidiaries incurred, but we are unpersuaded that the record compels that finding. "A corporation is not a biological entity for which it can be presumed that any act which extends its existence is beneficial to it." *Bloor v. Dansker (In re Investors Funding Corp. of New York Sec. Litig.)*, 523 F.Supp. 533, 541 (S.D.N.Y.1980). In other words, not every transfer that decreases the odds of bankruptcy for a corporation can be justified. The bankruptcy court considered the potential benefits of the transaction and found that they were nowhere close to its expected costs. In the light of all the evidence, we are not "left with the definite and firm conviction that" the bankruptcy court clearly erred. *In re Int'l Pharmacy & Disc. II, Inc.*, 443 F.3d 767, 770 (11th Cir. 2005).

The Transeastern Lenders and New Lenders argue that the record establishes that an adverse judgment in the Transeastern litigation would have caused TOUSA to file for bankruptcy, the revolving financing for the Conveying Subsidiaries to disappear, and the Conveying Subsidiaries to become liable for immediate payment of more than $1.3 billion to the revolving loan lenders and TOUSA bondholders. They contend that the bankruptcy court clearly erred when it found that the Conveying Subsidiaries could have survived a TOUSA bankruptcy. They argue that the bankruptcy court found that the Conveying Subsidiaries were insolvent before the transaction, and they argue that it is unlikely that the insolvent Conveying Subsidiaries could have obtained new financing. They also argue that the absence of standalone financial statements was a "clear obstacle" to new financing. They highlight that one of the experts for the Committee described the intercompany payables and receivables for TOUSA and the Conveying Subsidiaries as a "huge pile of tangled spaghetti." The Transeastern Lenders and New Lenders assert that it would have taken months, if not years, to sort through the mound of records, which proves that the Conveying Subsidiaries had no chance to receive standalone financing.

The bankruptcy court found this evidence to be irrelevant because, "even assuming that *all* of the TOUSA entities would have spiraled immediately into bankruptcy without the July 31 Transaction, the Transaction was *still* the more harmful option. ... [A]t most it delayed the inevitable." The bankruptcy court found that the benefits to the Conveying Subsidiaries were not close to being reasonably equivalent in value to the $403 million of obligations that they incurred. The Transeastern Lenders and New Lenders attack this finding as "hindsight reasoning ... at its most extreme," but the bankruptcy court based its extensive findings on a thorough review of public knowledge available before July 31, 2007; expert analysis of data available before July 31, 2007; and statements by TOUSA insiders made before July 31, 2007.

The Transeastern Lenders and New Lenders argue that the finding of an "inevitable" bankruptcy is against the weight of the evidence, but the only evidence they cite, in contrast with the thorough findings of the bankruptcy court, are the opinions of a TOUSA advisor that the company would remain viable after the transaction and statements from Tony Mon about a comprehensive strategy to shrink TOUSA after the transaction, shore up its finances, and rebuild the company. The Transeastern Lenders and New Lenders contend that the projections of TOUSA look unreasonable now only because weeks after the transaction, "a tragic global financial crisis of unprecedented proportions" began. They assert that the unexpected downturn was described by Alan Greenspan as "a once in a century credit tsunami" and by Warren Buffett as an "economic Pearl Harbor." The Transeastern Lenders and New Lenders argue that they cannot be held liable for failing to foresee the unforeseeable, that their actions were reasonable, and that the bankruptcy court clearly should have found that the transaction was a reasonable risk for the Conveying Subsidiaries to take.

The record supports a determination that the bankruptcy of TOUSA was far more like a slow-moving category 5 hurricane than an unforeseen tsunami. The bankruptcy court considered the evidence from outside advisors to TOUSA and found much of it suspect or based on faulty premises. The bankruptcy court considered and discounted Mon's deleveraging strategy for TOUSA in the light of the dire predictions he and other insiders made regarding the effects the transaction would have on TOUSA. And the bankruptcy court found that, even though Alan Greenspan and Warren Buffet could not foresee the general economic downturn that began in earnest in August 2007, numerous external observers and insiders at TOUSA recognized that the relevant housing markets for TOUSA had begun their free fall before the July 31 transaction. In contrast with the surprise attack at Pearl Harbor, the warnings about the collapse of TOUSA made that event as foreseeable as the bombing of Nagasaki after President Truman's ultimatum.

The opportunity to avoid bankruptcy does not free a company to pay any price or bear any burden. After all, "there is no reason to treat bankruptcy as a bogeyman, as a fate worse than death." *Olympia Equip. Leasing Co. v. W. Union Tel. Co.*, 786 F.2d 794, 802 (7th Cir.1986) (Easterbrook, J., concurring). The bankruptcy court correctly asked, "based on the circumstances that existed at the time the investment was contemplated, whether there was any chance that the investment would generate a positive return." *See In re R.M.L., Inc.*, 92 F.3d 139, 152 (3rd Cir.1996). And the record supports the negative answer found by the bankruptcy court.

The Bankruptcy Court Did Not Err When It Ruled That the Committee Could Recover from the Transeastern Lenders under Section 550(a)(1).

If a transfer is avoided under section 548 or one of several other provisions of the Bankruptcy Code, section 550(a)(1) allows the recovery of the property transferred or its value from the initial transferee or from an "entity for whose benefit such transfer was made." Although the liens of the Conveying Subsidiaries were transferred to secure loans to pay the Transeastern Lenders, the Transeastern Lenders argue that they are not covered by section 550 because they were subsequent transferees, not entities that benefitted from the initial transfer. Their argument is contradicted by the loan agreements, which required that the proceeds of the loans secured by the liens be transferred to the Transeastern Lenders. Under the plain language of section 550(a)(1) and the precedent of our Court, the Transeastern Lenders are entities for whose benefit the Conveying Subsidiaries transferred their liens.

To be sure, we have stated that "the paradigm case of a benefit under §550(a) is the benefit to a guarantor by the payment of the underlying debt of the debtor." *Reily v. Kapila (In re Int'l Mgmt. Assoc.)*, 399 F.3d 1288, 1292 (11th Cir.2005). The guarantor receives an immediate benefit when the debtor pays back a creditor, which reduces the liability of the guarantor. Although this relationship may be the paradigmatic case, it is not the only circumstance that can give rise to "for whose benefit" liability.

We have also held that a creditor similarly situated to the Transeastern Lenders can be liable as an entity for whose benefit a transfer was made. In *American Bank of Martin County v. Leasing Service Corp. (In re Air Conditioning, Inc. of Stuart)*, 845 F.2d 293 (11th Cir.1988), we ruled that §550(a)(1) allowed the trustee to recover the value of a $20,000 certificate of deposit from the creditor of a company that had transferred a security interest in the certificate of deposit to a bank, which had transferred a $20,000 letter of credit to the creditor. The company in *Air Conditioning* owed its creditor $20,000. When the company began falling behind on payments, the parties worked out a deal to keep the company in business. As part of the deal, the company issued a $20,000 promissory note to a bank secured by a $20,000 certificate of deposit. The bank, in turn, executed a $20,000 letter of credit to the creditor. After the company entered bankruptcy, we ruled that the transfer of the security interest in the certificate of deposit to the bank constituted an avoidable preference under section 547(b) because it was a transfer of property of the debtor to a creditor within 90 days of filing for bankruptcy that provided more value to the creditor than it would have received under chapter 7 of the Bankruptcy Code. See Bankruptcy Code §547(b). We then ruled that the bankruptcy trustee could recover the value of the certificate of deposit from the creditor because the company granted the security interest to the bank for the benefit of the creditor. We explained that the text of §550(a)(1) allows the trustee to recover from a creditor when it was an entity for whose benefit the transfer of the certificate of deposit was made.

Our decision in *Air Conditioning* controls this appeal. In *Air Conditioning,* the debtor transferred a lien to a lender who transferred funds to a creditor. The transfer of the lien was avoided and, under §550(a)(1), the creditor was an entity for whose benefit the transfer was made. In the same way, the Conveying Subsidiaries transferred liens to the New Lenders, who transferred funds to creditors, the Transeastern Lenders. The bankruptcy court avoided the transfer of the liens and, under §550(a)(1), the Transeastern Lenders were entities for whose benefit the transfer was made.

The Transeastern Lenders attempt to distinguish their appeal from *Air Conditioning* in two ways, but their arguments ignore the material similarities between the preference in that decision and the fraudulent transfer at issue in this appeal. First, the Transeastern Lenders contend that *Air Conditioning* involved a preference under §547 instead of a fraudulent transfer under 548, but "[t]he theory under which a transfer has been avoided is irrelevant to the liability of the transferee against whom the trustee seeks to recover [under §550]." *Danning v. Miller*, 922 F.2d 544, 546 n. 2 (9th Cir.1991). Second, the Transeastern Lenders argue that §550(a)(1) applied in *Air Conditioning* because a letter of credit was involved, but the Transeastern Lenders cannot provide a principled basis for limiting §550(a)(1) to factual scenarios that involve letters of credit.

The Transeastern Lenders also contend that they cannot be liable under §550(a)(1) because they benefitted from a subsequent transfer of funds from TOUSA, not from the initial transfer of the liens, but the record contradicts their assertion. The new loan agreements required that the loan proceeds be used to pay the Transeastern settlement, and the Transeastern settlement expressly depended on the new loans. When the liens were transferred to the New Lenders, the proceeds of the loans went to the Transeastern Lenders. The Transeastern Lenders assert that the funds passed from the New Lenders to a wholly-owned subsidiary of TOUSA before the funds were paid to the Transeastern Lenders, but the subsidiary that wired the money to the Transeastern Lenders did not have control over the funds. The loan documents required the subsidiary to wire the funds to the Transeastern Lenders immediately. Although the funds technically passed through the TOUSA subsidiary, this formality did not make the Transeastern Lenders subsequent transferees of the funds because TOUSA never had control over the funds. *See Nordberg v. Societe Generale (In re Chase & Sanborn Corp.)*, 848 F.2d 1196, 1199 (11th Cir.1988) (stating that courts must apply a "very flexible, pragmatic" test that "look[s] beyond the particular transfers in question to the entire circumstance of the transactions" when deciding whether debtors had controlled property later sought by their trustees); *Bonded Fin. Servs., Inc. v. European American Bank*, 838 F.2d 890, 893 (7th Cir.1988) (holding that a bank was not an initial transferee because it held funds "only for the purpose of fulfilling an instruction to make the funds available to someone else").

The Transeastern Lenders warn that our reading of section 550(a) would drastically expand the potential pool of entities that could be liable for any transaction, but these concerns are unsubstantiated. The Transeastern Lenders offer examples of a parent company taking out a loan secured by its subsidiaries with the specific intent of paying a contractor to build a building for the parent company or paying the dry cleaning bill of the parent company. The Transeastern Lenders caution that the contractor or dry cleaner could be forced to return their payments if the loan securing the money involved a fraudulent transfer, which would impose "extraordinary" duties of due diligence on the part of creditors accepting repayment. But every creditor must exercise some diligence when receiving payment from a struggling debtor. It is far from a drastic obligation to expect some diligence from a creditor when it is being repaid hundreds of millions of dollars by someone other than its debtor.

[The material on "Unreasonably Small Capital" in chapter 8C(2), which begins on *page 324*, should be supplemented by the following.]

Fraudulent conveyance attacks in bankruptcy on prebankruptcy transactions that exacerbate risk remain a potent tool in the hands of a bankruptcy trustee or debtor. And questions continue to arise on what it means for a debtor to be inadequately capitalized for the purposes of fraudulent conveyance law. See, for example, In re Iridium Operating LLC, 373 B.R. 283 (Bankr. S.D.N.Y. 2007), where the court held that there was insufficient evidence of inadequate capitalization despite the debtor's ultimate failure and warned against hindsight bias.

[The material on "Good-Faith Transferee" in chapter 8C(3), which begins on *page 341*, should be supplemented by the following.]

The bankruptcy court's decision in Manhattan Investment Company was affirmed on its general analysis of the law but reversed in its grant of summary judgment on the issue of good faith. See In re Manhattan Investment Fund, Ltd., 397 B.R. 1 (S.D.N.Y. 2007). The court held that a factual dispute existed on the question of whether Bear Stearns was diligent in its investigation once it had reason to be suspicious of Berger's activities. If Bear Stearns could show that it was diligent, it would not be found to have acted in bad faith and would be entitled to the protection of Bankruptcy Code §548(c). Ultimately, Bear Stearns prevailed on the diligence question and escaped liability. Nevertheless, this case strikes fear in financial intermediaries everywhere.

The case of In re Taneja, 743 F.3d 423 (4th Cir. 2014), explores the contours of a good faith defense under §548(c). The court took a flexible approach to how a transferee can establish such a defense.

IX. MANAGING THE ESTATE

[The material on "Sale of Assets" in chapter 9C(2), which begins on *page 447*, should be supplemented by the following.]

The sale of a debtor's important assets in lieu of a traditional reorganization process has become more common recently, and more controversial. The next cases, *Chrysler* and *RadLAX*, offer a deeper and broader view of what is at stake in the modern sales cases.

Chrysler is potentially important in its own right and as a blueprint for the much larger General Motors bankruptcy, which followed shortly thereafter (and broke little new ground). The case, from the Second Circuit, presents not only a sale of the debtor's business as a going concern, but a sale orchestrated by the DIP lender to an entity partly owned by a subset of the debtor's prebankruptcy creditors, those favored by the lender. The question arises whether the sale was an illegitimate *sub rosa* plan. The case more generally tests the bounds, if any, of what a DIP lender, here the United States government, can permissibly demand of the bankruptcy process—restricting the length and terms of an auction, e.g.—and highlights how contract can be used to anticipate and defuse bankruptcy conflict among creditors. (Regarding the latter point, see also Beal Savings Bank v. Sommer, 8 N.Y.3d 318 (2007), which enforced a collective action clause in a loan agreement and raises the question of whether such clauses can substitute for Bankruptcy Code provisions designed to quell minority dissent.) Observe also that Chrysler addresses the issue at the heart of *TWA*, the extent to which a sale can free assets from encumbrances beyond a traditional lien, but note that on this and all other legal issues, the Second Circuit's *Chrysler* opinion is no longer binding precedent (though the bankruptcy court opinion apparently remains), because the Supreme Court vacated the opinion as moot.

Lurking in the background of *Chrysler* is the question of whether a debtor may sell property under §363 free and clear of an undersecured loan without the consent of the secured creditor. The argument that such sale is not permitted comes from §363(f)(3), which permits a sale free and clear of a lien if "the price at which such property is to be sold is greater than the aggregate value of all liens on such property." By implication, a free and clear sale is permitted *only* if the price is greater than the aggregate value of the liens, and so the provision is not meaningless, "value" refers to the amount of the loans rather than the value of the security interests, which are determined by the value of the collateral itself. This, in any case, is the holding of In re PW, LLC, 391 B.R. 25 (9th Cir. BAP 2008), though courts are not unanimous in this view. *Chrysler* was able to sidestep this issue because the court deemed all secured creditors to have consented to the sale.

RadLAX addresses a twist on cases such as *Lionel* and *Chrysler*, which featured challenges to the legitimacy of a §363 sale in lieu of disposition under the Chapter 11 process. In *RadLAX*, a sale of the debtors' assets was conducted not under §363, but as part of the Chapter 11 process. As a consequence, it was contended, secured lenders could be deprived of their right to credit bid, a technique that has traditionally been used by illiquid senior lenders to protect their priority in their debtors' assets. In *RadLAX*, the Supreme Court rejects this contention.

Technical analysis aside, consider, although the *RadLAX* Court declined to do so, whether a restriction on credit bids serves any legitimate policy objective. In this regard, contemplate the case of In re Fisker Automotive Holdings, Inc., 510 B.R. 55 (D. Del. 2014), which limited the amount a secured lender could credit bid "for cause" under Bankruptcy Code §363(k). The stated cause was to promote a robust auction for the debtor's assets, but one might wonder why the court or any other creditor should have reason to object when an undersecured creditor forestalls an auction with a bid for the full amount of its lien.

These are not the only recent cases that explore the judicial authority to structure sales of a debtor's assets over the objection of a claim or interest holder. For another, see In re Texas Rangers, 431 B.R. 706 (Bankr. N.D. Tex. 2010). Among other issues, *Texas Rangers* addresses the propriety of a breakup fee for an initial bidder in an auction for a debtor's business. For another case on the topic of sale structure, see, e.g., American Safety Razor Co LLC, 2010 WL 7427449, (Bankr. D. Del. 2010).

IN RE CHRYSLER LLC

United States Court of Appeals, Second Circuit, 2009
576 F.3d 108, vacated as moot 558 U.S. 1087

JACOBS, CHIEF JUDGE

The Indiana State Police Pension Trust, the Indiana State Teachers Retirement Fund, and the Indiana Major Moves Construction Fund (collectively, the "Indiana Pensioners" or "Pensioners"), along with various tort claimants and others, appeal from an order entered in the United States Bankruptcy Court for the Southern District of New York, Arthur J. Gonzalez, Bankruptcy Judge, dated June 1, 2009 (the "Sale Order"), authorizing the sale of substantially all of the debtor's assets to New CarCo Acquisition LLC ("New Chrysler"). On June 2, 2009 we granted the Indiana Pensioners' motion for a stay and for expedited appeal directly to this Court, pursuant to 28 U.S.C. §158(d)(2). On June 5, 2009 we heard oral argument, and ruled from the bench and by written order, affirming the Sale Order "for the reasons stated in the opinions of Bankruptcy Judge Gonzalez," stating that an opinion or opinions would follow. This is the opinion.

In a nutshell, Chrysler LLC and its related companies (hereinafter "Chrysler" or "debtor" or "Old Chrysler") filed a pre-packaged bankruptcy petition under Chapter 11 on April 30, 2009. The filing followed months in which Chrysler experienced deepening losses, received billions in bailout funds from the Federal Government, searched for a merger partner, unsuccessfully sought additional government bailout funds for a stand-alone restructuring, and ultimately settled on an asset-sale transaction pursuant to §363 (the "Sale"), which was approved by the Sale Order. The key elements of the Sale were set forth in a Master Transaction Agreement dated as of April 30, 2009: substantially all of Chrysler's operating assets (including manufacturing plants, brand names, certain dealer and supplier relationships, and much else) would be transferred to New Chrysler in exchange for New Chrysler's assumption of certain liabilities and $2 billion in cash. Fiat S.p.A agreed to provide New Chrysler with certain fuel-efficient vehicle platforms, access to its worldwide distribution system, and new management that is experienced in turning around a failing auto company. Financing for the sale transaction—$6 billion in senior secured financing, and debtor-in-possession financing for 60 days in the amount of $4.96 billion—would come from the United States Treasury and from Export Development Canada. The agreement describing the United States Treasury's commitment does not specify the source of the funds, but it is undisputed that prior funding came from the Troubled Asset Relief Program ("TARP"), and that the parties expected the Sale to be financed through the use of TARP funds. Ownership of New Chrysler was to be distributed by membership interests, 55% of which go to an employee benefit entity created by the United Auto Workers union, 8% to the United States Treasury and 2% to Export Development Canada. Fiat, for its contributions, would immediately own 20% of the equity with rights to acquire more (up to 51%), contingent on payment in full of the debts owed to the United States Treasury and Export Development Canada.

At a hearing on May 5, 2009, the bankruptcy court approved the debtor's proposed bidding procedures. No other bids were forthcoming. From May 27 to May 29, the bankruptcy court held hearings on whether to approve the Sale. Upon extensive findings of fact and conclusions of law, the bankruptcy court approved the Sale by order dated June 1, 2009.

After briefing and oral argument, we affirmed the bankruptcy court's order on June 5, but we entered a short stay pending Supreme

Court review. The Supreme Court, after an extension of the stay, declined a further extension. The Sale closed on June 10, 2009.

The factual and procedural background is set out in useful detail in the opinions of Bankruptcy Judge Gonzalez. This opinion is confined to a discussion of the arguments made for vacatur or reversal ... . First, it is contended that the sale of Chrysler's auto-manufacturing assets, considered together with the associated intellectual property and (selected) dealership contractual rights, so closely approximates a final plan of reorganization that it constitutes an impermissible "sub rosa plan," and therefore cannot be accomplished under §363(b). We consider this question first, because a determination adverse to Chrysler would have required reversal. Second, we consider the argument by the Indiana Pensioners that the Sale impermissibly subordinates their interests as secured lenders and allows assets on which they have a lien to pass free of liens to other creditors and parties, in violation of §363(f). We reject this argument on the ground that the secured lenders have consented to the Sale, as per §363(f)(2) ... . Finally, we consider and reject the arguments advanced by present and future tort claimants. * * *

The Indiana Pensioners characterize the Sale as an impermissible, sub rosa plan of reorganization. As the Indiana Pensioners characterize it, the Sale transaction "is a 'Sale' in name only; upon consummation, new Chrysler will be old Chrysler in essentially every respect. It will be called 'Chrysler.' ... Its employees, including most man-agement, will be retained.... It will manufacture and sell Chrysler and Dodge cars and minivans, Jeeps and Dodge Trucks.... The real substance of the transaction is the underlying reorganization it implements.

Section 363(b) of the Bankruptcy Code authorizes a Chapter 11 debtor-in-possession to use, sell, or lease estate property outside the ordinary course of business, requiring in most circumstances only that a movant provide notice and a hearing. We have identified an "apparent conflict" between the expedient of a §363(b) sale and the otherwise applicable features and safeguards of Chapter 11. Committee of Equity Security Holders v. Lionel Corp. (In re Lionel Corp.), 722 F.2d 1063, 1071 (2d Cir. 1983).

In *Lionel*, we consulted the history and purpose of §363(b) to situate §363(b) transactions within the overall structure of Chapter 11. The origin of §363(b) is the Bankruptcy Act of 1867, which permitted a sale of a debtor's assets when the estate or any part thereof was "of a perishable nature or liable to deteriorate in value." Lionel, 722 F.2d at

1066. Typically, courts have approved §363(b) sales to preserve " 'wasting asset[s].' " Id. at 1068 (quoting Mintzer v. Joseph (In re Sire Plan, Inc.), 332 F.2d 497, 499 (2d Cir.1964)). Most early transactions concerned perishable commodities; but the same practical necessity has been recognized in contexts other than fruits and vegetables. "[T]here are times when it is more advantageous for the debtor to begin to sell as many assets as quickly as possible in order to insure that the assets do not lose value." Fla. Dep't of Revenue v. Piccadilly Cafeterias, Inc.,554 U.S. 33,57 (2008) (Breyer, J., dissenting) (internal quotation marks omitted); see also In re Pedlow, 209 F. 841, 842 (2d Cir.1913) (upholding sale of a bankrupt's stock of handkerchiefs because the sale price was above the appraised value and "Christmas sales had commenced and ... the sale of handkerchiefs depreciates greatly after the holidays"). Thus, an automobile manufacturing business can be within the ambit of the "melting ice cube" theory of §363(b). As *Lionel* recognized, the text of §363(b) requires no "emergency" to justify approval. For example, if "a good business opportunity [is] presently available," which might soon disappear, quick action may be justified in order to increase (or maintain) the value of an asset to the estate, by means of a lease or sale of the assets. Accordingly, *Lionel* "reject[ed] the requirement that only an emergency permits the use of §363(b)." "[I]f a bankruptcy judge is to administer a business reorganization successfully under the Code, then ... some play for the operation of both § 363(b) and Chapter 11 must be allowed for."

At the same time, *Lionel* "reject[ed] the view that §363(b) grants the bankruptcy judge carte blanche." Id. at 1069. The concern was that a quick, plenary sale of assets outside the ordinary course of business risked circumventing key features of the Chapter 11 process, which afford debt and equity holders the opportunity to vote on a proposed plan of reorganization after receiving meaningful information. Pushed by a bullying creditor, a §363(b) sale might evade such requirements as disclosure, solicitation, acceptance, and confirmation of a plan. If unfettered use of § 363(b) had been intended, there would have been no need for the requirement of notice and hearing prior to approval.

To balance the competing concerns of efficiency against the safeguards of the Chapter 11 process, Lionel required a "good business reason" for a § 363(b) transaction:

> [A bankruptcy judge] should consider all salient factors pertaining to the proceeding and, accordingly, act to further the diverse interests of the debtor, creditors and equity holders, alike. [A bankruptcy judge] might, for example, look to such

relevant factors as the proportionate value of the asset to the estate as a whole, the amount of elapsed time since the filing, the likelihood that a plan of reorganization will be proposed and confirmed in the near future, the effect of the proposed disposition on future plans of reorganization, the proceeds to be obtained from the disposition vis-a-vis any appraisals of the property, which of the alternatives of use, sale or lease the proposal envisions and, most importantly perhaps, whether the asset is increasing or decreasing in value. This list is not intended to be exclusive, but merely to provide guidance to the bankruptcy judge. 722 F.2d at 1071.

After weighing these considerations, the Court in *Lionel* reversed a bankruptcy court's approval of the sale of Lionel Corporation's equity stake in another corporation, Dale Electronics, Inc. ("Dale"). The Court relied heavily on testimony from Lionel's Chief Executive Officer, who conceded that it was "only at the insistence of the Creditors' Committee that Dale stock was being sold and that Lionel 'would very much like to retain its interest in Dale,' " as well as on a financial expert's acknowledgment that the value of the Dale stock was not decreasing. Since the Dale stock was not a wasting asset, and the proffered justification for selling the stock was the desire of creditors, no sufficient business reasons existed for approving the sale.

In the twenty-five years since Lionel, §363(b) asset sales have become common practice in large-scale corporate bankruptcies. A law review article recounts the phenomenon:

> Corporate reorganizations have all but disappeared.... TWA filed only to consummate the sale of its planes and landing gates to American Airlines. Enron's principal assets, including its trading operation and its most valuable pipelines, were sold within a few months of its bankruptcy petition. Within weeks of filing for Chapter 11, Budget sold most of its assets to the parent company of Avis. Similarly, Polaroid entered Chapter 11 and sold most of its assets to the private equity group at BankOne. Even when a large firm uses Chapter 11 as something other than a convenient auction block, its principal lenders are usually already in control and Chapter 11 merely puts in place a preexisting deal.

Douglas G. Baird & Robert K. Rasmussen, *The End of Bankruptcy*, 55 Stan. L. Rev. 751, 751-52 (2002). In the current economic crisis of 2008-09, §363(b) sales have become even more useful and customary.

The "side door" of §363(b) may well "replace the main route of Chapter 11 reorganization plans." Jason Brege, Note, An Efficiency Model of Section 363(b) Sales, 92 Va. L.Rev. 1639, 1640 (2006).

Resort to §363(b) has been driven by efficiency, from the perspectives of sellers and buyers alike. The speed of the process can maximize asset value by sale of the debtor's business as a going concern. Moreover, the assets are typically burnished (or "cleansed") because (with certain limited exceptions) they are sold free and clear of liens, claims and liabilities. A §363 sale can often yield the highest price for the assets because the buyer can select the liabilities it will assume and purchase a business with cash flow (or the near prospect of it). Often, a secured creditor can "credit bid," or take an ownership interest in the company by bidding a reduction in the debt the company owes.

This tendency has its critics. The objections are not to the quantity or percentage of assets being sold: it has long been understood sales may encompass all or substantially all of a debtor's assets. Rather, the thrust of criticism remains what it was in Lionel: fear that one class of creditors may strong-arm the debtor-in-possession, and bypass the requirements of Chapter 11 to cash out quickly at the expense of other stakeholders, in a proceeding that amounts to a reorganization in all but name, achieved by stealth and momentum. See, e.g., Motorola, Inc. v. Official Comm. of Unsecured Creditors and JPMorgan Chase Bank, N.A. (In re Iridium Operating LLC), 478 F.3d 452, 466 (2d Cir.2007) ("The reason sub rosa plans are prohibited is based on a fear that a debtor-in-possession will enter into transactions that will, in effect, short circuit the requirements of Chapter 11 for confirmation of a reorganization plan."

Chapter 11 bankruptcy proceedings ordinarily culminate in the confirmation of a reorganization plan. But in some cases, as here, a debtor sells all or substantially all its assets under §363(b)(1) before seeking or receiving plan confirmation. In this scenario, the debtor typically submits for confirmation a plan of liquidation (rather than a traditional plan of reorganization) providing for the distribution of the proceeds resulting from the sale.

As §363(b) sales proliferate, the competing concerns identified in *Lionel* have become harder to manage. Debtors need flexibility and speed to preserve going concern value; yet one or more classes of creditors should not be able to nullify Chapter 11's requirements. A balance is not easy to achieve, and is not aided by rigid rules and prescriptions.

Lionel's multi-factor analysis remains the proper, most comprehensive framework for judging the validity of §363(b) transactions.

Adopting the Fifth Circuit's wording in *Braniff*, 700 commentators and courts—including ours—have sometimes referred to improper §363(b) transactions as "sub rosa plans of reorganization." *Braniff* rejected a proposed transfer agreement in large part because the terms of the agreement specifically attempted to "dictat[e] some of the terms of any future reorganization plan. The [subsequent] reorganization plan would have to allocate the [proceeds of the sale] according to the terms of the [transfer] agreement or forfeit a valuable asset." 700 F.2d at 940. As the Fifth Circuit concluded, "[t]he debtor and the Bankruptcy Court should not be able to short circuit the requirements of Chapter 11 for confirmation of a reorganization plan by establishing the terms of the plan sub rosa in connection with a sale of assets." Id.

The term "sub rosa" is something of a misnomer. It bespeaks a covert or secret activity, whereas secrecy has nothing to do with a §363 transaction. Transactions blessed by the bankruptcy courts are openly presented, considered, approved, and implemented. Braniff seems to have used "sub rosa" to describe transactions that treat the requirements of the Bankruptcy Code as something to be evaded or subverted. But even in that sense, the term is unhelpful. The sale of assets is permissible under §363(b); and it is elementary that the more assets sold that way, the less will be left for a plan of reorganization, or for liquidation. But the size of the transaction, and the residuum of corporate assets, is, under our precedent, just one consideration for the exercise of discretion by the bankruptcy judge(s), along with an open-ended list of other salient factors.

Braniff's holding did not support the argument that a § 363(b) asset sale must be rejected simply because it is a sale of all or substantially all of a debtor's assets. Thus a §363(b) sale may well be a reorganization in effect without being the kind of plan rejected in *Braniff*. Although *Lionel* did not involve a contention that the proposed sale was a sub rosa or de facto reorganization, a bankruptcy court confronted with that allegation may approve or disapprove a §363(b) transfer that is a sale of all or substantially all of a debtor's assets, using the analysis set forth in *Lionel* in order to determine whether there was a good business reason for the sale.

The Indiana Pensioners argue that the Sale is a sub rosa plan chiefly because it gives value to unsecured creditors (i.e., in the form of the ownership interest in New Chrysler provided to the union benefit funds) without paying off secured debt in full, and without complying with the procedural requirements of Chapter 11. However, Bankruptcy Judge Gonzalez demonstrated proper solicitude for the priority between creditors and deemed it essential that the Sale in no way upset that priority. The lien holders' security interests would attach to all proceeds of the Sale: "Not one penny of value of the Debtors' assets is going to anyone other than the First-Lien Lenders." As Bankruptcy Judge Gonzalez found, all the equity stakes in New Chrysler were entirely attributable to new value-including governmental loans, new technology, and new management-which were not assets of the debtor's estate.

The Indiana Pensioners' arguments boil down to the complaint that the Sale does not pass the discretionary, multifarious *Lionel* test. The bankruptcy court's findings constitute an adequate rebuttal. Applying the *Lionel* factors, Bankruptcy Judge Gonzalez found good business reasons for the Sale. The linchpin of his analysis was that the only possible alternative to the Sale was an immediate liquidation that would yield far less for the estate-and for the objectors. The court found that, notwithstanding Chrysler's prolonged and well-publicized efforts to find a strategic partner or buyer, no other proposals were forthcoming. In the months leading up to Chrysler's bankruptcy filing, and during the bankruptcy process itself, Chrysler executives circled the globe in search of a deal. But the Fiat transaction was the only offer available. Sale Opinion at 6; see id. at 16-17 ("Notwithstanding the highly publicized and extensive efforts that have been expended in the last two years to seek various alliances for Chrysler, the Fiat Transaction is the only option that is currently viable. The only other alternative is the immediate liquidation of the company.").

The Sale would yield $2 billion. According to expert testimony—not refuted by the objectors—an immediate liquidation of Chrysler as of May 20, 2009 would yield in the range of nothing to $800 million. Crucially, Fiat had conditioned its commitment on the Sale being completed by June 15, 2009. While this deadline was tight and seemingly arbitrary, there was little leverage to force an extension. To preserve resources, Chrysler factories had been shuttered, and the business was hemorrhaging cash. According to the bankruptcy court, Chrysler was losing going concern value of nearly $100 million each day.

On this record, and in light of the arguments made by the parties, the bankruptcy court's approval of the Sale was no abuse of discretion. With its revenues sinking, its factories dark, and its massive debts growing, Chrysler fit the paradigm of the melting ice cube. Going concern value was being reduced each passing day that it produced no cars, yet was obliged to pay rents, overhead, and salaries. Consistent with an underlying purpose of the Bankruptcy Code—maximizing the value of the bankrupt estate—it was no abuse of discretion to determine that the Sale prevented further, unnecessary losses.

The Indiana Pensioners exaggerate the extent to which New Chrysler will emerge from the Sale as the twin of Old Chrysler. New Chrysler may manufacture the same lines of cars but it will also make newer, smaller vehicles using Fiat technology that will become available as a result of the Sale—moreover, at the time of the proceedings, Old Chrysler was manufacturing no cars at all. New Chrysler will be run by a new Chief Executive Officer, who has experience in turning around failing auto companies. It may retain many of the same employees, but they will be working under new union contracts that contain a six-year no-strike provision. New Chrysler will still sell cars in some of its old dealerships in the United States, but it will also have new access to Fiat dealerships in the European market. Such transformative use of old and new assets is precisely what one would expect from the § 363(b) sale of a going concern. * * *

The Indiana Pensioners next challenge the Sale Order's release of all liens on Chrysler's assets. In general, under §363(f), assets sold pursuant to §363(b) may be sold "free and clear of any interest" in the assets when, inter alia, the entity holding the interest consents to the sale. The bankruptcy court ruled that, although the Indiana Pensioners did not themselves consent to the release, consent was validly provided by the collateral trustee, who had authority to act on behalf of all first-lien credit holders.

We agree. Through a series of agreements, the Pensioners effectively ceded to an agent the power to consent to such a sale; the agent gave consent; and the Pensioners are bound. Accordingly, questions as to the status or preference of Chrysler's secured debt are simply not presented in this case.

The first-lien holders—among them, the Indiana Pensioners—arranged their investment in Chrysler by means of three related agreements: a First Lien Credit Agreement, a Collateral Trust Agreement, and a Form of Security Agreement. Together, these agreements create a framework for the control of collateral property. The collateral is held by a designated trustee for the benefit of the various lenders (including the Indiana Pensioners). In the event of a bankruptcy, the trustee is empowered to take any action deemed necessary to protect, preserve, or realize upon the collateral. The trustee may only exercise this power at the direction of the lenders' agent; but the lenders are required to authorize the agent to act on their behalf, and any action the agent takes at the request of lenders holding a majority of Chrysler's debt is binding on all lenders, those who agree and those who do not.

When Chrysler went into bankruptcy, the trustee had power to take any action necessary to realize upon the collateral—including giving consent to the sale of the collateral free and clear of all interests under §363. The trustee could take such action only at the direction of the lenders' agent, and the agent could only direct the trustee at the request of lenders holding a majority of Chrysler's debt. But if those conditions were met—as they were here—then under the terms of the various agreements, the minority lenders could not object to the trustee's actions since they had given their authorization in the first place.

The Indiana Pensioners argue that, by virtue of a subclause in one of the loan agreements, Chrysler required the Pensioners' written consent before selling the collateral assets. The clause in question provides that the loan documents themselves could not be amended without the written consent of all lenders if the amendment would result in the release of all, or substantially all, of the collateral property. This clause is no help to the Indiana Pensioners. The §363(b) Sale did not entail amendment of any loan document. To the contrary, the §363(b) sale was effected by implementing the clear terms of the loan agreements—specifically, the terms by which (1) the lenders assigned an agent to act on their behalf, (2) the agent was empowered, upon request from the majority lenders, to direct the trustee to act, and (3) the trustee was empowered, at the direction of the agent, to sell the collateral in the event of a bankruptcy. Because the Sale required no amendment to the loan documents, Chrysler was not required to seek, let alone receive, the Pensioners' written consent.

Anticipating the consequence of this contractual framework, the Indiana Pensioners argue as a last resort that the majority lenders were intimidated or bullied into approving the Sale in order to preserve or enhance relations with the government, or other players in the transaction. Absent this bullying, the Pensioners suggest, the majority lenders would not have requested the agent to direct the sale of the collateral, and the Sale would not have gone through. The Pensioners argue that this renders the lenders' consent ineffective or infirm.

The record before the bankruptcy court, and the record before this Court, does not support a finding that the majority lenders were coerced into agreeing to the Sale. On the whole, the record (and findings) support the view that they acted prudently to preserve substantial value rather than risk a liquidation that might have yielded nothing at all. Moreover, it is not at all clear what impact a finding of coerced consent would have on the validity of the consent given, or whether the bankruptcy court would have jurisdiction—or occasion—to adjudicate the Indiana Pensioners' allegation. Because the facts alleged by the Indiana Pensioners are not substantiated in this record, their arguments based on those allegations provide no ground for relief in this proceeding, and we decline to consider whether the allegations might give rise to some independent cause of action. * * *

Finally, several objectors appeal from that portion of the Sale Order extinguishing all existing and future claims against New Chrysler, that "(a) arose prior to the Closing Date, (b) relate[ ] to the production of vehicles prior to the Closing Date or (c) otherwise [are] assertable against the Debtors or [are] related to the Purchased Assets prior to the closing date." The objectors can be divided into three groups: (1) plaintiffs with existing product liability claims against Chrysler; (2) plaintiffs with existing asbestos-related claims against Chrysler; and (3) lawyers undertaking to act on behalf of claimants who, although presently unknown and unidentified, might have claims in the future arising from Old Chrysler's production of vehicles. We consider each group's arguments in turn … .

Section 363(f) provides, in relevant part, that a "trustee may sell property ... free and clear of *any interest in such property*," under certain circumstances. The objectors argue that personal injury claims are not "interests in property," and that the district court's reliance on In re Trans World Airlines, Inc., 322 F.3d 283 (3d Cir.2003) ("*TWA*"), which advances a broad reading of "interests in property," was misplaced.

We have never addressed the scope of the language "any interest in such property," and the statute does not define the term.

In *TWA*, the Third Circuit considered whether (1) employment discrimination claims and (2) a voucher program awarded to flight attendants in settlement of a class action constituted "interests" in property for purposes of § 363(f). The Third Circuit began its analysis by noting that bankruptcy courts around the country have disagreed about whether "any interest" should be defined broadly or narrowly. The

Third Circuit observed, however, that "the trend seems to be toward a more expansive reading of 'interests in property' which 'encompasses other obligations that may flow from ownership of the property.' "

The Third Circuit reasoned that "to equate interests in property with only in rem interests such as liens would be inconsistent with section 363(f)(3), which contemplates that a lien is but one type of interest." 322 F.3d at 290. After surveying its owns precedents and the Fourth Circuit's decision in United Mine Workers of Am.1992 Benefit Plan v. Leckie Smokeless Coal Co. (In re Leckie Smokeless Coal Co.), 99 F.3d 573 (4th Cir.1996), the *TWA* court held that "[w]hile the interests of the [plaintiffs] in the assets of TWA's bankruptcy estate are not interests in property in the sense that they are not in rem interests, ... they are interests in property within the meaning of section 363(f) in the sense that they arise from the property being sold." 322 F.3d at 290 (emphasis added).

Shortly after *TWA* was decided, the Southern District of California concluded that *TWA* applied to tort claimants asserting personal injury claims. See Myers v. United States, 297 B.R. 774, 781-82 (S.D. Cal. 2003). *Myers* involved claims arising from the negligent handling of toxic materials transported pursuant to a government contract. Applying *TWA*, the *Myers* court ruled that the plaintiff's "claim for personal injury does arise from the property being sold, i.e. the contracts to transport toxic materials."

Appellants argue that these decisions broadly construing the phrase "any interest in such property" fail to account for the language of §1141(c), a provision involving confirmed plans of reorganization. Section 1141(c) provides that "except as otherwise provided in the [reorganization] plan or in the order confirming the plan, after confirmation of a plan, the property dealt with by the plan is free and clear of *all claims and interests* of creditors, equity security holders, and of general partners in the debtor." §1141(c) (emphasis added). Appellants argue that Congress must have intentionally included the word "claims" in §1141(c), and omitted the word from §363(f), because it was willing to extinguish tort claims in the reorganization context, but unwilling to do so in the §363 sale context. Appellants account for this discrepancy on the basis that reorganization provides unsecured creditors procedural rights that are not assured in a §363(b) sale.

We do not place such weight on the absence of the word "claims" in §363(f). The language and structure of §1141(c) and §363(f) differ in many respects. Section 1141(c), for example, applies to all reorganization plans; §363(f), in contrast, applies only to classes of property that satisfy one of five criteria. Thus, while §363 sales do not afford many of the procedural safeguards of a reorganization, §363(f) is limited to specific classes of property.

Given the expanded role of §363 in bankruptcy proceedings, it makes sense to harmonize the application of §1141(c) and §363(f) to the extent permitted by the statutory language. See In re Golf, LLC, 322 B.R. 874, 877 (Bankr. D. Neb.2004) (noting that, while §363(f) requires less notice and provides for less opportunity for a hearing than in the reorganization process, "as a practical matter, current practice seems to have expanded §363(f)'s use from its original intent"). Courts have already done this in other contexts. For example, §1141(c) does not explicitly reference the extinguishment of liens, while §363(f) does. Notwithstanding this distinction, courts have uniformly held that confirmation of a reorganization can act to extinguish liens.

We agree with *TWA* and *Leckie* that the term "any interest in property" encompasses those claims that "arise from the property being sold." By analogy to *Leckie* (in which the relevant business was coal mining), "[appellants'] rights are grounded, at least in part, in the fact that [Old Chrysler's] very assets have been employed for [automobile production] purposes: if Appellees had never elected to put their assets to use in the [automobile] industry, and had taken up business in an altogether different area, [appellants] would have no right to seek [damages]." Leckie, 99 F.3d at 582.

"To allow the claimants to assert successor liability claims against [the purchaser] while limiting other creditors' recourse to the proceeds of the asset sale would be inconsistent with the Bankruptcy Code's priority scheme." TWA, 322 F.3d at 292. Appellants ignore this overarching principle and assume that tort claimants faced a choice between the Sale and an alternative arrangement that would have assured funding for their claims. But had appellants successfully blocked the Sale, they would have been unsecured creditors fighting for a share of extremely limited liquidation proceeds. Given the billions of dollars of outstanding secured claims against Old Chrysler, appellants would have fared no better had they prevailed.

The possibility of transferring assets free and clear of existing tort liability was a critical inducement to the Sale. As in *TWA*, "a sale of the assets of [Old Chrysler] at the expense of preserving successor liability claims was necessary in order to preserve some [55],000 jobs, ... and to provide funding for employee-related liabilities, including retirement benefits [for more than 106,000 retirees]." TWA, 322 F.3d at 293.

It is the transfer of Old Chrysler's tangible and intellectual property to New Chrysler that could lead to successor liability (where applicable under state law) in the absence of the Sale Order's liability provisions. Because appellants' claims arose from Old Chrysler's property, § 363(f) permitted the bankruptcy court to authorize the Sale free and clear of appellants' interest in the property … .

The Sale Order extinguished the right to pursue claims "on any theory of successor or transferee liability, whether known or unknown as of the Closing, now existing or hereafter arising, asserted or unasserted, fixed or contingent, liquidated or unliquidated." Sale Order at 40-41. This provision is challenged on the grounds that: (1) the Sale Order violates the due process rights of future claimants by extinguishing claims without providing notice; (2) a bankruptcy court is not empowered to trump state successor liability law; (3) future, unidentified claimants with unquantifiable interests could not be compelled "to accept a money satisfaction," Bankruptcy Code §363(f)(5); and (4) future causes of action by unidentified plaintiffs based on unknown events cannot be classified as "claims" under the Bankruptcy Code.

We affirm this aspect of the bankruptcy court's decision insofar as it constituted a valid exercise of authority under the Bankruptcy Code. However, we decline to delineate the scope of the bankruptcy court's authority to extinguish future claims, until such time as we are presented with an actual claim for an injury that is caused by Old Chrysler, that occurs after the Sale, and that is cognizable under state successor liability law. * * *

We have considered all of the objectors-appellants' contentions on these appeals and have found them to be without merit. For the foregoing reasons, we affirm the June 1, 2009 order of the bankruptcy court authorizing the Sale.

RADLAX GATEWAY HOTEL, LLC V. AMALGAMATED BANK

United States Supreme Court, 2012
132 S.Ct. 2065

SCALIA, JUSTICE

We consider whether a Chapter 11 bankruptcy plan may be confirmed over the objection of a secured creditor pursuant to Bankruptcy

Code §1129(b)(2)(A) if the plan provides for the sale of collateral free and clear of the creditor's lien, but does not permit the creditor to "credit-bid" at the sale.

I

In 2007, petitioners RadLAX Gateway Hotel, LLC, and RadLAX Gateway Deck, LLC (hereinafter debtors), purchased the Radisson Hotel at Los Angeles International Airport, together with an adjacent lot on which the debtors planned to build a parking structure. To finance the purchase, the renovation of the hotel, and construction of the parking structure, the debtors obtained a $142 million loan from Longview Ultra Construction Loan Investment Fund, for which respondent Amalgamated Bank (hereinafter creditor or Bank) serves as trustee. The lenders obtained a blanket lien on all of the debtors' assets to secure the loan.

Completing the parking structure proved more expensive than anticipated, and within two years the debtors had run out of funds and were forced to halt construction. By August 2009, they owed more than $120 million on the loan, with over $1 million in interest accruing every month and no prospect for obtaining additional funds to complete the project. Both debtors filed voluntary petitions for relief under Chapter 11 of the Bankruptcy Code.

A Chapter 11 bankruptcy is implemented according to a "plan," typically proposed by the debtor, which divides claims against the debtor into separate "classes" and specifies the treatment each class will receive. See Bankruptcy Code §1123. Generally, a bankruptcy court may confirm a Chapter 11 plan only if each class of creditors affected by the plan consents. See §1129(a)(8). Section 1129(b) creates an exception to that general rule, permitting confirmation of nonconsensual plans—commonly known as "cramdown" plans—if "the plan does not discriminate unfairly, and is fair and equitable, with respect to each class of claims or interests that is impaired under, and has not accepted, the plan." Section 1129(b)(2)(A), which we review in further depth below, establishes criteria for determining whether a cramdown plan is "fair and equitable" with respect to secured claims like the Bank's.

In 2010, the RadLAX debtors submitted a Chapter 11 plan to the United States Bankruptcy Court for the Northern District of Illinois. The plan proposed to dissolve the debtors and to sell substantially all of their assets pursuant to procedures set out in a contemporaneously filed "Sale and Bid Procedures Motion." Specifically, the debtors sought to auction their assets to the highest bidder, with the initial bid submitted by a "stalking horse"—a potential purchaser who was willing to make an advance bid of $47.5 million. The sale proceeds would be used to fund the plan, primarily by repaying the Bank. Of course the Bank itself might wish to obtain the property if the alternative would be receiving auction proceeds that fall short of the property's full value. Under the debtors' proposed auction procedures, however, the Bank would not be permitted to bid for the property using the debt it is owed to offset the purchase price, a practice known as "credit-bidding." Instead, the Bank would be forced to bid cash. Correctly anticipating that the Bank would object to this arrangement, the debtors sought to confirm their plan under the cramdown provisions of § 1129(b)(2)(A).

The Bankruptcy Court denied the debtors' Sale and Bid Procedures Motion, concluding that the proposed auction procedures did not comply with §1129(b)(2)(A)'s requirements for cramdown plans. The Bankruptcy Court certified an appeal directly to the United States Court of Appeals for the Seventh Circuit. That court accepted the certification and affirmed, holding that §1129(b)(2)(A) does not permit debtors to sell an encumbered asset free and clear of a lien without permitting the lienholder to credit-bid..

II

A

A Chapter 11 plan confirmed over the objection of a "class of secured claims" must meet one of three requirements in order to be deemed "fair and equitable" with respect to the nonconsenting creditor's claim. The plan must provide:

(i)(I) that the holders of such claims retain the liens securing such claims, whether the property subject to such liens is retained by the debtor or transferred to another entity, to the extent of the allowed amount of such claims; and (II) that each holder of a claim of such class receive on account of such claim deferred cash payments totaling at least the allowed amount of such claim, of a value, as of the effective date of the plan, of at least the value of such holder's interest in the estate's interest in such property;

(ii) for the sale, subject to section 363(k) of this title, of any property that is subject to the liens securing such claims, free and clear of such liens, with such liens to attach to the proceeds of such sale, and the treatment of such liens on proceeds under clause (i) or (iii) of this subparagraph; or

(iii) for the realization by such holders of the indubitable equivalent of such claims.

11 U.S.C. § 1129(b)(2)(A).

Under clause (i), the secured creditor retains its lien on the property and receives deferred cash payments. Under clause (ii), the property is sold free and clear of the lien, "subject to section 363(k)," and the creditor receives a lien on the proceeds of the sale. Section 363(k), in turn, provides that "unless the court for cause orders otherwise the holder of such claim may bid at such sale, and, if the holder of such claim purchases such property, such holder may offset such claim against the purchase price of such property"—*i.e.,* the creditor may credit-bid at the sale, up to the amount of its claim.[2] Finally, under clause (iii), the plan provides the secured creditor with the "indubitable equivalent" of its claim.

The debtors in this case have proposed to sell their property free and clear of the Bank's liens, and to repay the Bank using the sale proceeds—precisely, it would seem, the disposition contemplated by clause (ii). Yet since the debtors' proposed auction procedures do not permit the Bank to credit-bid, the proposed sale cannot satisfy the requirements of clause (ii).[3] Recognizing this problem, the debtors instead seek plan confirmation pursuant to clause (iii), which—unlike clause (ii)—does not expressly foreclose the possibility of a sale without credit-bidding. According to the debtors, their plan can satisfy clause (iii) by ultimately providing the Bank with the "indubitable equivalent" of its secured claim, in the form of cash generated by the auction.

We find the debtors' reading of §1129(b)(2)(A)—under which clause (iii) permits precisely what clause (ii) proscribes—to be hyper-

---

[2] The ability to credit-bid helps to protect a creditor against the risk that its collateral will be sold at a depressed price. It enables the creditor to purchase the collateral for what it considers the fair market price (up to the amount of its security interest) without committing additional cash to protect the loan. That right is particularly important for the Federal Government, which is frequently a secured creditor in bankruptcy and which often lacks appropriations authority to throw good money after bad in a cash-only bankruptcy auction.

[3] Bankruptcy Code §363(k)—and by extension clause (ii)—provides an exception to the credit-bidding requirement if "the court for cause orders otherwise." The Bankruptcy Court found that there was no "cause" to deny credit-bidding in this case, and the debtors have not appealed that disposition.

literal and contrary to common sense. A well-established canon of statutory interpretation succinctly captures the problem: "[I]t is a commonplace of statutory construction that the specific governs the general." *Morales v. Trans World Airlines, Inc.,* 504 U.S. 374, 384 (1992). That is particularly true where, as in §1129(b)(2)(A), "Congress has enacted a comprehensive scheme and has deliberately targeted specific problems with specific solutions." *Varity Corp. v. Howe,* 516 U.S. 489, 519 (1996) (Thomas, J., dissenting); see also *HCSC–Laundry v. United States,* 450 U.S. 1, 6 (1981) *(per curiam)* (the specific governs the general "particularly when the two are interrelated and closely positioned, both in fact being parts of [the same statutory scheme]").

The general/specific canon is perhaps most frequently applied to statutes in which a general permission or prohibition is contradicted by a specific prohibition or permission. To eliminate the contradiction, the specific provision is construed as an exception to the general one. But the canon has full application as well to statutes such as the one here, in which a general authorization and a more limited, specific authorization exist side-by-side. There the canon avoids not contradiction but the superfluity of a specific provision that is swallowed by the general one, "violat[ing] the cardinal rule that, if possible, effect shall be given to every clause and part of a statute." *D. Ginsberg & Sons, Inc. v. Popkin,* 285 U.S. 204, 208 (1932). The terms of the specific authorization must be complied with. For example, in the last cited case a provision of the Bankruptcy Act prescribed in great detail the procedures governing the arrest and detention of bankrupts about to leave the district in order to avoid examination. The Court held that those prescriptions could not be avoided by relying upon a general provision of the Act authorizing bankruptcy courts to " 'make such orders, issue such process, and enter such judgments in addition to those specifically provided for as may be necessary for the enforcement of the provisions of [the] Act.' " *Id.,* at 206 (quoting Bankruptcy Act of 1898, § 2(15), 30 Stat. 546). The Court said that "[g]eneral language of a statutory provision, although broad enough to include it, will not be held to apply to a matter specifically dealt with in another part of the same enactment." 285 U.S., at 208. ... Or as we said in a much earlier case:

> It is an old and familiar rule that, where there is, in the same statute, a particular enactment, and also a general one, which, in its most comprehensive sense, would include what is embraced in the former, the particular enactment must be operative, and the general enactment must be taken to affect only such cases within its general language as are not within the

provisions of the particular enactment. This rule applies wherever an act contains general provisions and also special ones upon a subject, which, standing alone, the general provisions would include.

United States v. Chase, 135 U.S. 255, 260 (1890).

Here, clause (ii) is a detailed provision that spells out the requirements for selling collateral free of liens, while clause (iii) is a broadly worded provision that says nothing about such a sale. The general/specific canon explains that the "general language" of clause (iii), "although broad enough to include it, will not be held to apply to a matter specifically dealt with" in clause (ii). *D. Ginsberg & Sons, Inc., supra,* at 208.

Of course the general/specific canon is not an absolute rule, but is merely a strong indication of statutory meaning that can be overcome by textual indications that point in the other direction. The debtors point to no such indication here. One can conceive of a statutory scheme in which the specific provision embraced within a general one is not superfluous, because it creates a so-called safe harbor. The debtors effectively contend that that is the case here—clause (iii) ("indubitable equivalent") being the general rule, and clauses (i) and (ii) setting forth procedures that will always, *ipso facto,* establish an "indubitable equivalent," with no need for judicial evaluation. But the structure here would be a surpassingly strange manner of accomplishing that result—which would normally be achieved by setting forth the "indubitable equivalent" rule first (rather than last), and establishing the two safe harbors as provisos to that rule. The structure here suggests, to the contrary, that (i) is the rule for plans under which the creditor's lien remains on the property, (ii) is the rule for plans under which the property is sold free and clear of the creditor's lien, and (iii) is a residual provision covering dispositions under all other plans—for example, one under which the creditor receives the property itself, the "indubitable equivalent" of its secured claim. Thus, debtors may not sell their property free of liens under §1129(b)(2)(A) without allowing lienholders to credit-bid, as required by clause (ii).

B

None of the debtors' objections to this approach is valid.

The debtors' principal textual argument is that §1129(b)(2)(A) "unambiguously provides three distinct options for confirming a Chapter 11 plan over the objection of a secured creditor." Brief for Petitioners.

With that much we agree; the three clauses of §1129(b)(2)(A) are connected by the disjunctive "or." The debtors contend that our interpretation of §1129(b)(2)(A) "transforms 'or' into 'and.' " Reply Brief for Petitioners. But that is not so. The question here is not whether debtors must comply with more than one clause, but rather which one of the three they must satisfy. Debtors seeking to sell their property free of liens under §1129(b)(2)(A) must satisfy the requirements of clause (ii), not the requirements of *both* clauses (ii) and (iii).

The debtors make several arguments against applying the general/specific canon. They contend that clause (ii) is no more specific than clause (iii), because the former provides a procedural protection to secured creditors (credit-bidding) while the latter provides a substantive protection (indubitable equivalence). As a result, they say, clause (ii) is not "a limiting subset" of clause (iii), which (according to their view) application of the general/specific canon requires. Brief for Petitioners. To begin with, we know of no authority for the proposition that the canon is confined to situations in which the entirety of the specific provision is a "subset" of the general one. When the conduct at issue falls within the scope of *both* provisions, the specific presumptively governs, whether or not the specific provision also applies to some conduct that falls outside the general. In any case, we think clause (ii) is entirely a subset. Clause (iii) applies to *all* cramdown plans, which include all of the plans within the more narrow category described in clause (ii).[4] That its requirements are "substantive" whereas clause (ii)'s are "procedural" is quite beside the point. What counts for application of the general/specific canon is not the *nature* of the provisions' prescriptions but their *scope*.

Finally, the debtors contend that the Court of Appeals conflated approval of bid procedures with plan confirmation. They claim the right to pursue their auction now, leaving it for the Bankruptcy Judge to determine, at the confirmation stage, whether the resulting plan (funded by auction proceeds) provides the Bank with the "indubitable equivalent" of its secured claim. Under our interpretation of §1129(b)(2)(A), however, that approach is simply a nonstarter. As a matter of law, no

---

[4] We are speaking here about whether clause (ii) is a subset for purposes of determining whether the canon applies. As we have described earlier, *after* applying the canon—*ex post,* so to speak—it ceases to be a subset, governing a situation to which clause (iii) will no longer be deemed applicable.

bid procedures like the ones proposed here *could* satisfy the requirements of §1129(b)(2)(A), and the distinction between approval of bid procedures and plan confirmation is therefore irrelevant.

III

The parties debate at some length the purposes of the Bankruptcy Code, pre-Code practices, and the merits of credit-bidding. To varying extents, some of those debates also occupied the attention of the Courts of Appeals that considered the question presented here. But nothing in the generalized statutory purpose of protecting secured creditors can overcome the specific manner of that protection which the text of §1129(b)(2)(A) contains. As for pre-Code practices, they can be relevant to the interpretation of an ambiguous text, but we find no textual ambiguity here. And the pros and cons of credit-bidding are for the consideration of Congress, not the courts.

The Bankruptcy Code standardizes an expansive (and sometimes unruly) area of law, and it is our obligation to interpret the Code clearly and predictably using well established principles of statutory construction. Under that approach, this is an easy case. Because the RadLAX debtors may not obtain confirmation of a Chapter 11 cramdown plan that provides for the sale of collateral free and clear of the Bank's lien, but does not permit the Bank to credit-bid at the sale, we affirm the judgment of the Court of Appeals.

[The material on "Debtor-in-Possession Financing" in chapter 9D(1), which begins on **page 479**, should be supplemented by the following.]

In re Barbara K. Enterprises, Inc., 2008 WL 2439649 (Bankr. S.D.N.Y 2008), is a case that rejected an aggressive request for favorable terms on a proposed DIP loan. The would-be DIP lender wanted to prime the security interests of prebankruptcy lenders, one of whom strenuously objected. The court held that the prospects of the debtor's success with or without the new loan were not great enough to justify putting the earlier secured creditors' return at risk even if that meant that the debtor could no longer operate as a going concern. The debtor in *Barbara K. Enterprises* was not a large business, but the principle established has broad implications: there are some loans that a debtor cannot take even as the only means to survive.

[The material on "Administrative Expenses" in chapter 9D(2), which begins on ***page 494***, should be supplemented by the following.]

In re Goody's Family Clothing, Inc., 610 F.3d 812 (3rd Cir. 2010), holds that a debtor's obligation to make post-petition payments on non-residential real estate leases under Bankruptcy Code §365(d)(3) does not supplant a lessor's administrative expense priority for a debtor's post-petition use of the leased premises. At issue was the debtor's unpaid obligation for "stub" rent, that is, rent for the portion of the month after the date of the bankruptcy petition but before the next payment was due under the lease.

X. PRIORITIES IN DISTRIBUTION

[The material on "Judicial Subordination" in chapter 10B, which begins on ***page 538***, should be supplemented by the following.]

Not every sort of judicial subordination is accomplished formally. Consider the case of *National Gas Distributors*, reproduced above on page 48 of this supplement, in which the court countenances bankruptcy decisions based on consideration of a business affiliate's welfare but denies that such consideration amounts to substantive consolidation of the entities in the affiliate. For another recent case that addresses implicit substantive consolidation, see In re Adelphia Communications, Corp., 544 F.3d 420 (2nd Cir. 2011) (stating in dicta that de facto substantive consolidation would in that case be unobjectionable so long as any adversely affected class approved the plan).

Turning now to the question of direct subordination (or disallowance) of claims, the court in In re Washington Mutual, 461 B.R. 200 (Bankr. D. Del. 2011), held that equity holders have standing to bring an action for equitable disallowance—as distinguished from equitable subordination—against claim holders who trade in a debtor's securities with the benefit of nonpublic information gained through the bankruptcy negotiation process. The point of disallowance, as opposed to subordination, is that the former, but not the latter, allows equity holders to benefit from the demotion of a creditor's claims. This holding, though vacated after settlement, 2012 WL 1563889, may well give pause to parties who simultaneously trade and negotiate over a debtor's securities.

Another case that involved misbehavior by a party in a claims trade is In re Lightsquared, Inc., 2014 WL 2612312 (Bankr. S.D.N.Y. 2014). A person in control of participants in the debtor's industry purchased enough debt to manipulate the debtor's bankruptcy process with an objective, the court believed, to privately benefit, directly or through other holdings, at the expense of the debtor's creditors as a whole. Although the court had previously determined (in conflict with *Washington Mutual*) that the Bankruptcy Code does not permit equitable disallowance, 504 B.R. 321, the court announced that it would *subordinate* the purchased debt to an extent to be determined.

An additional potential pitfall for claim purchasers is the risk of loss based on the misconduct of the seller. In re Noblehouse Technologies, Inc., 2013 WL 6816129 (Bankr. N.D.N.Y. 2013), observed that claims purchased in the case were "subject to all defenses and liabilities, including equitable subordination."

On the matter of more traditional equitable subordination, a seemingly appropriate basis is creditor predation. Predatory lending is typically associated with consumer transactions, where lenders are accused of persuading unsophisticated borrowers to take loans that they cannot easily afford to repay, but on which lenders can profit despite a high risk of default. In the next case, *Yellowstone Mountain Club*, the court treats what it sees as predatory loans in a business context as a basis for subordination. Consider whether this decision is sensible as a business law precedent. That is, consider whether the incentives created are productive or counterproductive.

IN YELLOWSTONE MOUNTAIN CLUB, LLC

United States Bankruptcy Court, D. Montana, 2009
2009 WL 3094930

KIRSCHER, BANKRUPTCY JUDGE

Various pleadings introduced in this Adversary Proceeding and in the main bankruptcy case state that in 1992, Plum Creek Timber Co., a subsidiary of Northern Pacific Railroad Company sold its land in the Gallatin National Forest to Blixseth and the McDougal brothers, foresters from Oregon. Blixseth consolidated his land holdings with three deals with the federal government to swap 100,000 acres he had just bought for the acreage that now encompasses the Debtors' real estate holdings known as the Yellowstone Club located in Madison County, Montana. The deal with the government also included additional land in several other Montana counties, plus 250 million feet of salable timber. The land swaps required two separate acts of Congress. The first, known as the Gallatin Preservation Act of 1993, covered 38,000 acres and was President Clinton's first major piece of environmental legislation. The second act, in 1998, is known as Gallatin II and involved another 54,000-acre swap. The public acquired another 8,100 acres in a third swap that was not subject to Congressional approval. Soon after the assemblage was completed, Blixseth and the McDougals dissolved their partnership. The timberland was distributed to the McDougal brothers and Blixseth retained the acreage that could be developed.

Blixseth and his former wife, Edra Blixseth ("Edra"), formed the Debtor corporations and on the land that Blixseth retained from his partnership with the McDougal brothers, began development in late 1999 of the world's only private ski and golf community, commonly referred to as the Yellowstone Club. The Yellowstone Club is a membership only master-planned unit development, situated on 13,500 acres of private land in Madison County, Montana near the northwest corner of Yellowstone National Park.

The Blixseths originally contemplated that the Yellowstone Club would consist of seven planned residential areas or neighborhoods comprised of roughly 864 fee dwelling units in 2,700 acres of development pods. To get the Yellowstone Club off the ground, the Blixseths sold equity interests in the Yellowstone Club to various persons, who were referred to as Pioneer and Frontier Members. The 25 Pioneer and 15 Frontier memberships were sold at substantially reduced prices. * * *

On September 30, 2005, the Debtors were controlled by Blixseth as the sole Class A Shareholder through his holding company, Blixseth Group, Inc. ("BGI"). Approximately 13% of the Club was owned by Class B Members who were referred to as the Class B Shareholders or the "Bs" in this litigation. BGI was an Oregon sub-S corporation, which was solely owned by Blixseth as President and CEO from 1999 to mid-August of 2008.

In or around December of 2004, Jeffrey Barcy ("Barcy"), a Director in Credit Suisse's Investment Banking Division, made several attempts to send Blixseth and his secretary or assistant emails that contained a two to three-page teaser, providing Blixseth with a brief overview of Credit Suisse and its new loan product referred to as a syndicated term loan, which was described to Blixseth as something akin to a "home-equity loan." Blixseth eventually responded to Barcy's emails by calling Barcy on the telephone. Blixseth and Barcy had a brief phone conversation and following the telephone conversation, the "next marketing step [for Barcy and his team] was a trip up to the Yellowstone Club[.]" Following the initial meeting at the Yellowstone Club, Barcy testified that although he could not remember exact details, he and Blixseth "had a number of phone conversations and probably emails back and forth as to why it would be interesting for [Blixseth] to potentially do a loan on the Club."

Credit Suisse was specifically trying to "break new ground with a product by doing real estate loans in the corporate bank loan market." Through its new syndicated term loans, Credit Suisse was able to offer a loan product the size of which had previously been unavailable to borrowers. Barcy testified that Credit Suisse's syndicated loan product had previously been marketed to other master-planned residential and recreational communities such as Tamarack Resort, Promontory, Ginn, Turtle Bay, and Lake Las Vegas. Each of the above entities received a syndicated loan from Credit Suisse's Cayman Islands branch, which allowed the equity holders in said entities to take sizeable distributions from all or part of the Credit Suisse loan proceeds. According to Steve Yankauer ("Yankauer"), a Managing Director at Credit Suisse, Credit Suisse's Cayman Islands branch was created in 2005 to facilitate the syndicated loan product and to Yaunkauer's knowledge, Credit Suisse never had a physical presence in the Cayman Islands.

Blixseth originally declined Credit Suisse's loan offer, but then contacted Barcy a couple months later and "said that he might have a use of the proceeds for the loan and would be interested in talking again." Following Blixseth's call, Barcy and another person from Credit Suisse met Blixseth at Blixseth's home in Palm Springs, California. Blixseth initially agreed to take a loan of only $150 million. After several months of negotiations between Credit Suisse First Boston and Blixseth, the proposed amount of the loan grew from $150 million to $375 million.

Credit Suisse, Cayman Islands Branch, and Blixseth, on behalf of the Debtors, eventually entered into a credit agreement dated September 30, 2005 ("Credit Agreement"). In the time leading up to September 20, 2005, Barcy testified that Credit Suisse did "a fair amount of due diligence." Such due diligence included doing a background check on Blixseth and hiring an appraisal firm to provide an "independent assessment" of the Yellowstone Club's cash flows and a law firm to "do a separate legal investigation into the Club to make sure that the entities we were financing against truly held the assets that we believed we were financing."

Curiously, Credit Suisse never requested audited financial statements from the Debtors and in fact, appears to have relied exclusively on the historical and future projections provided by Blixseth and the Debtors. Credit Suisse's financial due diligence instead consisted, as stated above, of commissioning Cushman & Wakefield to do an analysis of the Debtors' cash flows. Cushman & Wakefield was originally hired to do a fair market appraisal of the Debtors. However, the terms of engagement were eventually altered to provide that Cushman & Wakefield would perform a total net value analysis of the Debtors. Barcy explained that Credit Suisse's capital market group suggested and then developed, in conjunction with Cushman & Wakefield, a new form of appraisal methodology, which Credit Suisse termed "total net value." The Total Net Value methodology was first developed when Credit Suisse was selling its syndicated loan product to Lake Las Vegas. Credit Suisse's Total Net Value methodology does not comply with the Financial Institutions Recovery Reform Act of 1989 ("FIRREA"), but that was not important to Credit Suisse because Credit Suisse was seeking to sell its syndicated loans "to nonbank institutions."

Barcy also testified that he was aware of a prior limited appraisal of the Debtors' property that Cushman & Wakefield did on behalf of American Bank. In that limited appraisal, as of September 21, 2004, Cushman & Wakefield determined that the "as-is market value" of those assets that later served as collateral for Credit Suisse's $375 million loan was $420 million. The $420 million as-is valuation was based on a discount rate of 18.5 percent. Barcy and Credit Suisse apparently gave little, if any, regard to Cushman & Wakefield's September 21, 2004, appraisal and instead placed their reliance solely on Credit Suisse's newly created Total Net Value valuation.

Similar to the syndicated loans to Tamarack Resort, Promontory, Ginn, Turtle Bay and Lake Las Vegas, the Yellowstone Club Credit Agreement was originally drafted to provide that the proceeds of the loan would be used, in part, for "distributions" to members of the Borrower for purposes unrelated to the Yellowstone Development. During the same period of time that Blixseth was negotiating with Credit Suisse for his loan, Blixseth was also attempting to buy the interests of the B shareholders under the guise that Blixseth wanted to repurchase the "B" shares for estate planning purposes and to involve his children in ownership of the Yellowstone Club. Not all the B shareholders agreed to Blixseth's proposed purchase and thus, Blixseth purchased none of the B shareholders' interests because his offer was an all or nothing deal.

Coincidentally, in late August of 2005 or early September of 2005, about the same time that Blixseth was unsuccessful in buying the B shareholders' interests, Blixseth was allegedly advised by his attorneys and accountants that he would have to take the Credit Suisse loan proceeds as a loan rather than a distribution. The reasoning was two-fold. First, Blixseth would have tax consequences on a distribution. Second, recording such a large distribution on the Debtors' books would result in negative owners' equity accounts.

Barcy testified that Credit Suisse knew that "there were a number of minority investors in the Club." However, Barcy was not concerned when Blixseth contacted Credit Suisse sometime between August 22, 2005, and September 4, 2005, and requested that the Credit Agreement be modified to provide that the loan proceeds could be used: "(I) for distribution or loans up to [$ _____] to affiliates of the borrower for purposes unrelated to the Yellowstone Development[.]" Between September 4, 2005, and September 30, 2005, the recitals were once again amended to finally provide that the proceeds of the loan would be used "(I) for distribution or loans up to $209,000,000 to members of the Borrower for purposes unrelated to the Yellowstone Development, (ii) for investments up to $142,000,000 into Unrestricted Subsidiaries for purposes unrelated to the Yellowstone Development, (iii) to pay the Transaction Costs, (iv) to refinance the Existing Indebtedness, (v) to finance a portion of the development and construction costs associated with the Yellowstone Development in accordance with the Financial Plan[.]" Barcy testified that it was Blixseth's "responsibility to figure out what he had to do internally to make those distributions or not make those distributions. And as a controlling shareholder of the Yellowstone Club, that was in his court."

Nothing in the record suggests that the loan between Credit Suisse and Blixseth (disregarding, however, the minority shareholders) was not at arm's length. For instance, Credit Suisse originally sought a transaction fee of 3 percent, but Blixseth wanted the transaction fee reduced to 2 percent. Credit Suisse, via Barcy, and Blixseth ultimately agreed to "flip a coin" to decide the rate. Credit Suisse lost the toss, and Blixseth was thus successful in reducing the transaction fee to 2 percent.

After several months of negotiations, Credit Suisse and Blixseth finally came to an agreement on the terms of the Credit Agreement and executed the same. The Credit Agreement provided for the disbursement of $375 million in loan proceeds to be distributed in two significant ways after payment of $7.5 million in fees to Credit Suisse and other expenses attributable to the loan. First, the Credit Agreement designated up to $209 million of the loan proceeds to be used as "distributions or loans" for "purposes unrelated" to the Yellowstone Club. Additionally, up to $142 million was authorized to be used for investments into "unrestricted subsidiaries" for "purposes unrelated" to Yellowstone Club development. Thus, the bulk of the loan proceeds, up to $351 million, were designated to be used for purposes outside of, and unrelated to, the Yellowstone Club.

In the years leading up to the Credit Agreement, the Yellowstone Club carried a debt load ranging from a low of approximately $4 to $5 million to a high of approximately $60 million on a revolving line of credit. The day before the Loan Transaction, the Yellowstone Club carried approximately $19 to $20 million in debt on its books, consisting of a combination of a revolving line of credit and a term loan with American Bank. The majority of this debt was related to the construction of the Warren Miller Lodge, which was already underway.

The Debtors had also experienced negative cash flows in several of the years leading up to the Credit Agreement with Credit Suisse. Several of the witnesses made reference to EDITDA, which is earnings before interest, taxes, depreciation and amortization. Kent Mordy ("Mordy"), a certified public accountant and a certified insolvency and reorganization advisor, calculated that the Debtors' Cash EBITDA was a negative $15,701,772 in 2002, a positive $20,369,766 in 2003, and a negative $45,910,598 in 2004. According to Mordy, the Debtors projected Cash EBITDA of $83,500,000 in 2005 but realized Cash EBITDA of only $19 million. Dr. John S. Hekman ("Hekman"), who has a Ph.D in economics and is employed by LECG to provide expert witness testimony in the area of real estate and real estate finance, also did an EBITDA calculation. Hekman's EBITDA calculation for 2005 was $39 million. Mordy explained that his Cash EBITDA numbers were different from Hekman's EBITDA calculations, which were positive for 2003, 2004 and 2005, because Hekman did not subtract capital expenditures and development costs. Yankauer disputed Hekman's and Mordy's EBITDA calculations for 2005, arguing that such figure was closer to $55,610,953. Whatever the accurate number, it is clear that even though the Debtors' had nine months of operations under their belt before the September 30, 2005, Credit Agreement, they missed their profitability projections by a substantial amount. Such numbers show that Debtors' projections for the future, upon which Credit Suisse relied without question, had no foundation in historical reality.

Hekman also testified that the Federal Reserve aggressively lowered interest rates in 2001 to counteract the 2001 recession. As a result of the low interest rates, Hekman characterized 2003 and 2004 as the peak years for real estate. However, due to concerns about the housing bubble, the Federal Reserve began raising interest rates in 2005, which caused the beginning of a slowdown in the real estate markets.

Despite all the red flags, the Credit Agreement was consummated and $342,110,262.53 was wired to the Yellowstone Club. This amount reflected the total loan amount of $375 million less fees, administrative costs, and a $24,241,910.98 takeout to payoff preexisting debt. On the same date that $342,110,262.53 was transferred to the Debtors, approximately $209 million was transferred out of the Yellowstone Club by Blixseth to BGI. As previously noted, the transfer of loan proceeds out of the Yellowstone Club was a key feature of the product that Credit Suisse used to sell the loan. Yankauer testified that the cornerstone of this loan product was that it allowed preferred resort owners, such as Blixseth, to capitalize on the value of their asset.

The immediate transfer of funds out of the Yellowstone Club to BGI and then to Blixseth was not memorialized in any contemporaneous loan documents but was simply reflected on the Debtors' books with a journal entry. Blixseth, right around the time the B shareholders were threatening suit against Blixseth and the Yellowstone Club, drafted a two-page promissory note in the amount of $209 million. The $209 million unsecured demand note, payable by BGI to the Debtors, was created in May 2006, and backdated to September 30, 2005.

Roughly all of the $209 million proceeds that were transferred to BGI were then disbursed to various personal accounts and payoffs benefitting Tim and Edra Blixseth personally. Blixseth testified that the Debtors had no interest in any of these accounts or payoffs. The Debtors, under Blixseth' direction, never made demand of BGI on the demand notes, even when the Yellowstone Club needed cash.

From 2005 through the filing of the bankruptcy, the Yellowstone Club was persistently behind in its accounts payable. When the need for cash would become imperative, Moses Moore ("Moore"), who worked as a Senior Accountant and then later Comptroller for the Yellowstone Club, would request money from George Mack ("Mack"), who served at that time as the Yellowstone Club's outside accountant. Mack was a go-between between Blixseth and Moore when Moore needed money to pay the bills at the Yellowstone Club. After Moore would make a request for funds, Moore testified that money may or may not appear in the Yellowstone Club's accounts. Moore testified that it was not uncommon to have to shuffle the Yellowstone Club's accounts payables due to a lack of money, and creditor and vendor invoices would often go unpaid for 90 days or more.

When funds were tight, rather than make a demand on the BGI promissory note, Blixseth would instead seek to obtain operating funds from various members of the Yellowstone Club. One such member that Blixseth approached was Samuel T. Byrne ("Byrne"). Byrne, the founder and managing partner of CrossHarbor, first visited the Yellowstone Club in 2004 or 2005 as a guest of another Yellowstone Club member. As a result of his visit, Byrne purchased two Yellowstone Club lots in 2005. Blixseth approached Byrne and asked whether he would be interested in making a bulk purchase of Yellowstone Club lots at a substantially reduced price. Byrne made his first bulk purchase in 2006 by taking over the 58 unit Sunrise Ridge Condominium Development for a price of $60 million. In August of 2007, Blixseth again approached Byrne to purchase 31 lots on the golf course. That sale was consummated in August of 2007 at a price of $54 million.

The foregoing facts form the basis for the Court's decision regarding the Debtors' and the Committee's equitable subordination claim. The Court has carefully reviewed the case law under Bankruptcy Code §510(c), and concludes that equitable subordination is an appropriate remedy in this case. Under § 510(c), a court may, based upon equitable considerations, subordinate for purposes of distribution all or a part of a claim or interest to all or part of another. * * *

When the remedy of equitable subordination involves a non-insider, non-fiduciary, "the level of pleading and proof is elevated: gross and egregious conduct will be required before a court [can] equitably subordinate a claim." [In re First Alliance Mortg. Co., 497 F.3d 977, 1006 (9th Cir.2006).] * * *

As Judge Easterbrook pointed out in Kham & Nate's Shoes No. 2, Inc. v. First Bank, 908 F.2d 1351, 1356 (7th Cir. 1990), "[c]ases subordinating the claims of creditors that dealt at arm's length with the debtor are few and far between." The dearth of cases subordinating the claims of non-insiders is readily explained by the high threshold of misconduct that must be established by the objectant in non-insider cases.

In In re Osborne, 42 B.R. 988, 996 (W.D.Wis. 1984), the court discussed the conduct required for equitable subordination in non-insider cases:

> [The degree of misconduct] has been variously described as "very substantial" misconduct involving "moral turpitude or some breach of duty or some misrepresentation whereby other creditors were deceived to their damage" or as gross misconduct amounting to fraud, overreaching or spoliation. * * *

Although courts have struggled to articulate the misconduct that must be established to subordinate non-insider claims, it is clear that the non-insider's misconduct must be "gross or egregious." Thus, "[a] mere statement that the creditor is guilty of 'inequitable conduct' will not suffice." In re W.T. Grant, 4 B.R. 53, 75-76 (Bankr. S.D.N.Y. 1980), aff 'd, 699 F.2d 599 (2d Cir. 1983). Rather, the plaintiff must prove gross misconduct tantamount to "fraud, overreaching or spoliation." … In summary, the "gross or egregious misconduct" needed to subordinate claims of non-insiders is much greater than the "inequitable conduct" that warrants subordination of insiders and fiduciaries.

Credit Suisse's actions in the case were so far overreaching and self-serving that they shocked the conscience of the Court.

In Cushman & Wakefield's July 1, 2005, appraisal, the Debtors had purportedly sold 243 lots or units, and another 42 lots were listed under contract. The lot sales for 2000 through 2005 are summarized by closing date, lot number, price and type in Addendum B to the appraisal. Dean R. Paauw ("Paauw"), a certified Member of the Appraisal Institute ("MAI") who prepared Cushman & Wakefield's July 1, 2005, appraisal of the Yellowstone Club, states on page 65, in discussing an overview of the Yellowstone Club's current and recent real estate pricing, that there were five remaining lots in inventory in Pine Ridge, a subdivision at the Yellowstone Club. The five remaining Pine Ridge Lots were listed for sale at asking prices ranging from $1,950,000 to $4,000,000. Paauw went on to state that "[t]he developer typically achieves his asking price on his inventory, and [the Pine Ridge] lots are expected to be sold within the next 12 months." Paauw's July 1, 2005, appraisal also concludes that "[a]bsorption in Yellowstone Club has historically been hurt by limited availability in product."

In 2005, Credit Suisse was offering a new financial product for sale. It was offering the owners of luxury second-home developments the opportunity to take their profits up front by mortgaging their development projects to the hilt. Credit Suisse would loan the money on a non-recourse basis, earn a substantial fee, and sell off most of the credit to loan participants. The development owners would take most of the money out as a profit dividend, leaving their developments saddled with enormous debt. Credit Suisse and the development owners would benefit, while their developments—and especially the creditors of their developments—bore all the risk of loss. This newly developed syndicated loan product enriched Credit Suisse, its employees and more than one luxury development owner, but it left the developments too thinly capitalized to survive. Numerous entities that received Credit Suisse's syndicated loan product have failed financially, including Tamarack Resort, Promontory, Lake Las Vegas, Turtle Bay and Ginn. If the foregoing developments were anything like this case, they were doomed to failure once they received their loans from Credit Suisse.

Credit Suisse, Barcy, Yankauer and others on the Credit Suisse team only earned fees if they sold loans. Credit Suisse thus devised a loan scheme whereby it encouraged developers of high-end residential resorts, such as Blixseth, to take unnecessary loans. The higher the loan amount, the fatter the fee to Credit Suisse. This program essentially puts the fox in charge of the hen house and was clearly self-serving for Credit Suisse.

The fee structure was undoubtedly the catalyst that led to the most shocking aspect of Credit Suisse's newly developed loan product. As noted earlier, Credit Suisse's new loan product was marketed to developers on grounds that developers were authorized to take a substantial portion of their Credit Suisse loan proceeds as a distribution, or as Blixseth argues, a loan. In this case, Credit Suisse had not a single care how Blixseth used a majority of the loan proceeds, and in fact authorized Blixseth to take $209 million and use it for any purpose unrelated to the Yellowstone Club. Blixseth, however, had a problem in this case because he was not the sole owner of the Yellowstone Club and he did not want to share the loan proceeds with the B shareholders. Thus, Blixseth booked the $209 proceeds that he took from the Yellowstone Club as a loan months after he actually took the proceeds. Blixseth claims he always intended to repay the $209 million BGI note, but Blixseth's former wife Edra testified to the contrary.

Blixseth testified that he always intended to take the $209 loan proceeds as a loan rather than a distribution because booking the transaction as a distribution would have caused his owner's equity account to have a negative balance. The negative owner's equity would have appeared as a qualification on the Debtors' audited financial statements and may have caused the Debtors' to be out of compliance with the

Credit Agreement. A sophisticated lender such as Credit Suisse had to have known what a distribution would do to the Debtors' financial statements, and in particular, their balance sheets, yet Credit Suisse proceeded with the loan, and thus earned its large fee.

In addition to turning a blind eye to Debtors' financial statements, Credit Suisse's due diligence with respect to the $375 million loan was almost all but non-existent. Credit Suisse spent a fair amount of money on legal bills to ascertain that the Debtors did in fact own the property at the Yellowstone Club, and Credit Suisse also spent a fair amount ensuring that it was not violating any laws with its loan product. Credit Suisse, however, did little financial due diligence. Barcy testified that Credit Suisse was aware that Cushman & Wakefield had appraised Debtors' assets in 2004 and thus either knew or should have known that the collateral that Blixseth proposed for the Credit Suisse loan had a fair market value of $420 million in 2004. The Court highly doubts that Credit Suisse could have successfully syndicated the Yellowstone Club loan if the loan to value ratio was 90 percent. Thus, Credit Suisse instead commissioned Cushman & Wakefield to employ its newly devised valuation methodology. In applying the new valuation methodology, Credit Suisse relied almost exclusively on the Debtors' future financial projections, even though such projections bore no relation to the Debtors' historical or present reality.

Moreover, the Debtors' past debt had bounced between $4 to $5 million on the low end to $60 million on the high end. Credit Suisse proposed to increase the Debtors' debt load by at least six times. Barcy, Yankauer and the rest of the Credit Suisse syndicated loan team could not have believed under any set of circumstances that the Debtors could service such an increased debt load, particularly when the Debtors had several years of net operating losses, mixed with a couple years of net operating revenues.

The only plausible explanation for Credit Suisse's actions is that it was simply driven by the fees it was extracting from the loans it was selling, and letting the chips fall where they may. Unfortunately for Credit Suisse, those chips fell in this Court with respect to the Yellowstone Club loan. The naked greed in this case combined with Credit Suisse's complete disregard for the Debtors or any other person or entity who was subordinated to Credit Suisse's first lien position, shocks the conscience of this Court. While Credit Suisse's new loan product resulted in enormous fees to Credit Suisse in 2005, it resulted in financial ruin for several residential resort communities. Credit Suisse lined its pockets on the backs of the unsecured creditors. The only equitable remedy to compensate for Credit Suisse's overreaching and predatory lending practices in this instance is to subordinate Credit Suisse's first lien position to that of CrossHarbor's superpriority debtor-in-possession financing and to subordinate such lien to that of the allowed claims of unsecured creditors.

The Debtors have provided for the membership claims in their proposed Chapter 11 plan. Accordingly, the Court declines to equitably subordinate Credit Suisse's secured claim to those of the members, including members of the Ad Hoc Committee of Yellowstone Club Members or the Ad Hoc Group of Class B Unit Holders.

For purposes of the upcoming auction of Debtors' assets scheduled for May 13, 2009, Credit Suisse shall be allowed to submit a credit bid for the amount of its allowed secured claim of $232 million. However, because Credit Suisse's claim is equitably subordinated, Credit Suisse must provide, as a component of its credit bid, sufficient funds to pay the CrossHarbor debtor-in-possession financing, the administrative fees and costs of the Debtors' bankruptcy estate and the allowed unsecured claims of non-member creditors. For the reasons discussed herein,

IT IS ORDERED that a separate and final memorandum of decision and judgment will follow this partial and interim order, wherein judgment will be entered in favor of the Debtors and the Committee and against Credit Suisse; and pursuant to Bankruptcy Code §510(c), Credit Suisse's allowed secured claim of $232 million is equitably subordinated to: (1) CrossHarbor's debtor-in-possession financing; (2) approved administrative fees and costs of the bankruptcy estate; and (3) the allowed claims of unsecured creditors. Credit Suisse's $232 million secured claim is not subordinated with respect to the claims of members resulting from their membership agreements and is not subordinated to any claims of the Class "B" minority shareholder members.

XI. THE FRESH START FOR INDIVIDUAL DEBTORS

[The material on "Unbundling Interests in Property" in chapter 11A, which begins on *page 565*, should be supplemented by the following.]

In re Ryan, 725 F.3d 623, 626 (7th Cir. 2013), held that *Dewsnup* cannot be limited to Chapter 7 cases or there would be "lien stripping without any of the safeguards set forth in §§1129(b), 1225, and 1325 governing the treatment of secured claims and lien rights." That is, according to the court, while lien stripping may be available under specific provisions of the Bankruptcy Code, such stripping will occur, if at all, under those specific provisions, not by virtue of §506 alone.

[The material on "Exempt Property" in chapter 11B, which begins on *page 583*, should be supplemented by the following.]

In Law v. Siegel, 134 S.Ct. 1188 (2014), a debtor fabricated a lien on his home in order to deny actual creditors property value in excess of the debtor's homestead exemption. The bankruptcy trustee challenged the phony lien and when he prevailed surcharged the homestead exemption for the expense of the litigation. The Supreme Court held that the surcharge exceeded the trustee's authority under the Bankruptcy Code. The holding may be cold comfort to future debtors who attempt the same scam because, as the Court observed, in addition to direct penalties available to combat swindlers, a fraudulent debtor may be denied a discharge. The case may be significant nonetheless as a signal of general limitation on a bankruptcy court's equitable powers.

In the case of In re Abdul-Rahim, 720 F.3d 710 (8th Cir. 2013), the court held that although Missouri in practice exempts a debtor's personal injury claims from creditor collection, because such claims are not listed or otherwise provided for by the Missouri exemption statute, the claims are not exempt under Bankruptcy Code §522(b)(3).

[The material on "Scope of Discharge" in chapter 11C, which begins on *page 600*, should be supplemented by the following.]

Section 523(a)(4) of the Bankruptcy Code denies a debtor a discharge on any debt "for fraud or defalcation while acting in a fiduciary capacity, embezzlement, or larceny." In Bullock v. BankChampaign, N.A., 133 S.Ct. 1754, 1759 (2013), the Supreme Court held that where a debtor's conduct "does not involve bad faith, moral turpitude, or other immoral conduct," the term "defalcation" in this context requires an "intentional wrong," which includes a conscious disregard or willful blindness to a "substantial and unjustifiable risk" that the conduct "will turn out to violate a fiduciary duty."

Section 523(a)(8) excludes from discharge educational loans "unless excepting such debt from discharge under this paragraph would impose an undue hardship on the debtor." Krieger v. Educational Credit

Management Corp., 713 F.3d 882 (7th Cir. 2013), addresses what constitutes "undue hardship" and considers—in a disagreement between majority and concurrence—the consequences of a debtor's failure to enroll in a program that would have reduced her monthly obligations.

XII. ADJUSTMENT OF INDIVIDUAL DEBT IN CHAPTER 13

[The material on "Repayment Obligation on Unsecured Claims" in chapter 12A, which begins on **page 625**, should be supplemented by the following.]

Lanning has been affirmed at every level of the appellate process, ultimately by the Supreme Court in Hamilton v. Lanning, 506 U.S. 505 (2010). On the question of whether a court should employ a mechanical or a flexible approach to the calculation of disposable income, the Court held that although a court should begin with a mechanical approach, it is "in unusual cases that a court may go further and take into account other known or virtually certain information about the debtor's future income or expenses." Id. At 519.

This said, *Lanning* does not resolve all ambiguities related to disposable income under Chapter 13. In re Flores, 735 F.3d 855 (9th Cir. 2013), for example, considers whether Bankruptcy Code §1325(b)(4), which defines an "applicable commitment period," prescribes a minimum length for a Chapter 13 plan or merely establishes a metric for the calculation of the minimum payments under the plan, the latter a function of projected disposable income. As *Flores* explains, there are the two polar positions and also a hybrid approach, that while §1325(b)(4) does generally set a minimum plan length, five years for above-median debtors, that length is inapplicable to debtors without any projected disposable income. *Flores* takes the majority position that the applicable commitment period prescribes a minimum length without regard to disposable income. See also Piller v. Stearns, 747 F.3d 260 (4th Cir. 2014).

[The material on "Treatment of Secured Claims" in chapter 12B, which begins on **page 644**, should be supplemented by the following.]

Although the Bankruptcy Reform Act of 2005 was designed in significant part to protect the interests of mortgagees, at least some courts have been creative in finding loopholes. Consider In re Davis, 716 F.3d 331 (4th Cir. 2013). In *Davis*, debtors filed a Chapter 13 bankruptcy petition within four years of a Chapter 7 petition that resulted in a discharge, which meant that under the Reform Act the debtors were ineligible for another discharge. But the debtors did not need a discharge in the Chapter 13 case, having just received one in the Chapter 7 case. What the debtors sought from Chapter 13 was to strip junior liens from their property, including a home. This, the debtors argued, could be done under Bankruptcy Code §1322(b)(2), notwithstanding §1325(a), which requires that the holder of a secured claim retain a lien until payment in full or the debtor's discharge, and notwithstanding *Nobelman* (summarized in the casebook), which prohibits the modification of a lien on a debtor's principal residence. The debtors contended that because the amount of senior liens was greater than the value of the collateral, after the application of §506(a), the holders of the junior liens had *no* secured claim. According to the debtors, this meant that both §1325(a) and *Nobelman* were inapplicable (the latter because a strip *down* to the value of a creditor's interest in collateral was different from a strip *off* where there is no such value). The court accepted the debtors' reasoning and stripped the liens, though the court observed that not all courts would accept each step in its analysis.

Turning to another issue in connection with the Bankruptcy Reform Act of 2005, there continues the interpretive struggle over the enigmatic hanging paragraph of §1325(a), discussed by *Wright*. See, e.g., In re Ford, 574 F.3d 1279 (10th Cir. 2009) (negative equity part of secured creditor's purchase money security interest); In re Miller, 570 F.3d 633 (5th Cir. 2009) (deficiency must be treated as an unsecured claim); In re Pruitt, 401 B.R. 546 (Bankr. D. Ct. 2009) (surrender of vehicle constitutes full satisfaction).

XIII. CORPORATE REORGANIZATIONS IN CHAPTER 11

[The material on "Plan of Reorganization," in Chapter 13A, which begins on ***page 678***, should be supplemented by the following.]

Plan support agreements are sometimes adopted among creditors who seek to arrange a prenegotiated reorganization. Those who oppose the resulting plan may challenge the agreement as a violation of Bankruptcy Code §1125, which provides for disclosure and plan solicitation. Observing that sophisticated parties who enter a plan support agreement are not the sorts of creditors who Congress intended to protect with §1125, In re Indianapolis Downs, LLC, 486 B.R. 286 (Bankr. D. Del. 2013), denied a plan opponents' objections. See also, In re Residential Capital, LLC, 2013 WL 3286198 (Bankr. S.D.N.Y. 2013).

On another matter relevant to the plan of reorganization, in the case of In re Tribune, 464 B.R. 126 (Bankr. D. Del. 2011), the court held that absent substantive consolidation a joint reorganization plan must satisfy Bankruptcy Code §1129(a)(10) on a per debtor basis rather than merely once for the plan. The provision itself does not expressly address this point and the case describes contrary precedent.

Turning to the effects of a confirmed plan, in the case of In re S. White Transp., Inc., 725 F3d 494 (5th Cir. 2013), the court held that Bankruptcy Code §1141(c) does not operate automatically to strip a lien on property dealt with under a plan unless the affected creditor participates in the reorganization through "more than mere passive receipt of effective notice." As observed in the case, other courts assert that passive notice is sufficient. This difference of opinion aside, it is noteworthy that the judicial participation requirement for the operation of §1141(c) does not limit the debtor's authority expressly to modify a lien under other provisions of the Bankruptcy Code. See, e.g., §1123(b).

[The material on the "Classification" in chapter 13A(1), which begins on *page 687*, should be supplemented by the following.]

A debtor can use classification in an attempt to engineer plan confirmation through either strategic formation of classes or strategic payments to classes. The latter includes what is referred to as "artificial impairment," where the debtor chooses to modify the payments of claims in a class, rather than pay the claims on original terms, not because the debtor lacks the resources to pay but because the modification leaves the class impaired under Bankruptcy Code §1124 and a candidate to satisfy §1129(a)(10), which requires that if there is an impaired class of claims at least one such class accept the reorganization plan. Through artificial impairment, a debtor may barely, if at all, reduce the value of claims as compared to reinstatement, which would leave them unimpaired under §1124. As a result, the debtor may garner plan acceptance by that class, thus removing what otherwise would be a veto by an objecting class or classes.

As observed by the recent case of In re Village at Camp Bowie I, LP, 710 F.3d 239 (5th Cir. 2013), courts are divided on whether artificial impairment without more constitutes a lack of good faith under §1129(a)(3). As observed in the case, however, even courts that reject artificial impairment as per se bad faith may take the debtor's motive into account as part of a broader good faith determination.

Also on the topic of class payment under a plan, the next case, *Journal Register*, addresses the question of whether some, but not all, creditors within a reorganization plan class can legitimately receive payments under the plan from funds conceded by creditors from outside the class. You'll note that this case distinguishes *Armstrong World Industries*, the district court opinion in which is reproduced in chapter 13A(3) of the casebook (affirmed 432 F.3d 507 (3rd Cir. 2005)). The difference, according to the *Journal Register* court is that in *Armstrong* the proposed distribution would violate interclass priority, while in *Journal Register*, the differences in distribution would be within a class. Consider whether this distinction justifies different outcomes in the cases. Consider too whether the common classification of favored and disfavored creditors in *Journal Register* was of any significance given the court's observation that "both the favored and the disfavored members of the class have voted overwhelmingly to accept" the plan. Also, reconsider this case after reading *DBSD*, reproduced below on page 127 of this update.

IN RE JOURNAL REGISTER CO.

United States Bankruptcy Court, S.D.N.Y., 2009
407 B.R. 520

GROPPER, BANKRUPTCY JUDGE

Formally established in 1997, the Debtors are a national media company that own and operate daily newspapers and non-daily publications, news and employment websites, and commercial printing facilities. The Debtors operate in six geographical "clusters": greater Philadelphia; metropolitan Detroit and other areas of Michigan; Connecticut; Ohio; and the Capital-Saratoga and Mid-Hudson regions of New York. As of the Petition Date, the Debtors operated 20 daily newspapers, 159 non-daily publications, 148 local news and information websites, and 14 printing facilities. They had 3,465 employees, 18% of whom were employed pursuant to collective bargaining agreements.

The Debtors have approximately $695 million in outstanding prepetition indebtedness to the Secured Lenders under credit agreements (the "Credit Agreements") secured by first priority liens on substantially all of the Debtors' assets. The validity and enforceability of the Secured Lenders' liens are undisputed. In March 2009, the Court approved a stipulation for the use of cash collateral in which the Debtors stipulated that the Secured Lenders' liens were properly perfected and valid, and provided the Creditors Committee with a period of time after its appointment to investigate and challenge the liens. The Creditors Committee, appointed on March 3, 2009, did not challenge the validity or perfection of the Secured Lenders' liens, and the time to do so has lapsed.

The Debtors' unsecured debt is estimated at $27 million, $6.6 million of which is allegedly owed to trade creditors. Equity is comprised of one class of common stock, with approximately 48 million shares outstanding. The Debtors' common stock was publicly traded until July 2008, when SEC registration terminated. * * *

The Debtors have sustained net operating losses for at least the last two years. They attribute the losses to an industry-wide decline in readership, circulation and revenue, caused by increased competition from other forms of media (such as the internet), the global recession, and weak advertising demand. In the fall of 2007, the Debtors began efforts to reduce operating costs, and by early 2008 they had closed 53 unprofitable publications and eliminated approximately $6.4 million in annual expenses. Between 2006 and 2008 the Debtors reduced their labor force by approximately 1,475 full-time positions.

In spite of their cost-cutting efforts, the Debtors were unable to comply with certain financial covenants under their Credit Agreements. In July 2008, the Debtors and the Secured Lenders entered into a forbearance agreement that required the Debtors to retain a restructuring advisor and deliver a five-year business plan along with a term sheet setting forth the terms of a comprehensive restructuring plan for the company. In exchange, the Secured Lenders agreed to waive the Debtors' defaults until October 31, 2008. The Debtors retained Conway, Del Genio, Gries & Co., LLC ("CDG") to provide restructuring management services and Robert Conway to act as their chief restructuring officer. On the Petition Date, Robert Conway became the Debtors' interim chief operating officer.

Assisted by CDG, the Debtors delivered a five-year business plan and negotiated an extension for the completion of the term sheet to February 6, 2009. On February 13, 2009, after further negotiations with the Secured Lenders, the Debtors delivered a term sheet, which served as the basis for a plan support agreement entered into with a super-majority of the Secured Lenders (the "Consenting Lenders"). This support agreement, in turn, led to the chapter 11 plan of reorganization the Debtors filed with the Court on the Petition Date, and indirectly to the amended version presented for confirmation. * * *

As more fully explained below, the Debtors' Plan proposes, among other things, to (i) deleverage the Debtors by converting the Secured Lenders' debt into 100% of the new equity of the Reorganized Debtors and new tranche A and B secured loans; (ii) make certain distributions to the unsecured creditors class; (iii) cancel the old equity; and (iv) establish a Post-Emergence Incentive Plan. As one of the "means of execution" of the Plan, but not as a matter of Plan classification and distribution, it is also proposed that there be a further payment to certain of the unsecured creditors, the so-called "trade creditors," from a purported "gift" of the Secured Lenders. . . .

Claims and interest are divided into six classes. Classes 1 and 3 are comprised of Priority Non-Tax Claims and Other Secured Claims in the estimated amounts of $0.59 million and $2.6 million, respectively. Under the Plan, both classes would receive full payment. Existing Equity Interests and Existing Securities Laws Claims are classified in classes 5 and 6, respectively. The Plan provides no distribution to these two classes and for the cancellation of the existing shareholders' stock.

Class 2 of the Plan encompasses the Secured Lenders, who, as previously stated, hold estimated claims of approximately $695 million, which aggregates approximately 96% of the total debt, secured by substantially all of the Debtors' assets. The members of this class are to receive the following distribution under the Plan in full satisfaction of their claims: (i) 100% of the new common stock of the Reorganized Debtors; (ii) assumption by the Reorganized Debtors of new indebtedness, consisting of tranche A and B loans in the aggregate amount of $225 million, secured by first and third liens on all the assets of the Reorganized Debtors, bearing interest of up to 15% per annum and maturing in four and five years from the effective date of the Plan, respectively; and (iii) payment in cash of any fees due to the Secured Lenders' professionals in connection with these cases. The Debtors' financial advisor, Eric R. Mendelsohn, a managing director of Lazard Frères & Co., LLC, testified without contradiction at the confirmation hearing that the mid-point of the estimated enterprise value of the Reorganized Debtors was at most $300 million. It is therefore undisputed on the record of the confirmation hearing that based on these values the package of consideration made available to the members of Class 2 would constitute a recovery of only 42% of their claims. Using the liquidation analysis that the Debtors included as part of their Disclosure Statement and that was also unchallenged, in a chapter 7 liquidation the Secured Lenders would receive a distribution on their claims of less than 20%.

The Plan provides for a pro rata distribution of $2 million to all of the Debtors' general unsecured creditors, who are classified in Class 4. It is estimated that the general unsecured creditors are owed approximately $27 million, and that a pro rata distribution would result in an approximate 9% recovery to each general unsecured creditor. In addition, as mentioned above, the Secured Lenders have also agreed to fund an additional "gift," which has been labeled as a "Trade Account Distribution" and will be payable to certain unsecured creditors in accordance with the following criteria: (i) the creditor holds a "Trade Unsecured Claim," as defined in the Plan; (ii) the creditor does not object to the confirmation of the Plan; and (iii) the creditor consents to the release of any claim against the Debtors and the Secured Lenders arising during these cases or from confirmation of the Plan. The Debtors' Disclosure Statement states that "[t]he grant of such releases to the Lenders by the creditors that will receive the Trade Account Distributions is the linchpin of such Lenders' willingness to contribute such funds that they would otherwise retain on account of their Secured Claims." At the confirmation hearing, Robert Conway testified that the Trade Account Distribution was critically important to the future of the Reorganized Debtors and their ability to fulfill their business plan, in that it would ensure the goodwill and survival of certain trade creditors that were under severe financial stress themselves and were essential to the Debtors' daily operations and long-term survival.

This additional "gift" will be placed in a so-called trade account that "shall not constitute property of the Debtors or the Reorganized Debtors" and "[a]fter all Trade Claim Payments have been distributed … the undistributed portion of the Trade Account Distribution, if any, shall become the sole and exclusive property" of the Lenders. The Plan provides authority to the Court to resolve any dispute that relates to the Trade Account Distribution, if necessary. An "Unsecured Claim Distribution Agent" is to make the pro rata distribution to unsecured creditors with Class 4 claims, and a "Plan Distribution Agent" would be responsible for the additional Trade Account Distribution and all other Plan distributions. It is estimated that the additional Trade Account Distribution will aggregate approximately $6.6 million. * * *

The Plan also establishes a so-called Post-Emergence Incentive Plan (the "Incentive Plan") for the benefit of certain employees of the Reorganized Debtors. The Incentive Plan provides bonuses if the employees achieve certain goals the Debtors and the Consenting Lenders established in the plan support agreement. The Debtors' Disclosure Statement describes the Incentive Plan, as follows:

The Post-Emergence Incentive Plan was designed to incentivize those employees that were critical to the Company's efforts to implement the initial stages of the Business Plan, and to expeditiously confirm and consummate a plan of reorganization. To that end, the Performance Objectives for which Key Employees will receive an award under the Post-Emergence Incentive Plan are as follows: (i) the "shutdown objective," which was achieved upon the shutdown of substantially all of the publications slated for elimination in the Business Plan due to such publications' negative performance; (ii) the "Cost-Reduction Objective," which was achieved upon the targeted reduction of certain additional salary-related expenses as a result of the elimination and associated reconfiguration of operations and publications; and (iii) the "Emergence Objective," which will be earned upon consummation of a plan of re-organization for the Debtors. * * *

Post-effective date obligations and working capital needs of the Reorganized Debtors are to be funded primarily with cash from operations, which according to Robert Conway's testimony and CDG's projections will be sufficient to service annual debt obligations and capital expenditures of approximately $26 million and $10 million, respectively. The Reorganized Debtors have also obtained exit financing in the *528 form of a $25 million three-year revolving credit facility that will provide liquidity and working capital. The revolving credit facility will be secured by first and second priority liens on certain assets of the Reorganized Debtors. * * *

[Five] objections have been filed to confirmation of the Plan. One of the objections, filed by Central States, relies on Bankruptcy Code §§1122 and 1129(b) of the Bankruptcy Code and contends that the Plan discriminates unfairly among Class 4 unsecured creditors by allowing the Secured Lenders to provide a "gift" to some but not all of the members of that class. The Guild and the State of Connecticut oppose only that part of the Plan that provides the above-described Incentive Plan. The Minority Shareholders filed the other two objections to confirmation on grounds that assert, insofar as relevant to confirmation, that (i) the Plan is not feasible, and (ii) fails the best interests test. * * *

Central States objects to the "gift" conferred on the trade creditors, arguing that the proposal constitutes unfair discrimination. This objection presents the principal challenge to confirmation of the Debtors' Plan, and it raises an issue as to the application of the so-called "gift doctrine." * * *

The gift doctrine dates from Official Unsecured Creditors Committee v. Stern (In re SPM Manufacturing, Corp.), 984 F.2d 1305 (1st Cir. 1993), a converted chapter 7 case in which the Court of Appeals for the First Circuit held that a secured creditor is free to "gift" its bankruptcy proceeds to junior creditors without regard to the distribution scheme of the Bankruptcy Code. There, a creditors committee, formed when the case was still in chapter 11, negotiated a co-operation agreement with the debtor's secured creditor, providing for the formulation of a joint plan of reorganization and for the sharing of proceeds resulting from either confirmation of a plan or a liquidation of the debtor's assets. Efforts to reorganize the debtor failed, and the assets of the debtor were sold for less than the debt owed to the secured creditor. Two days after the sale, a previously-entered order went into effect, granting relief from the automatic stay to the secured lender and converting the case to a chapter 7 liquidation.

When the creditors committee and the secured creditor requested distribution of the sale proceeds in accordance with their agreement, objections were filed by the debtor and its principal officers, who would be personally liable for unpaid taxes the debtor owed. The objections argued that the distribution proposed in the agreement violated the priority scheme of the Bankruptcy Code by providing payments to general unsecured creditors ahead of a priority tax debt. In reversing the lower courts, the Circuit Court concluded:

> Any sharing between [the secured creditor] and the general, unsecured creditors was to occur *after* distribution of the estate property, having no effect whatever on the bankruptcy distribution to other creditors. … Section 726 and the other Code provisions governing priorities of creditors apply only to distribution of property of the estate. The Code does not govern the rights of creditors to transfer or receive nonestate property. While the debtor and the trustee are not allowed to pay nonpriority creditors ahead of priority creditors, creditors are generally free to do whatever they wish with the bankruptcy dividends they receive, including to share them with other creditors. … There is nothing in the Code forbidding [secured creditors] to have voluntarily paid parts of these monies to some or all of the general, unsecured creditors after the bankruptcy proceeding finished.

SPM Manufacturing, 984 F.2d at 1312-13 (emphasis in the original).

Application of the gift doctrine in chapter 11 cases has divided the courts. … A few courts have generally rejected the doctrine, asserting that in the context of chapter 11:

> [t]o accept [the] argument that a secured lender can, without any reference to fairness, decide which creditors get paid and how much those creditors get paid, is to reject the historical foundation of equity receiverships and to read § 1129(b) out of the Code. … To accept that argument is simply to start down a slippery slope that does great violence to history and to positive law.

In re Sentry Operating Co. of Texas, Inc., 264 B.R. 850, 865 (Bankr. S.D. Tex. 2001).

Other courts have invalidated certain applications of the gift doctrine without rejecting it. In In re Armstrong World Indus., Inc., 432 F.3d 507 (3d Cir. 2005), a debtor had proposed a chapter 11 plan that divided unsecured creditors into two classes: an asbestos claimants class and a general unsecured creditors class. The plan required asbestos claimants to share a portion of their plan distribution with equity holders, but it did not provide full payment to the members of the general unsecured creditors class. The official creditors committee in the case objected to confirmation, arguing that the proposed distribution violated the absolute priority rule of §1129(b) by providing value to equity over the objection of an impaired class of unsecured creditors. The debtors argued that the distributions were coming from proceeds otherwise payable to another group with its consent as allowed by the gift doctrine.

The Third Circuit agreed with the creditors committee and, in denying confirmation of the Plan as contrary to the absolute priority rule, stated that the gift doctrine cases "do not stand for the unconditional proposition that creditors are generally free to do whatever they wish with the bankruptcy proceeds they receive." 432 F.3d at 514. The Third Circuit, however, did not reject the doctrine out of hand.

Finally, some courts reject application of the doctrine only when it is used for ulterior, improper ends. In In re Scott Cable Communications, Inc., 227 B.R. 596, 603-04 (Bankr.D.Conn.1998), a debtor proposed to sell its assets pursuant to a plan of liquidation that provided for payments to all administrative, priority, and unsecured creditors from recoveries that were otherwise payable to secured creditors. However, the plan did not provide payment for capital gain taxes attributable to the sale. The Court denied confirmation on the ground that the principal purpose of the plan was the avoidance of taxes, contrary to §1129(d), and it refused to approve the plan on the basis of the gift doctrine, distinguishing *SPM Manufacturing* as a chapter 7 case not subject to the confirmation requirements of §1129.

The Court of Appeals for the Second Circuit has not decided the validity or scope of the gift doctrine in the plan confirmation context. In In re Iridium Operating LLC, 478 F.3d 452 (2d Cir. 2007), the issue was whether a settlement based on a gift theory was consistent with the priority rules of the Bankruptcy Code. The Court reserved the question whether the gift doctrine "could ever apply to Chapter 11 settlements." On the other hand, the Court rejected a per se rule that another Circuit had adopted on the issue, and it remanded to the Bankruptcy Court for further findings of fact. . . .

Central States ... relies on that part of §1129(b) that prohibits non-consensual or "cramdown" plans from discriminating unfairly against dissenting impaired classes. See Bankruptcy Code §1129(b). This provision prohibits unfair discrimination between classes of creditors with the same level of bankruptcy priority. The rule "looks at the treatment of a particular class of claims or interests, and compares it with other classes." 7 Collier on Bankruptcy at ¶1129.04[4]. It is concerned with plan treatment between classes—not within classes. In these cases there is no charge of unfair discrimination between classes of creditors. Therefore §1129(b) is not violated by the Plan on the ground of unfair discrimination.

Section 1129(b) of the Bankruptcy Code also requires that a cramdown plan satisfy the fair and equitable or absolute priority rule. This was the rule at issue in Armstrong, and the fact that the so-called gift had the effect of undermining the priority principles of the Code was the principal factor that the Circuit Court relied on in reversing. Here, there is no forced distribution from one class to a junior class over the objection of an intervening dissenting or objecting class. The "gift" by a small group of Secured Lenders is wholly consensual on their part, and there is no contention that they are making the "gift" to another class over the dissent of an intervening class.

The only objection to plan confirmation that could be made by a creditor such as Central States that claims to be damaged by unequal treatment when compared to members of its class is under §1123(a)(4). This section advances the policy of equality of distribution of estate property in bankruptcy law by requiring that a plan "provide the same treatment for each claim or interest of a particular class, unless the holder of a particular claim or interest agrees to a less favorable treatment of such particular claim or interest." Bankruptcy Code §1123(a)(4).

It is undisputed that the Debtors' Plan establishes only one class of unsecured creditors (Class 4), who are to share pro rata the same distribution of $2 million. There is no creation of a separate class of unsecured creditors that receives an unequal distribution. Further, and contrary to the argument of Central States, the funds in the Trade Account are not property of the estate. The Plan provides that the Trade Account is the property of the Secured Lenders, with any undistributed portion to revert to the Secured Lenders.

Nevertheless, it is also undisputed that the payment that certain "trade creditors" in Class 4 are to receive subsequent to confirmation of the Plan is intended to be higher than that of other unsecured creditors in Class 4, and that the Plan contains certain "means of execution" that facilitate this intended disparity. Therefore, the question under §1123(a)(4) is whether the payment that creates the difference is provided "under the Plan," and whether the principles of the Bankruptcy Code are undermined notwithstanding that the distribution comes from a "gift" of the Secured Lenders.

It is concluded that under the facts of these cases the existence of plan provisions that facilitate the Trade Account Distribution do not result in a classification issue or provide any other reason to deny confirmation of this Plan. We start with the proposition that members of an unsecured creditors class may have rights to payment from third parties, such as joint obligors, sureties and guarantors, and these rights may entitle them to a disproportionate recovery compared to other creditors of the same class (up to a full recovery). The existence of such additional rights to payment does not create a classification problem under §1123(a). Indeed, a debtor is entitled to voluntarily repay a debt, provided the repayment is truly voluntary. This may result in the debtor providing a benefit to certain creditors that is disproportionate to the plan recovery, but it has never been thought to raise any question of plan classification.

Since there is no principle that would preclude the Secured Lenders from making the "gift" totally outside the Plan and the chapter 11 process, the further question is whether the fact that certain provisions of the Plan facilitate the "gift" and provide that it is one of the "means of execution of the Plan" should cause the Court to invalidate it. Under the circumstances, the provisions of the Plan relating to the Trade Account Distribution are immaterial and do not cause it to be an inappropriate distribution "under the Plan." The fact that the Plan provides for an administrator to make the distribution and for the Court to resolve any disputes does not implicate the classification scheme under the Plan. Indeed, if the Court excised the gift provision from the Plan, the recoveries of the "disfavored" Class 4 creditors would not be increased. This would only put the "gift" at risk by providing the Secured Lenders with an opportunity to withdraw their offer. It would also make it much more difficult to resolve disputes as to who is a trade creditor, since the Court would have no jurisdiction over the issue, and the process would be carried out by the Secured Lenders alone or be subject to an expensive and extended proceeding under State law. This would not benefit any party.

A more negative result would take place if the Court were to deny confirmation of the Plan altogether on grounds that it provides unequal treatment to unsecured creditors. At least two possibilities would arise under this scenario: (i) the Debtors and the Secured Lenders could propose another Plan that provides no recovery for the general unsecured class as a whole, and the Secured Lenders could then pay the trade creditors after confirmation of that Plan if they chose to do so; or (ii) the Secured Lenders could decide not to pay any other party and perhaps attempt to foreclose outside chapter 11 altogether. This would jeopardize the recoveries of all general unsecured creditors who overwhelmingly voted to accept the proposed Plan and create the possibility of a result that would contravene the over-riding purpose behind chapter 11 of maximizing the going concern value of a debtor's business for the benefit of its stakeholders.

Moreover, it is equally important that the Secured Lenders' "gift" is not being used for an "ulterior purpose," to use the Second Circuit's term in *Iridium*. The Court credits the testimony of the Debtors' chief restructuring officer, Robert Conway, who testified that the "gift" is necessary to ensure the goodwill of trade creditors essential to the Debtors' post-confirmation survival. The goal of the "gift" is in accordance with the overriding purpose of chapter 11 that going concern value be preserved or enhanced.

In the first version of the Plan, filed with the petitions, it was proposed that the unsecured creditors receive no distribution and be deemed a class that automatically rejected the plan. This reflected the provisions of the prepetition plan support agreement that committed the Secured Lenders to paying a subset of the unsecured creditors in full, without providing any recovery to the unsecured creditors as a class. The Court expressed concern that this could put the Creditors Committee in an untenable position, in that some of its members might not want to jeopardize their recovery and the Committee might be deterred from fulfilling its statutory duty of attempting to negotiate a plan that would benefit the entire class. In its objection to Plan confirmation, Central States relies heavily on the Court's previously expressed concerns.

The Court is satisfied that the Creditors Committee acted appropriately and ably in these cases and that the "gift" is not being made for ulterior purposes. As for the role of the Creditors Committee, it has three members: one trade creditor and two non-trade creditors, one of which is Central States itself. It thus has a majority of disfavored creditors. The Committee, represented by an experienced and able law firm, negotiated an amendment to the Debtors' original plan that provides for an approximate 9% distribution to all unsecured creditors, notwithstanding that the Secured Lenders are undersecured by more than $350 million and that their liens are not subject to challenge. The Committee's actions dispel any concerns about its bona fides.

As for the question of ulterior purposes, Class 4 has been given the opportunity to vote on the Plan, and both the favored and the disfavored members of the class have voted overwhelmingly to accept it. The Debtors and the Secured Lenders have explained why certain creditors have been favored. There has not been any contention that the Plan has not been proposed in "good faith," as required by §1129(a)(3), and the facts of record dispel any such concerns. Central States' objection is accordingly denied. * * *

As stated above, the Incentive Plan will be paid after the effective date of the Plan from assets that will be owned by the Secured Lenders. The Debtors' Disclosure Statement and the Plan fully disclosed the Incentive Plan, giving the holders of unsecured claims an opportunity to factor the payments into their decision whether to accept the Plan, which they did overwhelmingly. Moreover, the Creditors Committee endorsed the Incentive Plan as reasonable, and the Debtors' chief operating officer, who is an experienced restructuring professional, testified without contradiction that the Incentive Plan is reasonable. There is no suggestion that it is not in line with the market for compensation of the top executives of similar companies. Compliance with §1129(a)(4) has been established. * * *

Compliance with the so-called best interests test is also necessary for confirmation of a chapter 11 reorganization plan. ... There is no dispute in these cases that substantially all of the Debtors' assets are fully encumbered by valid first priority liens, and that the value of those assets is substantially less than the debt secured. The Debtors have presented credible documentary evidence and expert testimony that the secured creditors of the estate would receive less than a 20% recovery on their claims in a chapter 7 liquidation, leaving no proceeds available for distribution to unsecured creditors or to shareholders. The Minority Shareholders have presented no evidence to the contrary. Since all creditors are receiving at least as much or more than they would receive in a liquidation, and Classes 5 and 6 would receive nothing in a liquidation, the Debtors' Plan complies with the best interests test. * * *

The Plan satisfies the requirements of §1129. An appropriate Confirmation Order will be entered herewith.

[The material on the "Voting" in chapter 13A(2), which begins on **page 697**, should be supplemented by the following. The principal case, *DBSD* can also be covered in connection with "Absolute Priority" in chapter 13A(3), which begins on **page 707**.]

In re Texas Rangers, 434 B.R. 393 (Bankr. N.D. Tex. 2010), is a recent case that addressed the definition of impairment under Bankruptcy Code §1124. The court held that a plan could impair a class of claims through the alteration of contractual rights even if such alteration did not deprive the claims of full repayment plus post-petition interest. The court noted that ordinarily full payment in cash of claims plus interest is sufficient to deem the claims unimpaired, as other courts have held. But in this case, the court believed that such payment would not sufficient to avoid impairment because the contractual rights in question—the power to veto a sale of the debtor's assets—were independent of the amount of the claims in the class. Somewhat mysteriously, however, the court held that a sale of the debtor's assets prior to plan confirmation, even over the creditors' objection, would not impair the claims in the class if the plan provided an adequate remedy for the breach of the claim holders' contractual rights.

The principal case reproduced below, *DBSD*, addresses (in the second half of the opinion) the issue of vote or claim designation under Bankruptcy Code §1126(e). The context is a creditor's attempt to vote claims purchased for just that purpose. This case relies on and revisits the *Allegheny* decision described in Note 13A.4. *DBSD* also reaches the related issue of how a court should treat a class all of the claims in which have been designated.

IN RE DBSD NORTH AMERICA, INC.

United States Court of Appeals, Second Circuit, 2011
634 F.3d 79

LYNCH, CIRCUIT JUDGE

These consolidated appeals arise out of the bankruptcy of DBSD North America, Incorporated and its various subsidiaries (together, "DBSD"). The bankruptcy court confirmed a plan of reorganization for DBSD over the objections of the two appellants here, Sprint Nextel Corporation ("Sprint") and DISH Network Corporation ("DISH").

Before us, Sprint argues that the plan improperly gave shares and warrants to DBSD's owner—whose interest lies below Sprint's in priority—in violation of the absolute priority rule of Bankruptcy Code §1129(b)(2)(B). DISH, meanwhile, argues that the bankruptcy court erred when it found DISH did not vote "in good faith" under §1126(e) and when, because of the §1126(e) ruling, it disregarded DISH's class for the purposes of counting votes under §1129(a)(8). * * *

ICO Global Communications founded DBSD in 2004 to develop a mobile communications network that would use both satellites and land-based transmission towers. In its first five years, DBSD made progress toward this goal, successfully launching a satellite and obtaining certain spectrum licenses from the FCC, but it also accumulated a large amount of debt. Because its network remained in the developmental stage and had not become operational, DBSD had little if any revenue to offset its mounting obligations.

On May 15, 2009, DBSD (but not its parent ICO Global), filed a voluntary petition in the United States Bankruptcy Court for the Southern District of New York, listing liabilities of $813 million against assets with a book value of $627 million. Of the various claims against DBSD, three have particular relevance here:

1. *The First Lien Debt:* a $40 million revolving credit facility that DBSD obtained in early 2008 to support its operations, with a first-priority security interest in substantially all of DBSD's assets. It bore an initial interest rate of 12.5%.

2. *The Second Lien Debt:* $650 million in 7.5% convertible senior secured notes that DISH issued in August 2005, due August 2009. These notes hold a second-priority security in-

terest in substantially all of DBSD's assets. At the time of filing, the Second Lien Debt had grown to approximately $740
million. It constitutes the bulk of DBSD's indebtedness.

3. *Sprint's Claim:* an unliquidated, unsecured claim based
on a lawsuit against a DBSD subsidiary. Sprint had sued seeking reimbursement for DBSD's share of certain spectrum re-
location expenses under an FCC order. At the time of DBSD's
filing, that litigation was pending in the United States District
Court for the Eastern District of Virginia and before the FCC.
In the bankruptcy case, Sprint filed a claim against each of the
DBSD entities jointly and severally, seeking $211 million.
The bankruptcy court temporarily allowed Sprint's claim in
the amount of $2 million for voting purposes.

After negotiations with various parties, DBSD proposed a plan of
reorganization which, as amended, provided for "substantial de-lever-
aging," a renewed focus on "core operations," and a "continued path as
a development-stage enterprise." The plan provided that the holders of
the First Lien Debt would receive new obligations with a four-year maturity date and the same 12.5% interest rate, but with interest to be paid
in kind ("PIK"), meaning that for the first four years the owners of the
new obligations would receive as interest more debt from DBSD rather
than cash. The holders of the Second Lien Debt would receive the bulk
of the shares of the reorganized entity, which the bankruptcy court estimated would be worth between 51% and 73% of their original claims.
The holders of unsecured claims, such as Sprint, would receive shares
estimated as worth between 4% and 46% of their original claims. Finally, the existing shareholder (effectively just ICO Global, which
owned 99.8% of DBSD) would receive shares and warrants in the reorganized entity. * * *

Sprint raises only one issue on appeal: it asserts that the plan improperly gives property to DBSD's shareholder without fully satisfying
Sprint's senior claim, in violation of the absolute priority rule. That rule
provides that a reorganization plan may not give "property" to the holders of any junior claims or interests "on account of" those claims or
interests, unless all classes of senior claims either receive the full value
of their claims or give their consent. Because the existing shareholder
received shares and warrants on account of its junior interest, Sprint
argues, Sprint's class of general unsecured creditors had a right to receive "full satisfaction of their claims" or at least "an amount sufficient
to obtain approval from the class." But the plan provided neither, and

so Sprint asks us to vacate the order confirming it or to provide other relief that would satisfy Sprint's claim. * * *

Sprint argues that the plan violated the absolute priority rule by giving shares and warrants to a junior class (the existing shareholder) although a more senior class (Sprint's class) neither approved the plan nor received the full value of its claims. The appellees respond, and the courts below held, that the holders of the Second Lien Debt, who are senior to Sprint and whom the bankruptcy court found to be under-secured, were entitled to the full residual value of the debtor and were therefore free to "gift" some of that value to the existing shareholder if they chose to. We recently avoided deciding the viability of this "gifting doctrine" in a similar context, but we now face the question squarely. * * *

Long before anyone had imagined such a thing as Chapter 11 bankruptcy, it was already "well settled that stockholders are not entitled to any share of the capital stock nor to any dividend of the profits until all the debts of the corporation are paid." Chicago, Rock Island & Pac. Railroad v. Howard, 74 U.S. (7 Wall) 392, 409-10 (1868). In the days of the railroad barons, however, parties observed this rule in the breach. Senior creditors and original shareholders often cooperated to control the reorganization of a failed company, sometimes to make the process go smoothly—to encourage the old shareholders to provide new capital for the reorganization or to keep them from engaging in costly and delaying litigation—or sometimes simply because the senior creditors and the old shareholders were the same parties. For their cooperation, the old owners would often receive or retain some stake in whatever entity arose from the reorganization. Junior creditors, however, often received little or nothing even though they technically stood above the old shareholders in priority.

In response to this practice, the Supreme Court developed a "fixed principle" for reorganizations: that all "creditors were entitled to be paid before the stockholders could retain [shares] for any purpose whatever." Northern Pacific Railway v. Boyd, 228 U.S. 482, 507-08 (1913). "[A] plan of reorganization," the Court later stated, "would not be fair and equitable which … admitted the stockholders to participation, unless" at very least "the stockholders made a fresh contribution in money or in money's worth in return for 'a participation reasonably equivalent to their contribution.' " Marine Harbor Props., Inc. v. Mfrs. Trust Co., 317 U.S. 78, 85 (1942), quoting Case v. Los Angeles Lumber Products. Co., 308 U.S. 106, 121 (1939). Courts came to call this the "absolute priority rule." Ecker v. Western Pacific Railroad, 318 U.S. 448, 484

(1943). The Bankruptcy Code incorporates a form of the absolute priority rule in its provisions for confirming a Chapter 11 plan of reorganization. For a district court to confirm a plan over the vote of a dissenting class of claims, the Code demands that the plan be "fair and equitable, with respect to each class of claims … that is impaired under, and has not accepted, the plan." §1129(b)(1). The Code does not define the full extent of "fair and equitable," but it includes a form of the absolute priority rule as a prerequisite. * * *

Absent the consent of all impaired classes of unsecured claimants, therefore, a confirmable plan must ensure either (i) that the dissenting class receives the full value of its claim, or (ii) that no classes junior to that class receive any property under the plan on account of their junior claims or interests.

Under the plan in this case, Sprint does not receive "property of a value … equal to the allowed amount" of its claim. Rather, Sprint gets less than half the value of its claim. The plan may be confirmed, therefore, only if the existing shareholder, whose interest is junior to Sprint's, does "not receive or retain" "any property" "under the plan on account of such junior … interest." We hold that the existing shareholder did receive property under the plan on account of its interest, and that the bankruptcy court therefore should not have confirmed the plan.

[W]e conclude that the existing shareholder received "property," that it did so "under the plan," and that it did so "on account of" its prior, junior interest.

The Supreme Court's interpretations of §1129(b)(2)(B) give us confidence in ours. Although that Court has not addressed the exact scenario presented here under the codified absolute priority rule, its two post-Code cases on the rule are instructive. In both cases, the prior owners tried to avoid the absolute priority rule by arguing that they received distributions not on account of their prior interests but rather on account of the new value that they would contribute to the entity. In both cases, the Supreme Court rejected those arguments. Although dictum in an earlier case had suggested that contributing new value could allow prior shareholders to participate in the reorganized entity, the Court refused to decide whether §1129(b)(2)(B) permitted such new-value exchanges. Instead, the Court held that neither "future labor, experience and expertise," Sce Norwest Bank Worthington v. Ahlers, 485 U.S. 197, 199 (1989) (quotation marks omitted), nor capital contributions "without benefit of market valuation," See Bank of America National

Trust & Savings Ass'n v. 203 N. LaSalle St. Partnership, 526 U.S. 434, 458 (1999), could suffice to escape the absolute priority rule, even assuming the ongoing validity of the *Case* dictum.

203 North LaSalle and *Ahlers* indicate a preference for reading the rule strictly. Given that the Supreme Court has hesitated to allow old owners to receive new ownership interests even when contributing new value, it is doubtful the Court would allow old owners to receive new ownership without contributing any new value, as in this case. As the Court explained in *Ahlers*, "the statutory language and the legislative history of §1129(b) clearly bar any expansion of any exception to the absolute priority rule beyond that recognized in our cases at the time Congress enacted the 1978 Bankruptcy Code." Ahlers, 485 U.S. at 206. The Supreme Court has never suggested any exception that would cover a case like this one.

The appellees, unsurprisingly, see the case in a different light. They contend that, under the "gifting doctrine," the shares and warrants rightfully belonged to the secured creditors, who were entitled to share them with the existing shareholder as they saw fit. Citing In re SPM Manufacturing Corp., 984 F.2d 1305 (1st Cir. 1993), the appellees argue that, until the debts of the secured creditors "are paid in full, the Bankruptcy Code's distributional priority scheme, as embodied in the absolute priority rule, is not implicated." DBSD was not worth enough, according to the bankruptcy court's valuation, to cover even the secured lenders' claims, much less those of unsecured creditors like Sprint. Therefore, as the bankruptcy court stated in ruling for the appellees, "the 'Gifting' Doctrine—under which senior secured creditors voluntarily offer a portion of their recovered property to junior stakeholders (as the Senior Noteholders did here)—defeats Sprint's Absolute Priority Rule objection." We disagree.

Most fatally, this interpretation does not square with the text of the Bankruptcy Code. The Code extends the absolute priority rule to "any property," §1129(b)(2)(B)(ii), not "any property not covered by a senior creditor's lien." The Code focuses entirely on who "receive[s]" or "retain[s]" the property "under the plan," not on who *would* receive it under a liquidation plan. And it applies the rule to any distribution "under the plan on account of" a junior interest, regardless of whether the distribution could have been made outside the plan, and regardless of whether other reasons might support the distribution in addition to the junior interest.

We distinguish this case from *In re SPM* on several grounds. In that case, a secured creditor and the general unsecured creditors agreed to seek liquidation of the debtor and to share the proceeds from the liquidation. The bankruptcy court granted relief from the automatic stay and converted the case from Chapter 11 to a Chapter 7 liquidation. The bankruptcy court refused, however, to allow the unsecured creditors to receive their share under the agreement with the secured creditor, ordering instead that the unsecured creditors' share go to a priority creditor in between those two classes. The district court affirmed, but the First Circuit reversed, holding that nothing in the Code barred the secured creditors from sharing their proceeds in a Chapter 7 liquidation with unsecured creditors, even at the expense of a creditor who would otherwise take priority over those unsecured creditors.

The first and most important distinction is that *In re SPM* involved Chapter 7, not Chapter 11, and thus involved a liquidation of the debtor, not a reorganization. Chapter 7 does not include the rigid absolute priority rule of §1129(b)(2)(B). As the First Circuit noted, "the distribution scheme" of Chapter 7 "does not come into play until all valid liens on the property are satisfied." *In re SPM* repeatedly emphasized the "lack[ ]" of "statutory support" for the argument against gifting in the Chapter 7 context. Under Chapter 11, in contrast §1129(b)(2)(B) provides clear "statutory support" to reject gifting in this case, and the distribution scheme of Chapter 11 ordinarily distributes *all* property in the estate (as it does here), including property subject to security interests.

Furthermore, the bankruptcy court in *In re SPM* had granted the secured creditor relief from the automatic stay, and treated the property in question as no longer part of the estate. In a very real sense, the property belonged to the secured creditor alone, and the secured creditor could do what it pleased with it. Here, however, the relevant property has remained in the estate throughout, and has never belonged to the secured creditors outright. For these reasons, therefore, assuming without deciding that the First Circuit's approach was correct in the context of Chapter 7—a question not before us—we do not find it relevant to this case.

Even if the text of §1129(b)(2)(B) left any room for the appellees' view of the case, we would hesitate to accept it in light of the Supreme Court's long history of rejecting such views. That history begins at least as early as 1868, in Howard, 74 U.S. (7 Wall) 392. In that case, the stockholders and mortgagees of a failing railroad agreed to foreclose on the railroad and convey its property to a new corporation, with the old stockholders receiving some of the new shares. The agreement gave nothing, however, to certain intermediate creditors, who sought a share of the distribution in the courts.

The stockholders defended their agreement with nearly the exact logic the appellees employ here:

> The road was mortgaged for near three times its value .... If, then, these stockholders have got anything, it must be because the bondholders have *surrendered* a part of *their* fund to them. If the fund belonged to the bondholders, they had a right so to surrender a part or a whole of it. And if the bondholders did so surrender their own property to the stockholders, it became the private property of these last; a gift, or, if you please, a transfer for consideration from the bondholders .... What right have these complainants to *such* property in the hands of the stockholders?

Even in 1868, however, the Supreme Court found that "[e]xtended discussion of that proposition is not necessary." Id. at 414. "Holders of bonds secured by mortgages as in this case," the Court noted, "may exact the whole amount of the bonds, principal and interest, or they may, if they see fit, accept a percentage as a compromise in full discharge of their respective claims, but whenever their lien is legally discharged, the property embraced in the mortgage, or whatever remains of it, belongs to the corporation" for distribution to other creditors. *Id.* Similarly, in this case, the secured creditors could have demanded a plan in which they received all of the reorganized corporation, but, having chosen not to, they may not "surrender" part of the value of the estate for distribution "to the stockholder[ ]," as "a gift." *Id.* at 400. Whatever the secured creditors here did not take remains in the estate for the benefit of other claim-holders.

As the Court built upon *Howard* to develop the absolute priority rule, it continued to reject arguments similar to the ones the appellees make before us. For example, in *Louisville Trust Co. v. Louisville, New Albany & Chicago Railway Co.,* the Court noted that "if the bondholder wishes to foreclose and exclude inferior lienholders or general unsecured creditors and stockholders, he may do so; but a foreclosure which attempts to preserve any interest or right of the mortgagor in the property after the sale must necessarily secure and preserve the prior rights of general creditors thereof." 174 U.S. 674, 683-84 (1899). The Court rejected another similar argument in 1913 in *Boyd,* where it finally set down the "fixed principle" that we now call the absolute priority rule.

Those cases dealt with facts much like the facts of this one: an over-leveraged corporation whose undersecured senior lenders agree to give shares to prior shareholders while intermediate lenders receive less than the value of their claim. *See* Douglas G. Baird & Thomas H. Jackson, *Bargaining After the Fall and the Contours of the Absolute Priority Rule*, 55 U. Chi. L. Rev. 738, 739-44 (1988). And it was on the basis of those facts that the Supreme Court developed the absolute priority rule, with the aim of stopping the very sort of transaction that the appellees propose here. These old cases do not bind us directly, given that Congress has now codified the absolute priority rule. But if courts will not infer statutory abrogation of the common law without evidence that Congress intended such abrogation, it would be even less appropriate to conclude that Congress abrogated the more-than-a-century-old core of the absolute priority rule by passing a statute whose language explicitly adopts it.

We recognize the policy arguments against the absolute priority rule. Gifting may be a "powerful tool in accelerating an efficient and non-adversarial … chapter 11 proceeding," Leah M. Eisenberg, *Gifting and Asset Reallocation in Chapter 11 Proceedings: A Synthesized Approach*, 29 Am. Bankr. Inst. J. 50, 50 (2010), and no doubt the parties intended the gift to have such an effect here. As one witness testified below, "where … the equity sponsor is out of the money, … a tip is common to [e]nsure a consensual bankruptcy rather than a contested one." Enforcing the absolute priority rule, by contrast, "may encourage hold-out behavior by objecting creditors … even though the transfer has no direct effect on the value to be received by the objecting creditors." Harvey R. Miller & Ronit J. Berkovich, *The Implications of the Third Circuit's Armstrong Decision on Creative Corporate Restructuring: Will Strict Construction of the Absolute Priority Rule Make Chapter 11 Consensus Less Likely?*, 55 Am. U.L. Rev. 1345, 1349 (2006).

It deserves noting, however, that there are substantial policy arguments in favor of the rule. Shareholders retain substantial control over the Chapter 11 process, and with that control comes significant opportunity for self-enrichment at the expense of creditors. This case provides a nice example. Although no one alleges any untoward conduct here, it is noticeable how much larger a distribution the existing shareholder will receive under this plan (4.99% of all equity in the reorganized entity) than the general unsecured creditors put together (0.15% of all equity), despite the latter's technical seniority. Indeed, based on the debtor's estimate that the reorganized entity would be worth approximately $572 million, the existing shareholder will receive approximately $28.5 million worth of equity under the plan while the unsecured creditors must share only $850,000. And if the parties here were less scrupulous or the bankruptcy court less vigilant, a weakened absolute priority rule could allow for serious mischief between senior creditors and existing shareholders.

Whatever the policy merits of the absolute priority rule, however, Congress was well aware of both its benefits and disadvantages when it codified the rule in the Bankruptcy Code. The policy objections to the rule are not new ones; the rule has attracted controversy from its early days. Four Justices dissented from the Supreme Court's 1913 holding in *Boyd*, and that decision "was received by the reorganization bar and bankers with something akin to horror," James N. Rosenberg, *Reorganization—The Next Step,* 22 Colum. L. Rev. 14, 14 (1922). The Commission charged with reviewing the bankruptcy laws in the lead-up to the enactment of the Bankruptcy Code suggested loosening the absolute priority rule to allow greater participation by equity owners. *See Bruce A. Markell, Owners, Auctions, and Absolute Priority in Bankruptcy Reorganizations,* 44 Stan. L. Rev. 70, 87-89 & n.117 (1991). Yet, although Congress did soften the absolute priority rule in some ways, it did not create any exception for "gifts" like the one at issue here. We therefore hold that the bankruptcy court erred in confirming the plan of reorganization. * * *

DISH raises different objections to the bankruptcy court's order. First, DISH contends that the bankruptcy court should not have designated its vote as "not in good faith," Bankruptcy Code § 1126(e), and that, even after the designation, the bankruptcy court should not have disregarded the entire class that DISH's claim comprised. * * *

DISH, although not a creditor of DBSD before its filing, had purchased the claims of various creditors with an eye toward DBSD's spectrum rights. As a provider of satellite television, DISH has launched a number of its own satellites, and it also has a significant investment in TerreStar Corporation, a direct competitor of DSDB's in the developing field of hybrid satellite/terrestrial mobile communications. DISH desired to "reach some sort of transaction with [DBSD] in the future if [DBSD's] spectrum could be useful in our business."

Shortly after DBSD filed its plan disclosure, DISH purchased all of the First Lien Debt at its full face value of $40 million, with an agreement that the sellers would make objections to the plan that DISH could adopt after the sale. As DISH admitted, it bought the First Lien Debt not just to acquire a "market piece of paper" but also to "be in a position to take advantage of [its claim] if things didn't go well in a restructuring."

Internal DISH communications also promoted an "opportunity to obtain a blocking position in the [Second Lien Debt] and control the bankruptcy process for this potentially strategic asset." In the end, DISH (through a subsidiary) purchased only $111 million of the Second Lien Debt—not nearly enough to control that class—with the small size of its stake due in part to DISH's unwillingness to buy any claims whose prior owners had already entered into an agreement to support the plan.

In addition to voting its claims against confirmation, DISH reasserted the objections that the sellers of those claims had made pursuant to the transfer agreement, arguing, among other things, that the plan was not feasible under §1129(a)(11) and that the plan did not give DISH the "indubitable equivalent" of its First Lien Debt as required to cram down a dissenting class of secured creditors under §1129(b)(2)(A). Separately, DISH proposed to enter into a strategic transaction with DBSD, and requested permission to propose its own competing plan (a request it later withdrew).

DBSD responded by moving for the court to designate that DISH's "rejection of [the] plan was not in good faith." §1126(e). The bankruptcy court agreed, finding that DISH, a competitor to DBSD, was voting against the plan "not as a traditional creditor seeking to maximize its return on the debt it holds, but ... 'to establish control over this strategic asset.' " (quoting DISH's own internal presentation slides). The bankruptcy court therefore designated DISH's vote and disregarded DISH's wholly-owned class of First Lien Debt for the purposes of determining plan acceptance under §1129(a)(8). The court also rejected DISH's objections to the plan, finding that the plan was feasible and that, even assuming that DISH's vote counted, the plan gave DISH the "indubitable equivalent" of its First Lien Debt claim and could thus be crammed down over DISH's dissent. * * *

DISH contends that the bankruptcy court should not have designated its vote as "not in good faith," §1126(e), and that, even after the designation, the bankruptcy court should not have disregarded the entire class that DISH's claim comprised. Second, DISH argues that the plan should have been rejected in its entirety as not feasible. We address these arguments in turn. * * *

To confirm a plan of reorganization, Chapter 11 generally requires a vote of all holders of claims or interests impaired by that plan. This voting requirement has exceptions, however, including one that allows a bankruptcy court to designate (in effect, to disregard) the votes of "any entity whose acceptance or rejection of such plan was not in good faith." §1126(e).

The Code provides no guidance about what constitutes a bad faith vote to accept or reject a plan. Rather, §1126(e)'s "good faith" test effectively delegates to the courts the task of deciding when a party steps over the boundary. Case by case, courts have taken up this responsibility. No circuit court has ever dealt with a case like this one, however, and neither we nor the Supreme Court have many precedents on the "good faith" voting requirement in any context; the most recent cases from both courts are now more than 65 years old and address §1126(e)'s predecessor, § 203 of the Bankruptcy Act. Nevertheless, these cases, cases from other jurisdictions, legislative history, and the purposes of the good-faith requirement give us confidence in affirming the bankruptcy court's decision to designate DISH's vote in this case.

We start with general principles that neither side disputes. Bankruptcy courts should employ §1126(e) designation sparingly, as "the exception, not the rule." In re Adelphia Communications Corp., 359 Bankr. 54, 61 (Bankr. S.D.N.Y. 2006). For this reason, a party seeking to designate another's vote bears the burden of proving that it was not cast in good faith. Merely purchasing claims in bankruptcy "for the purpose of securing the approval or rejection of a plan does not of itself amount to 'bad faith.' " In re P-R Holding Corp., 147 F.2d 895, 897 (2d Cir. 1945). Nor will selfishness alone defeat a creditor's good faith; the Code assumes that parties will act in their own self interest and allows them to do so.

Section 1126(e) comes into play when voters venture beyond mere self-interested promotion of their claims. "[T]he section was intended to apply to those who were not attempting to protect their own proper interests, but who were, instead, attempting to obtain some benefit to which they were not entitled." In re Figter Ltd., 118 F.3d 635, 638 (9th Cir. 1997). A bankruptcy court may, therefore, designate the vote of a party who votes "in the hope that someone would pay them more than the ratable equivalent of their proportionate part of the bankrupt assets," Young v. Higbee Co., 324 U.S. 204, 211 (1945) or one who votes with an "ulterior motive," Revision of the Bankruptcy Act: Hearing on H.R. 6439 Before the House Comm. on the Judiciary, 75th Cong. 180 (1937) (statement of SEC Commissioner William O. Douglas), that is, with "an interest other than an interest as a creditor," In re P-R Holding, 147 F.2d at 897.

Here, the debate centers on what sort of "ulterior motives" may trigger designation under §1126(e), and whether DISH voted with such an impermissible motive. The first question is a question of law that we review *de novo*, and the second a question of fact that we review for clear error, recognizing that "a decision that someone did or did not act in good faith" hinges on "an essentially factual inquiry and is driven by the data of practical human experience," In re Figter, 118 F.3d at 638 (quotation marks omitted).

Clearly, not just any ulterior motive constitutes the sort of improper motive that will support a finding of bad faith. After all, most creditors have interests beyond their claim against a particular debtor, and those other interests will inevitably affect how they vote the claim. For instance, trade creditors who do regular business with a debtor may vote in the way most likely to allow them to continue to do business with the debtor after reorganization. And, as interest rates change, a fully secured creditor may seek liquidation to allow money once invested at unfavorable rates to be invested more favorably elsewhere. We do not purport to decide here the propriety of either of these motives, but they at least demonstrate that allowing the disqualification of votes on account of *any* ulterior motive could have far-reaching consequences and might leave few votes upheld.

The sort of ulterior motive that §1126(e) targets is illustrated by the case that motivated the creation of the "good faith" rule in the first place, Texas Hotel Securities Corp. v. Waco Development Co., 87 F.2d 395 (5th Cir. 1936). In that case, Conrad Hilton purchased claims of a debtor to block a plan of reorganization that would have given a lease on the debtor's property—once held by Hilton's company, later cancelled—to a third party. Hilton and his partners sought, by buying and voting the claims, to "force [a plan] that would give them again the operation of the hotel or otherwise reestablish an interest that they felt they justly had in the property." The district court refused to count Hilton's vote, but the court of appeals reversed, seeing no authority in the Bankruptcy Act for looking into the motives of creditors voting against a plan.

That case spurred Congress to require good faith in voting claims. As the Supreme Court has noted, the legislative history of the predecessor to §1126(e) "make[s] clear the purpose of the [House] Committee [on the Judiciary] to pass legislation which would bar creditors from a vote who were prompted by such a purpose" as Hilton's. Young, 324 U.S. at 211 n.10. As then-SEC Commissioner Douglas explained to the House Committee:

> We envisage that "good faith" clause to enable the courts to affirm a plan over the opposition of a minority attempting to block the adoption of a plan merely for selfish purposes. The *Waco* case ... was such a situation. If my memory does not serve me wrong it was a case where a minority group of security holders refused to vote in favor of the plan unless that group were given some particular preferential treatment, such as the management of the company. That is, there were ulterior reasons for their actions.

1937 Hearing, at 181-82. One year after Commissioner Douglas's testimony, and two years after the *Waco* case, Congress enacted the proposed good faith clause as part of the Chandler Act of 1938. The Bankruptcy Code of 1978 preserved this good faith requirement, with some rewording, as §1126(e).

Modern cases have found "ulterior motives" in a variety of situations. In perhaps the most famous case, and one on which the bankruptcy court in our case relied heavily, a court found bad faith because a party bought a blocking position in several classes after the debtor proposed a plan of reorganization, and then sought to defeat that plan and to promote its own plan that would have given it control over the debtor. See In re Allegheny International, Inc., 118 Bankr. 282, 289-90 (Bankr. W.D. Pa. 1990). In another case, the court designated the votes of parties affiliated with a competitor who bought their claims in an attempt to obstruct the debtor's reorganization and thereby to further the interests of their own business. See In re MacLeod Co., 63 Bankr. 654, 655-56 (Bankr. S.D. Ohio 1986). In a third case, the court found bad faith where an affiliate of the debtor purchased claims not for the purpose of collecting on those claims but to prevent confirmation of a competing plan. See In re Applegate Prop., Ltd., 133 Bankr. 827, 833-35 (Bankr. W.D. Tex. 1991).

Although we express no view on the correctness of the specific findings of bad faith of the parties in those specific cases, we think that this case fits in the general constellation they form. As the bankruptcy court found, DISH, as an indirect competitor of DBSD and part-owner of a direct competitor, bought a blocking position in (and in fact the entirety of) a class of claims, after a plan had been proposed, with the intention not to maximize its return on the debt but to enter a strategic transaction with DBSD and "to use status as a creditor to provide advantages over proposing a plan as an outsider, or making a traditional bid for the company or its assets." In effect, DISH purchased the claims as votes it could use as levers to bend the bankruptcy process toward its own strategic objective of acquiring DBSD's spectrum rights, not toward protecting its claim.

We conclude that the bankruptcy court permissibly designated DISH's vote based on the facts above. This case echoes the *Waco* case that motivated Congress to impose the good faith requirement in the first place. In that case, a competitor bought claims with the intent of voting against any plan that did not give it a lease in or management of the debtor's property. 87 F.2d at 397-99. In this case, a competitor bought claims with the intent of voting against any plan that did not give it a strategic interest in the reorganized company. The purchasing party in both cases was less interested in maximizing the return on its claim than in diverting the progress of the proceedings to achieve an outside benefit. In 1936, no authority allowed disregarding votes in such a situation, but Congress created that authority two years later with cases like *Waco* in mind. We therefore hold that a court may designate a creditor's vote in these circumstances.

We also find that, just as the law supports the bankruptcy court's legal conclusion, so the evidence supports its relevant factual findings. DISH's motive—the most controversial finding—is evinced by DISH's own admissions in court, by its position as a competitor to DBSD, by its willingness to overpay for the claims it bought, by its attempt to propose its own plan, and especially by its internal communications, which, although addressing the Second Lien Debt rather than the First Lien Debt at issue here, nevertheless showed a desire to "to obtain a blocking position" and "control the bankruptcy process for this potentially strategic asset."

The Loan Syndications and Trading Association (LSTA), as *amicus curiae,* argues that courts should encourage acquisitions and other strategic transactions because such transactions can benefit all parties in bankruptcy. We agree. But our holding does not "shut[ ] the door to strategic transactions," as the LSTA suggests. Rather, it simply limits the methods by which parties may pursue them. DISH had every right to propose for consideration whatever strategic transaction it wanted— a right it took advantage of here—and DISH still retained this right even after it purchased its claims. All that the bankruptcy court stopped DISH from doing here was using the votes it had bought to secure an advantage in pursuing that strategic transaction.

DISH argues that, if we uphold the decision below, "future creditors looking for potential strategic transactions with chapter 11 debtors will be deterred from exploring such deals for fear of forfeiting their rights as creditors." But our ruling today should deter only attempts to *"obtain* a blocking position" and thereby "control the bankruptcy process for [a] potentially strategic asset" (as DISH's own internal documents stated). We leave for another day the situation in which a *preexisting* creditor votes with strategic intentions. We emphasize, moreover, that our opinion imposes no categorical prohibition on purchasing claims with acquisitive or other strategic intentions. On other facts, such purchases may be appropriate. Whether a vote has been properly designated is a fact-intensive question that must be based on the totality of the circumstances, according considerable deference to the expertise of bankruptcy judges. Having reviewed the careful and fact-specific decision of the bankruptcy court here, we find no error in its decision to designate DISH's vote as not having been cast in good faith.

DISH next argues that the bankruptcy court erred when, after designating DISH's vote, it disregarded the entire class of the First Lien Debt for the purpose of determining plan acceptance under Bankruptcy Code §1129(a)(8). Section 1129(a)(8) provides that each impaired class must vote in favor of a plan for the bankruptcy court to confirm it without resorting to the (more arduous) cram-down standards of §1129(b). Faced with a class that effectively contained zero claims—because DISH's claim had been designated—the bankruptcy court concluded that "[t]he most appropriate way to deal with that [situation] is by disregarding [DISH's class] for the purposes of§1129(a)(8). We agree with the bankruptcy court. Common sense demands this result, which is consistent with (if not explicitly demanded by) the text of the Bankruptcy Code.

The Code measures the acceptance of a plan not creditor-by-creditor or claim-by-claim, but class-by-class. The relevant provision explains how to tally acceptances within a class of claims to arrive at the vote of the overall class:

> A class of claims has accepted a plan if such plan has been accepted by creditors, *other than any entity designated under subsection (e) of this section,* that hold at least two-thirds in amount and more than one-half in number of the allowed claims of such class held by creditors, *other than any entity designated under subsection (e) of this section,* that have accepted or rejected such plan.

Bankruptcy Code §1126(c) (emphasis added). For each class, then, the bankruptcy court must calculate two fractions based on the non-designated, allowed claims in the class. To arrive at the first fraction, the court divides the value of such claims that vote to accept the plan by the value of all claims that vote either way. For the second fraction, the court uses the number of claims rather than their value. If the first fraction equals two-thirds or more, and the second fraction more than one-half, then the class as a whole votes to accept the plan.

The arithmetic breaks down in cases like this one. Because the only claim in DISH's class belongs to DISH, whose vote the court designated, each fraction ends up as zero divided by zero. In this case, the plain meaning of the statute and common sense lead clearly to one answer: just as a bankruptcy court properly ignores designated *claims* when calculating the vote of a class, *see* §1126(c), so it should ignore a wholly designated *class* when deciding to confirm a plan under §1129(a)(8). We agree with the bankruptcy court that any other rule "would make [the] designation ruling meaningless" in this context. We therefore affirm the bankruptcy court's treatment of DISH's class.

[The material on the "Absolute Priority" in chapter 13A(3), which begins on ***page 707***, should be supplemented by the following.]

The Second Circuit's opinion in *DSBD*, reproduced above on page 127 of this update in connection with vote designation, addresses and rejects the controversial gifting doctrine, under which a senior class of claims sacrifices some of its return in a reorganization plan in favor of a junior class of claims or interests over the objection of an intermediate class. Compare *Journal Register*, reproduced above on page 115 of this update, and *Armstrong*, the district court opinion in which is reproduced in this part of the casebook (affirmed 432 F.3d 507 (3rd Cir. 2005)).

DSBD also addresses the so-called new value exception to the absolute priority rule at issue in *203 North LaSalle Street*. The next two cases, *RTJJ* and *Castleton*, are recent, and contrasting, developments in the doctrine of this exception.

IN RE RTJJ, INC.

United States Bankruptcy Court, W.D. North Carolina, 2013
2013 WL 462003

J. CRAIG WHITLEY, BANKRUPTCY JUDGE

The Debtor is a small family business, which owns sixty-two (62) rental houses, apartments and undeveloped residential building lots in Gastonia, North Carolina. Most of these are former single-family residences, colloquially "mill houses." More recently, these homes have been subdivided for rental as individual apartments. Thus, a single dwelling may be rented to multiple tenants. RTJJ's business is unique in the local market not just for this, but also because it rents furnished apartments on a weekly rental basis.

The family patriarch, Harrill Jones, started RTJJ's predecessor businesses (Harrill Jones, Inc. and Excelsior Group, Inc.) in the 1960's. Jones' businesses prospered and for years, the companies had a waiting list of tenants. These companies catered to textile worker tenants. In 1997, sons Rick, Todd, and Jeffrey Jones incorporated RTJJ and purchased many of the Properties from these predecessor companies.

Between 2000 and 2004, many Gaston County mills closed. The closings adversely affected the local economy and left one-third of the Jones' companies' rental units vacant. Meanwhile, Harrill Jones suffered other business and investment reversals. In 2005, Harrill Jones took his own life.

This unfortunate sequence of events left the Jones family businesses in a tough spot. Rick Jones, RTJJ's President, says his father's death left the businesses with $3,500,000 million in insurance proceeds but over $7,000,000 in debt, including a $650,000 federal tax debt.

In 2006, RTJJ purchased the remaining properties owned by Harrill Jones, Inc. and Excelsior Group, Inc. Community One financed these purchases as well as the company's tax debt.

Community One's debts exist under four notes and three separate deeds of trust, which give it a perfected mortgage debt on all but one of RTJJ's real properties. (Community One's collateral is the "Properties.") Creditor First National Bank of Shelby ("First National") holds a mortgage on that one other rental house. From what can be surmised, there never was much equity in the Properties over Community One's loan balance, if any. It may be that the Properties were over encumbered from the outset. Either way, Community One's secured position suffered dramatic erosion after the 2007 housing bubble bust and national real estate values plummeted.

Between these events and its then high vacancy rate, RTJJ was unable to make its monthly mortgage payments. It succeeded in obtaining a twelve month forbearance agreement from Community One. RTJJ used this time to remodel its properties, redirect its business, and attempt to return to profitability. Recognizing that the market for apartment rentals had changed, RTJJ converted a number of its one bedroom apartments into larger two bedroom apartments. This change improved the company's occupancy rate; however, RTJJ was still unable to make its full mortgage payments.

Community One then instituted foreclosure proceedings against the Properties. To stop the sale, on August 8, 2011, RTJJ filed Chapter 11.

According to its Schedules, RTJJ owed secured debt of $3,918,967.20 at the filing date, no priority debt, and $43,191.71 of general unsecured debt. The claims docket as of October 27, 2011 summarizes filed claims as follows: $2,534,209.02 secured; $453.67 priority; and $57,189.48 general unsecured. These differences are not material for present purposes. * * *

Since bankruptcy, RTJJ has continued to operate the Properties under an agreed cash collateral order with Community One. The Debtor's post petition operations have been quite successful. RTJJ's occupancy rate has increased from sixty-seven percent (67%) to ninety-five percent (95%), and has remained there for the past year. Effectively, the Properties are fully rented. RTJJ has made all of the agreed adequate protection payments to Community One. By October 2012, RTJJ's 2012 cash flow had exceeded 2011 levels with two months of the year to spare. The Debtor is showing an operating profit, albeit before debt service.

All concerned agree that RTJJ is a well-run company. From the two appraisers who testified at an earlier valuation hearing, to the Gastonia City manager, all agree that RTJJ has a very good reputation, is well run, and is compliant with applicable housing requirements. It is also undisputed that as the only area business of its sort, RTJJ serves a vital need in the Gastonia low-income housing market. Because RTJJ's Properties are located in fragile, poor neighborhoods, Gastonia believes that loss of this business would have a negative effect on the community, both in loss of low-income housing and the prospect of increased crime.

Unfortunately, even at full occupancy levels, the Properties do not generate sufficient revenues to service the mortgage debt of Community One and First National. Thus, reorganization is dependent on RTJJ being able to "smooth down" its secured debt to a level that the Properties can support. With First National, doing so has been relatively easy. RTJJ and First National agree that its single collateral property has a value (and therefore a secured claim) of $17,500, and an unsecured 'deficiency' of about $7,500. The two sides have agreed on the treatment of these claims in a plan.

The Community One situation is much more contentious. In its Schedules, RTJJ originally valued Community One's collateral at $864,710.00. However, Community One has maintained throughout the case that its collateral was worth more than its $2,453,838.88 debt. The proper valuation of the Properties and thus, Community One's secured claim has been the crucial issue in the case.

When RTJJ filed its original plan and disclosure Statement on January 18, 2012, it proposed to value Community One's collateral per §506(a) and bifurcate the debt between its secured and unsecured portions. The secured claim was to be re-amortized and paid in installments as a long term secured claim. The unsecured claim would be treated with other unsecured claims and receive a small dividend. The accompanying Disclosure Statement was approved on March 1, 2012 and the Plan was circulated for balloting on March 13, 2012. A balloting response deadline was set for April 3, 2012. However, Community One was the only creditor to file a timely ballot. It rejected the plan and further filed an objection to confirmation.

By agreement, confirmation was then delayed in order to have the Properties appraised. A valuation hearing was held on July 9, 2012. The Properties were ascribed a fair market value of $1,471,350. Per §506(a), Community One holds a secured claim of the same amount. Its remaining $982,487.00 debt is an unsecured claim. * * *

The Second Amended Plan contemplates that RTJJ will continue to operate its business and fund plan payments through future revenues.

Community One's $1,471,350 secured claim (Class 1) is to be repaid with interest at five percent per annum, in monthly installments of $8,599.32 under a twenty-five year amortization schedule and with a seven year call. As filed, the Second Amended Plan proposes to surrender three of the Properties in a "dirt for debt" provision. However, Community One objected to this treatment, and at the confirmation hearing, RTJJ withdrew this proposal. RTJJ currently proposes to retain all of the Properties and pay the full secured portion of the claims as above.

Meanwhile, Community One's $982,487 unsecured claim is treated in Class 4, together with the claims of Harill Jones, Inc., Patty M. Jones, and the Exclesior Group. Each is the unsecured portion of a mortgage claim. As filed, the Second Amended Plan proposes to give Class 4 claimants nonvoting Class B stock in satisfaction of their unsecured claims. Community One objected to this treatment, suggesting that the Class B stock is worthless and noting that §1123(a)(6) prohibits a reorganized debtor from issuing nonvoting stock. Again seeking to appease its lender, at the confirmation hearing RTJJ amended the Class 4 treatment to give Community One an immediate $50,000 cash payment in satisfaction of its Class 4 claim. All other class members (all are insiders) agreed to waive a distribution on their Class 4 claims.

Regarding First National, the $17,500 secured portion of its mortgage claim (Class 2) is to be paid in monthly installments with 4.25% interest, a twenty year amortization period and a five year call date. The remaining $7,500 balance of First National's debt is to be treated as a Class 5 unsecured claim.

All other unsecured claims are treated in Class 5. These holders are to receive two percent of their allowed claims payable over five years in equal annual installments, without interest.

RTJJ's outstanding stock will be cancelled. The Jones brothers will contribute $20,000 to the reorganized Debtor in exchange for new Class A Common Stock. Class A Common Stock is to receive no interest, dividends, or any other distributions while Community One's Class 1 secured claim is outstanding (and as filed, while the Class B Common Stock is outstanding). The Plan alternatively proposed to auction the Class A Common Stock at the confirmation hearing. Given the hearing amendment to Class 4 noted above, the stock restriction is no longer applicable. * * *

Community One has objected to confirmation of each iteration of the Plan, including the verbal amendments offered at hearing. It argues … this plan is not fair and equitable as to its Class 4 unsecured claim because it violates the absolute priority rule. Specifically, Community One objects to the Jones brothers receiving the new Class A stock and argues that their $20,000 payment does not constitute "new value." * * *

By contrast, the other two balloting, non-insider creditors, First National and Simonds, are satisfied with the Debtor's plan. They believe that their treatment under the Second Amended Plan (revised) while modest, is superior to what they could expect in either liquidation or foreclosure.

In this, they are correct. All of RTJJ's assets are subject to the liens of Community One, First National, or the subordinate mortgages of the other Class 4 creditors. Even at fair market values, these rental properties are upside down at least $2,500,000. (Fair market value of $1,470,000 as compared to mortgage debt of $3,918,967.00).

The two first priority lenders, Community One and First National, are greatly undersecured, even at fair market values. However, in a forced liquidation or foreclosure, the Properties would fetch far less than fair market value. The RTJJ houses are unique assets. Generally, they are old houses. Most have been extensively remodeled such that a single house typically contains multiple apartments. Because of this, these houses could not be resold for use as single-family residences without substantial modifications. Further, they are unlikely to be sold "as is" for use by other landlords. There are no other landlords in the Gastonia market who operate similar businesses (furnished units, multiple units per house, weekly rentals). The real estate market is weak. Because there are so many of these rental properties and the market is so small (population of Gastonia, N.C. is only 70,000), a forced sale of the Properties would flood the low-income real estate market and further depress already depressed values. In a Chapter 7 liquidation or foreclosure, the seller of the Properties would take an unbelievable "bath."

Meanwhile, RTJJ also owes administrative expenses of at least $45,313.00. Hypothetical Chapter 7 administrative expenses would run at least this much, even assuming that the lenders would consent to a short sale. In sum, in a liquidation or foreclosure, there will be no distribution to unsecured creditors. Secured creditors would recover much less than the secured portion of their claims.

Notwithstanding the obvious deleterious effects of a foreclosure, unless RTJJ can pay its entire $2.5 million debt, Community One wants to pursue this course. Its motivation appears to have little to do with RTJJ or the merits of the Second Amended Plan (rev.)

Like many community banks that before the real estate crash had made too many real estate and development loans, Community One has had its own problems of late. At the confirmation hearing, RTJJ introduced several pieces of evidence bearing on the bank's woes. Among this evidence, as of March 31, 2011, the Bank was categorized as "critically undercapitalized." and was almost closed by the Office of the Controller of the Currency ("OCC"). It, a sister bank, and their holding company have been operating under OCC supervision for some time. Given this, and because Community One's demands are alternatively unrealistic (the demand to be paid as a fully secured creditor per the original loan terms), or self destructive (the request to foreclose), RTJJ believes that the Bank's actions are based on regulatory pressures and not on the merits of the Plan. On this record, it appears that RTJJ is correct. * * *

Section 1129(b)(2) sets forth criteria that must be met in order for a plan to be considered fair and equitable as to a dissenting class of unsecured claims. Specifically, §1129(b)(2)(B) requires that the plan satisfy the "absolute priority rule." Under this rule, either (i) the plan must provide for payment in full of the allowed amount of the unsecured claims in the dissenting class, or (ii) the holder of any claim or interest junior to the dissenting class (i.e., equity owners in the debtor) may not receive or retain property on account of such claim or interest.

Clearly, control of a business and the right to future distributions based upon stock ownership are "property" under §1129(b)(2)(B)(ii). See Bank of America National Trust and Sav. Ass'n v. 203 N. LaSalle St. Partnership, 526 U.S. 434, 455 (1999); Norwest Bank Worthington v. Ahlers, 485 U.S. 197, 208 (1988); N. Pac. Ry. Co. v. Boyd, 228 U.S. 482, 508 (1913).

Community One argues that the Second Amended Plan is not fair and equitable to it as an unsecured creditor under §1129(b)(2)(B)(ii) because the Jones brothers, the existing shareholders, are afforded the exclusive right to purchase stock in the reorganized Debtor and to receive future distributions, based upon the newly issued Class A Common Stock.

RTJJ counters that the stock purchase proposal falls within the "new value exception" to the absolute priority rule. Under the new value exception, equity may retain an interest in a reorganized debtor over the objection of a class of creditors whose claims are not paid in full, in exchange for a fresh contribution of new capital. A plan that meets the new value exception does not violate §1129(b)(2)(B)(ii) because it does "not give old equity property 'on account of prior interests, but instead will allow the former owners to participate in the reorganized debtor on account of a substantial, necessary, and fair new value contribution."

The five requirements of 'new value' are that it be "1) new, 2) substantial, 3) money or money's worth, 4) necessary for a successful reorganization and 5) reasonably equivalent to the value or interest received."

In this case, the first and third requirements are not in dispute. The $20,000 that the Jones brothers are borrowing to contribute to RTJJ is undoubtedly new money.

However, Community One argues that the shareholders' contribution is not necessary, substantial, or reasonably equivalent to the equity interest in the reorganized debtor that the Shareholders are to receive. It points out that $20,000 is only two percent (2%) of its $982,487 unsecured claim. Community One also maintains that the contribution is grossly disproportionate to the value of the assets the reorganized debtor is to retain, which value, Community One characterizes as $1.5 million. Given the small dollar amount of the equity contribution, Community One suggests that it is not necessary. After all, the Debtor has other banked funds. Finally, the Bank suggests that the equity contribution has not been market tested.

On the facts presented, this Court disagrees. The equity contribution serves a necessary function in this particular case: this contribution is the only available funding available to pay administrative expenses, specifically RTJJ's attorneys fees. The Debtor is in a bit of quandary here. Payment of administrative expenses is required under §1129(a)(9) as a condition of confirmation. While the Debtor has some bank deposits, much of this is necessary to operations. Further, these monies derive from rents. Community One holds an assignment of rents on the Properties. Under §552(b)(2), post petition rents serve as additional collateral for Community One's mortgage debt. Absent consent, a debtor cannot fund its attorney's fees from an undersecured creditor's collateral. Community One opposes RTJJ's reorganization attempt and has not consented to RTJJ using rents to pay Mr. Henderson's fees. The $20,000 is certainly necessary.

Similarly, the contribution is substantial. Substantiality is the most controversial aspect of the new value exception, with courts struggling to define the term and commentators suggesting that it is unnecessary. All agree that the payment cannot be token or nominal but beyond this there is no consensus. As Community One suggests, some courts have measured substantiality by comparison to the total amount of unsecured claims. However, other courts warn against employing such mechanical tests. Collier's criticizes this approach as not be required by case precedent and also because it is unnecessary.

Here, the equity contribution is admittedly small as compared to outstanding unsecured debt. However, even at this level, this $20,000 infusion is significant to a small family business, bereft of unencumbered assets, and generally limited in its cash resources. This Debtor has only $36,000 of bank deposits, after tenant deposits and the $50,000 payment to be made on Community One's Class 4 claim. As compared to net available cash, $20,000 is significant. The proposed stock payment will satisfy administrative expense claims. [6]

This sum is also significant from the shareholders' perspective. The absolute priority rule dates back to railroad reorganizations of yesteryear. It was formulated to prevent bond and stockholders using bankruptcy to squeeze out intermediate unsecured debt. That is of course an appropriate restatement of the non-bankruptcy rule that creditors are paid before equity. However, there are no coupon clippers in this case. The Jones brothers are working people of modest means. For them, $20,000 is a sizeable sum; in fact, they will have to borrow to fund their contribution.

Finally, the fifth requirement, "reasonably equivalent to the value or interest received" is also satisfied. Community One compares the $20,000 equity contribution to the total asset value in the case, $1.5 million. However, it is ignoring the fact that these assets are over encumbered and have no net asset value. RTJJ is balance sheet insolvent by more than $2.5 million. Thus, what is being purchased with $20,000 is nothing more than the right to control a small family business that has no net asset value. On these facts, the new value is substantial.

This takes us to Community One's market testing argument. Community One suggests that the new value contribution hasn't been exposed to the market for competitive bidding. For cases still within the §1121 exclusivity period, this would be a problem. In *203 North LaSalle,* the Supreme Court found the absolute priority rule to be violated by a plan "provision for vesting equity in the reorganized business in the Debtor's partners without extending an opportunity to anyone

---

[6] Henderson is willing to accept a partial, rather than a full, payment of his administrative expense claim.

else either to compete for that equity *or to propose a competing reorganization plan.*" (emphasis added). Bank of Am. National. Trust and Savings Association v. 203 N. LaSalle St. Partnership, 526 U.S. 434, 436 (1999). Because "no one else could propose an alternative" plan, "the Debtor's partners necessarily enjoyed an exclusive opportunity that was in no economic sense distinguishable from the advantage of the exclusively entitled offeror or option holder." Id. at 455.

However, when exclusivity has expired and there is no option value to the right to propose a plan, the value of the property being retained should be determined based on normal valuation basis (i.e., the balance sheet of the reorganized debtor or by capitalizing its projected income). In re Red Mountain Mach., 448 Bankr. 1, 18 (Bankr. D. Ariz.2011).

In our current case, exclusivity expired many months before the confirmation hearing was held. During this period, any party, including Community One, could have filed a competing plan that proposed a different ownership of the business. No one has done so, and apart from Community One, no one has suggested there is retained value in the Class A stock in excess of $20,000. Even Community One has offered no evidence to support such a valuation. Its objection is formulaic and obviously intended to block confirmation so that it may foreclose on the Properties.

This Plan meets the new value exception. * * *

A plan "must literally be fair and equitable." Thus, courts have denied confirmation to plans that are "one-sided rearrangement[s]" that impose "substantial" risks on the secured creditor while providing "significant benefits" to equity who accept "only minimal risks." And a plan proponent seeking cram down "must carry the burden of showing that the terms of the plan treat the dissenting classes fairly." In re Grandfather Mountain Ltd. P'ship, 207 Bankr. 475, 487 (Bankr. M.D.N.C. 1996). Community One cites these cases in its brief, suggesting that RTJJ's Plan does not meet these standards. In point of fact, the opposite is true. Reorganization under the Second Amended Plan (as revised at hearing), is fair to all creditors. It is denial of confirmation and foreclosure that would be unfair and inequitable—to everyone, including Community One.

Reorganization offers benefits to all of RTJJ's creditors. The two partially secured creditors will derive the fair market value of their collateral, with interest. Unsecured creditors will receive a small distribution on their claims, but will also retain a customer and the prospect of future sales. RTJJ's employees will retain their jobs. Tenants will stay in their apartments. The Gastonia community will continue to enjoy low income housing provided by a reputable and lawful provider.

If confirmation is denied, relief from stay and foreclosure will follow. Unsecured creditors will receive nothing and some, like Simonds, will lose a good customer. RTJJ's employees will lose their jobs. Tenants are unlikely to remain in their apartments post foreclosure. Gastonia's housing concerns (loss of low income housing and an increase in crime due to absentee landlords) will probably come to fruition. A reputable low-income housing source will be lost.

Even Community One and First National will be disadvantaged by foreclosure. As noted, their collateral is unique and generally unmarketable. The Properties are not presently suited for resale as residences. There are no identified buyers for these assets. There are no other landlords of this type in this market. In foreclosure, the two secured creditors are assured of a tremendous loss of value.

First National recognizes this. Community One does not seem to care. Under pressure from federal regulators, Community One seeks to rid itself of this nonperforming loan, at any cost. Its aims are noneconomic-at least as to this Debtor-and are destructive. Reorganization is preferable.

With the minor amendments noted at hearing, the Second Amended Plan should be *Confirmed.*

IN RE CASTLETON PLAZA, LP

United States Court of Appeals, Seventh Circuit, 2013
707 F.3d 821

EASTERBROOK, CIRCUIT JUDGE

Creditors in bankruptcy are entitled to full payment before equity investors can receive anything. 11 U.S.C. § 1129(b)(2)(B)(ii). This is the absolute-priority rule. Equity investors sometimes contend that the value they receive from the debtor in bankruptcy is on account of new (post-bankruptcy) investments rather than their old ones. The Supreme Court held in Bank of America National Trust & Savings Ass'n v. 203 North LaSalle Street Partnership, 526 U.S. 434 (1999), that competition is the way to tell whether a new investment makes the senior creditors (and the estate as a whole) better off. A plan of reorganization that includes a new investment must allow other potential investors to bid. In this competition, creditors can bid the value of their loans. RadLAX

Gateway Hotel, LLC v. Amalgamated Bank, 132 S.Ct. 2065 (2012). The process protects creditors against plans that would give competing claimants too much for their new investments and thus dilute the creditors' interests.

This appeal presents the question whether an equity investor can evade the competitive process by arranging for the new value to be contributed by (and the new equity to go to) an "insider," as §101(31) defines that term. The bankruptcy judge answered yes; our answer is no. Competition is essential whenever a plan of reorganization leaves an objecting creditor unpaid yet distributes an equity interest to an insider.

The material facts are simple. Castleton Plaza, the debtor, owns a shopping center in Indiana. George Broadbent owns 98% of Castleton's equity directly and the other 2% indirectly. EL–SNPR Notes Holdings is its only secured lender. The note carries interest of 8.37% and has several features, such as lockboxes for tenants' rents and approval rights for major leases, designed for additional security. The note matured in September 2010, and Castleton did not pay. Instead it commenced a bankruptcy proceeding. About a year later Castleton proposed a plan of reorganization under which $300,000 of EL–SNPR's roughly $10 million secured debt would be paid now and the balance written down to roughly $8.2 million, with the difference treated as unsecured. The $8.2 million secured loan would be extended for 30 years, with little to be paid until 2021, and the rate of interest cut to 6.25%, exceptionally low for credit representing 97% of the estimated value of the borrower's assets. All of the note's extra security features, such as the rental lockbox and approval rights, would be abolished.

Unpaid creditors normally receive the equity in a reorganized business. Castleton proposed a plan that cut the creditors out of any equity interest. Since the plan pays EL–SNPR less than its contractual entitlement, §1129(b)(2)(B)(ii) provides that George Broadbent cannot retain any equity interest on account of his old investment—and *203 North LaSalle* requires an auction before he could receive equity on account of a new investment. The proposed plan of reorganization nominally left George empty-handed. But it provided that 100% of the equity in the reorganized Castleton would go to Mary Clare Broadbent, George's wife, who would invest $75,000. Mary Clare owns all of the equity in The Broadbent Company, Inc., which runs Castleton under a management contract. George is the CEO of The Broadbent Company and receives an annual salary of $500,000 for his services. The plan of reorganization provides that the management contract between Castleton and The Broadbent Company would be continued.

EL–SNPR believes that Castleton's assets have been undervalued—see 2011 Bankr.LEXIS 3804 (Bankr.S.D.Ind. Sept. 30, 2011) (estimating the real estate's value at $8.25 million)—and that, given the dramatic decrease in the amount Castleton owes on the loan, the equity in the reorganized business will be worth more than $75,000. It offered $600,000 for the equity and promised to pay all other creditors 100¢ on the dollar. (Castleton's plan, by contrast, offers only 15% on unsecured claims, paid over five years.) Castleton rejected this proposal, though a revised plan did increase Mary Clare Broadbent's investment to $375,000. EL–SNPR asked the bankruptcy judge to condition that plan's acceptance on Mary Clare making the highest bid in an open competition. But the bankruptcy judge held that competition is unnecessary and confirmed the plan as proposed. * * *

The bankruptcy court thought competition unnecessary because Mary Clare Broadbent does not own an equity interest in Castleton, and §1129(b)(2)(B)(ii) deals only with "the holder of any claim" that is junior to the impaired creditor's claim. Yet *203 North LaSalle* did not interpret the language of §1129(b)(2)(B)(ii), which does not speak to new-value plans. The Court devised the competition requirement to curtail evasion of the absolute-priority rule. A new-value plan bestowing equity on an investor's spouse can be just as effective at evading the absolute-priority rule as a new-value plan bestowing equity on the original investor. For many purposes in bankruptcy law, such as preference recoveries under §547, an insider is treated the same as an equity investor. Family members of corporate managers are insiders under §101(31)(B)(vi). In *203 North LaSalle* the Court remarked on the danger that diverting assets to insiders can pose to the absolute-priority rule. It follows that plans giving insiders preferential access to investment opportunities in the reorganized debtor should be subject to the same opportunity for competition as plans in which existing claimholders put up the new money.

There can be no doubt that George Broadbent would receive value from the equity that Mary Clare Broadbent stands to obtain under the plan of reorganization. One form of value would be the continuation of George's salary as CEO of The Broadbent Company. Another would come through an increase in the family's wealth. Indiana is not a community-property state, but one spouse usually receives at least an indirect benefit from another's wealth, and Indiana treats each spouse as having a presumptive interest in the other's wealth. The fact that each spouse's wealth benefits the whole family is a principal reason why the statutory definition of insider includes family members—and why federal judges must recuse themselves when spouses or children living in the household have financial interests in litigants. And we cannot overlook the fact that George Broadbent, through his control of Castleton, set the option's price at $75,000 (and then $375,000) rather than some higher number. The difference between $375,000 and the price the option would fetch in competition is value to the entire Broadbent family.

In tax law, the exercise of a general power of appointment is treated as income to the holder. Thus if George Broadbent had directed The Broadbent Company to remit some of his salary to his spouse, child, or the supplier of the family's new piano, the money still would be treated as income to George and taxed accordingly. Similarly, if George had a discretionary power under a trust, and could direct assets to either Mary Clare or himself, the value would be treated as income to George even if the trust paid Mary Clare. That's fundamentally what happened here. George had control over Castleton and used his authority to propose a plan that directed a valuable opportunity (an option to buy all of the equity in the reorganized firm) to his spouse. Since the exercise of a power of appointment is treated as income in tax law, it should be treated as income for the purpose of §1129(b)(2)(B)(ii) too. Thus, under the plan of reorganization, George receives value on account of his investment, which gave him control over the plan's details. The absolute-priority rule therefore applies despite the fact that Mary Clare had not invested directly in Castleton. This reinforces our conclusion that competition is essential. * * *

None of the considerations we have mentioned depends on whether Castleton proposed the plan during the exclusivity period. Nor does the rationale of *203 North LaSalle* depend on who proposes the plan. Competition helps prevent the funneling of value from lenders to insiders, no matter who proposes the plan or when. An impaired lender who objects to *any* plan that leaves insiders holding equity is entitled to the benefit of competition. If, as Castleton and the Broadbents insist, their plan offers creditors the best deal, then they will prevail in the auction. But if, as EL–SNPR believes, the bankruptcy judge has underestimated the value of Castleton's real estate, wiped out too much of the secured claim, and set the remaining loan's terms at below-market rates, then someone will pay more than $375,000 (perhaps a *lot* more) for the equity in the reorganized firm.

The judgment of the bankruptcy court is reversed, and the case is remanded with directions to open the proposed plan of reorganization to competitive bidding.

[The material on "Transnational Bankruptcy" in chapter 13B, which begins on *page 744*, should be supplemented by the following.]

To be recognized under Chapter 15 of the Bankruptcy Code, a foreign process must be either a foreign main proceeding or a foreign nonmain proceeding. A foreign main proceeding is afforded substantial assistance by the United States courts, while a foreign nonmain proceeding is provided some assistance. As the next case, *Gold & Honey*, demonstrates, however, a United States court has significant discretion in whether to recognize a foreign proceeding at all. In its decision, the court cited public policy, among other grounds, as support for its refusal to recognize a foreign government's receivership, which, the court held, violated the automatic stay of a bankruptcy case filed in the United States. Other cases also display a reticence by United States courts to cede control of the bankruptcy process, despite Chapter 15 and the United Nations Model Law on which it is based. See, for example, the case of In re Vitro, S.A.B. de C.V., 701 F.3d 1031 (5th Cir. 2012), where the court declined to implement in the United States a foreign reorganization plan that, in the court's view, allowed insiders to control creditor voting in a manner inconsistent with U.S. Law, that violated absolute priority, as determined under U.S. law, and that, in violation of U.S. law, extinguished creditor claims against the debtor's nondebtor subsidiaries.

This is not to say that cooperation is nonexistent. For example, in In re Sino-Forest Corp., 501 B.R. 655 (Bankr. S.D.N.Y. 2013), the court held that a Canadian court's release of a third-party nondebtor was entitled to comity under Chapter 15, and in the case of In re Metcalfe & Mansfield Alternative Investments, 421 B.R. 685 (Bankr. S.D.N.Y. 2010), the court found that a Canadian remedy should be enforced on comity grounds "whether or not the same relief could be ordered in a plenary case under [U.S. law]."

The specific points of contention in *Gold & Honey* include the legitimacy and nature of the foreign proceeding that the United States Bankruptcy Court was asked to recognize. Not at issue in the case was the debtor's center of main interests (or "COMI"), which is frequently important in a determination of whether a foreign proceeding is a main proceeding. The applicable principles in determining a debtor's COMI are described by the *Gold & Honey* court in a footnote reproduced below.

IN RE GOLD & HONEY, LTD.

United States Bankruptcy Court, E.D.N.Y., 2009
410 B.R. 357

TRUST, BANKRUPTCY JUDGE

Pending before the Court in each of these non-consolidated chapter 15 cases (collectively, the "Chapter 15 Cases") are the petitions for recognition filed by Petitioners Amir Bartov ("Bartov") and Aliza Sharon ("Sharon") (each a "Receiver" and together, the "Receivers"). The Receivers assert that they are acting as the persons appointed as co-receivers by the Tel-Aviv-Jaffa District Court of the State of Israel (the "Israeli Court"), pursuant to a receivership proceeding pending before the Israeli Court (the "Israeli Receivership Proceeding").

Additionally, the Receivers assert that they are co-receivers of the entities Gold & Honey, Ltd. ("GH Ltd."), a debtor before this Court, and non-debtor entity Lucky Seven Ltd. ("Lucky Seven"), as well as co-receivers over substantially all of the known assets located in the State of Israel of Gold & Honey (1995) L.P., also a debtor before this Court ("GH LP"). The named debtors in these Chapter 15 Cases are also debtors in administratively consolidated chapter 11 proceedings, which were pending before this Court at the time these Chapter 15 Cases were filed. GH LP is the debtor and debtor-in-possession in case number 08-75237, filed on September 23, 2008. GH Ltd. is the debtor and debtor-in-possession in case number 08-75240, filed on September 23, 2008.

For the reasons herein, the petitions for recognition in each of the Chapter 15 Cases will be denied. * * *

The Parties

Debtor GH LP, a New York limited partnership established on January 1, 1994, maintains an office at 16 South Maryland Avenue, Port Washington, New York.

Debtor GH Ltd., a corporation organized under the laws of the State of Israel, is a general partner of GH LP and 49.5% equity holder of GH LP. Debtor Almond Jewelers, a corporation organized under the laws of the State of New York, is a general partner of GH LP and a 49.5% equity holder of GH LP.

First International Bank of Israel ("FIBI"), a foreign banking corporation organized and existing under the laws of the State of Israel, is a pre-petition lender to GH Ltd. Those pre-petition loans were guaranteed by GH LP, and possibly by non-debtor entities. Although FIBI conducts business in many countries around the world and has business contacts with the United States, it has no offices or branches within the physical borders of the United States.

The Receivers, appointed by the Israeli Court after the commencement of the Chapter 11 Cases, are the petitioners in the Chapter 15 Cases.

Background of the Debtors

Almond Jewelers is a New York-based designer, manufacturer, and marketer of jewelry products made primarily from gold and other precious metals. Almond Jewelers has asserted that during the late 1980s it encountered various manufacturing difficulties resulting from the lack of skilled employees such as tool makers, and experienced competition from other manufacturers who utilized cheap labor in developing countries.

In or about 1993, one or more of the Debtors decided to move the manufacturing facility of precious metal components (the "Components") from Westbury, New York, to Israel. Debtors were attracted to Israel because, *inter alia,* they could obtain substantial governmental financial incentives to build a new factory for the mass production of the Components. In 1994, the Debtors invested close to $50 million (USD) in building a manufacturing plant in Israel. That investment was comprised of: (a) more than 30% from funds contributed or raised by Debtor; (b) approximately 30% in conditional grants from the Israeli government; and (c) approximately 40% through loans from the Israeli government. Abatement of the repayment of the Israeli grants was conditioned upon the Debtors continuing operations in Israel for a period of not less than seven (7) years. Initially, the grants and loans from the Israeli government were provided to GH Ltd., an Israeli corporation, due to the Israeli practice of not providing governmental incentives directly to foreign partnerships. This procedural hurdle was overcome in or about 1996, when the Israeli government agreed to the assignment of the ownership interest of the Israeli factory to GH LP. Thus, by 1996, the manufacturing plant for the mass production of Components in Israel had been completed, and operations in Israel began under the name of GH LP, which remained a New York limited partnership.

GH LP's Operations and Business Activities

GH LP's business consists of designing, manufacturing, and worldwide marketing and sales of moderately priced jewelry products, including earrings, bangles, pendants, charms, rings, bracelets and necklaces. Typically, GH LP designs, manufactures and sells jewelry directly to large retailers, large wholesalers, and to various other entities as a private label contractor. Debtors assert that the design and marketing were mainly done from GH LP's United States office in Port Washington, New York, where GH LP's overall management is located and the overall business decisions are allegedly made. Prior to filing the Chapter 11 Cases, GH LP produced the Components in Israel, which were then shipped to Thailand for the production of finished jewelry by Almond Thailand Ltd., an affiliated entity of the Debtors ("Almond Thailand"). Almond Thailand is not a debtor before this Court.

As a result of the post-petition continued prosecution of the Israeli Receivership Proceeding, as discussed, *infra,* GH LP and GH Ltd. no longer conduct business in Israel.

GH Ltd.'s and GH LP's Financial History with Israel and FIBI

In 1994, GH Ltd. obtained loans and conditional grants from the State of Israel and pledged a "floating" charge on all of its assets as collateral security for the repayment of these loans and grants. GH LP also made pledges of some of its machinery and equipment, tools and dies.

In or about 1996, the State of Israel agreed to guaranty a working capital line of credit in the principal amount of $12 million (USD) which would be provided to the Debtors (the "Working Capital Credit Line"). The Working Capital Credit Line was intended, among other uses, to provide GH Ltd. with immediate cash availability to purchase gold and other precious metals. With the backing of the Israeli government's guaranty, GH Ltd. sought a lending institution to fund the Working Capital Credit Line. In or about 1996, GH Ltd. selected FIBI to finance the Working Capital Credit Line, primarily due to FIBI offering a favorable interest rate, and due to FIBI having agreed to finance the Working Capital Credit Line without any guaranty from either the Israeli government or the owners of GH Ltd. FIBI agreed to lend GH Ltd. $9 million (USD). FIBI, as lender, and GH Ltd., as borrower, then executed the documents required to implement the Working Capital Credit Line.

At all relevant times since the inception of the Working Capital Credit Line, the Debtors maintained their primary bank accounts at FIBI. In or about April 1997, GH LP signed a guaranty in favor of FIBI as security for the repayment of the Working Capital Credit Line. In 2003, GH Ltd. and GH LP asked FIBI to increase the Working Capital Credit Line. FIBI agreed, and increased the Working Capital Credit Line to approximately $12 million (USD). As additional collateral for the repayment of the increased Working Capital Credit Line, FIBI required GH LP to pledge certain accounts receivables (the "Existing Contracts"). The pledge of the Existing Contracts was memorialized by appropriate documentation including a pledge agreement (the "Pledge Agreement"). FIBI purportedly recorded the Pledge Agreement as a lien against the Existing Contracts with the Israeli Pledge Registrar and/or the Israeli Companies Registrar.

In or about March 2008, the Working Capital Credit Line was increased to $16 million (USD). At that time, FIBI required additional collateral from GH Ltd. and GH LP. Consequently, at that time, GH LP provided FIBI with a pledge on certain machinery and equipment.

Summary of Litigation Between FIBI, GH LP and GH Ltd.

FIBI commenced litigation in Israel shortly after the Working Capital Credit Line was increased in March 2008. The following briefly summarizes the history of that litigation.

In late July 2008, FIBI seized substantially all of GH Ltd. and GH LP's assets and accounts, and commenced the Israeli Receivership Proceeding. Prior to the filing of the Chapter 11 Cases, a number of events occurred in the Israeli Receivership Proceeding, primarily resulting in the Israeli Court denying FIBI's emergency and *ex parte* applications for the appointment of a receiver.

On September 23, 2008 (the "Petition Date"), the Debtors filed the Chapter 11 Cases. Notice of the commencement of the Chapter 11 Cases was provided by Debtors to FIBI.

On October 2, 2008, notwithstanding the pendency of the Chapter 11 Cases, FIBI continued its application for the appointment of a temporary receiver before the Israeli Court. FIBI took the position before the Israeli Court that the automatic stay, which arose by virtue of the Chapter 11 Cases, did not apply to FIBI's actions or its attempt to obtain control over the property of the bankruptcy estates of GH Ltd. and GH LP. As a result of the proceedings before the Israeli Court, and with the agreement of GH Ltd. and GH LP, on October 2, 2008, Sharon was appointed as supervisor over the Debtors' businesses. The Israeli Court then adjourned the October 2 hearing and its decision on FIBI's application for the appointment of a temporary receiver until October 12, 2008.

On October 3, 2008, the Debtors applied to this Court for an order determining that the automatic stay applied to the Debtors' property wherever located and by whomever held, and, in particular, to the Israeli Receivership Proceeding. The hearing on this request was scheduled on an expedited basis before this Court for October 6, 2008 (the "October 6 Hearing"). FIBI specially appeared at the October 6 Hearing represented by both New York bankruptcy counsel in person, as well as its Israeli counsel, Bartov, who appeared via telephone. FIBI asserted that this Court had no jurisdiction over FIBI and had no jurisdiction over the Israeli Receivership Proceeding.

This Court determined at the October 6 Hearing, over FIBI's objection, that the automatic stay did, in fact, apply to the Debtors' property wherever located and by whomever held, and entered an Order to that effect (the "Stay Order"). Due to the expedited nature of the October 6 Hearing, however, this Court did not reach the issue of whether the automatic stay specifically applied to the Israeli Receivership Proceeding or whether this Court had *in personam* jurisdiction over FIBI. However, this Court advised FIBI that if it proceeded before the Israeli Court in the Israeli Receivership Proceeding, it did so at its own peril. The Stay Order includes the following pertinent paragraphs:

> ORDERED, that the automatic stay provided under section 362(a) of the Bankruptcy Code (the "Automatic Stay") is in full force and effect in this bankruptcy case; and it is further
>
> ORDERED, that the Automatic Stay stays, among other things, actions arising under section 362(a) of the Bankruptcy Code:
>
> (1) the commencement or continuation, including the issuance or employment of process, of a judicial, administrative, or other action or proceeding against the debtor that was or could have been commenced before the commencement of the case under this title, or to recover a claim against the debtor that arose before the commencement of the case under this title;
>
> (2) the enforcement, against the debtor or against property of the estate, of a judgment obtained before the commencement of the case under this title;

(3) any act to obtain possession of property of the estate or of property from the estate or to exercise control over property of the estate; and it is further

ORDERED, that property of the estate includes property of the Debtors "wherever located and by whomever held" pursuant to section 541(a) of the Bankruptcy Code.

Following the October 6 Hearing and entry of the Stay Order, FIBI chose to continue to prosecute the Israeli Receivership Proceeding. The Stay Order and the record of the October 6 Hearing were then presented to the Israeli Court. In a thoughtful and thorough opinion dated October 30, 2008 (the "October 30 Decision"), the Israeli Court declined to give effect to the automatic stay or the Stay Order, and determined that it could proceed, regardless of the pendency of the Chapter 11 Cases. However, the Israeli Court based its analysis partially on the presumed illegitimacy of the Chapter 11 Cases, partially on the failure of GH Ltd. and GH LP to properly register the Stay Order in the Israeli Receivership Proceeding, and partially on principles of comity. The Israeli Court also stated: "There is indeed no doubt that the Court in the United States is competent to make an order concerning a stay of proceedings, which applies to all the assets of the debtor wherever they are situated."

As a result of the post-petition proceedings before the Israeli Court, Sharon continued to act as supervisor over the Debtors' businesses.

Debtors then commenced [an] adversary proceeding against FIBI on October 30, 2008 (the "Adversary"), and sought a temporary restraining order (the "TRO Request"). This Court conducted a hearing on the TRO Request on November 6, 2008. Supplemental briefing was permitted to be filed by November 14, 2008, and a ruling conference was scheduled for December 10, 2008.

On November 30, 2008, the Israeli Court issued a judgment appointing Bartov, an Israeli attorney for FIBI, and Sharon, an accountant, as permanent receivers for GH LP and GH Ltd. in the Israeli Receivership Proceeding. FIBI filed a translation of the Israeli Court's ruling on December 4, 2008, with its motion to dismiss the Adversary for lack of personal jurisdiction (the "Motion to Dismiss").

On December 10, 2008, this Court held the previously scheduled ruling conference on the TRO Request (the "Ruling Conference"). At that time, this Court made its findings of fact and conclusions of law on the record, to the extent applicable, in accordance with Rule 7052 of the Federal Rules of Bankruptcy Procedure. As memorialized in a written Summary of Decision and Order entered on December 12, 2008, this Court stated as follows:

> After due consideration, this Court denies the issuance of a TRO for the following reasons:
>
> 1. A TRO would be redundant to the automatic stay, which is, and has been, in effect, and which prohibits FIBI from proceeding with the continuation of a judicial, administrative, or other action or proceeding against the Debtors that was commenced prior to the petition date herein, and which prohibits FIBI from proceeding to recover a claim against the Debtors that arose before the commencement of these cases, and which prohibits FIBI from any act to obtain possession of property of the estate or to exercise control over property of the estate, wherever located, and by whomever held;
>
> 2. FIBI has demonstrated that it can answer in damages, thus precluding this Court's determination of irreparable harm to Debtors, with such determination a likely prerequisite for the issuance of a specific TRO against FIBI.
>
> This Court does not, and need not, reach the issue of whether FIBI is subject to in personam jurisdiction in the United States. The issue of in personam jurisdiction will be determined in connection with FIBI's pending Motion to Dismiss this adversary proceeding.

On January 7, 2009, FIBI filed a motion for relief from the automatic stay or for abstention ("FIBI Lift Stay Motion") in the Chapter 11 Cases of GH LP and GH Ltd. FIBI requested this Court enter an order pursuant to Bankruptcy Code Section 362, subsections (d)(1) and (d)(2), vacating the automatic stay nunc pro tunc with respect to the Israeli Receivership Proceeding, vacating the stay to allow other creditors to take action in Israel or, in the alternative, enter an order pursuant to Section 305(a)(1) abstaining from exercising jurisdiction over and dismissing, the Chapter 11 Cases. Additionally, Bartov filed an affirmation in support of the FIBI Lift Stay Motion that included as exhibits, translations of the relevant Israeli law and certain of the various hearings held in Israel ("Bartov Declaration").

On January 28, 2009, the Receivers filed petitions for recognition in these Chapter 15 Cases. They seek recognition of the Israeli Receivership Proceeding as foreign main proceedings of GH LP and GH Ltd., pursuant to Chapter 15 of the Bankruptcy Code (the "Receivers' Petitions"). The Receivers each filed declarations in Support of the Receivers' Petitions (the "Receivers' Declarations"). This Court has received extensive briefing and submissions on the Receivers' Petitions as well as on the FIBI Motion to Dismiss the Adversary and the FIBI Lift Stay Motion. A ruling conference was held on those matters on July 29, 2009. That ruling conference is discussed, *infra.*

Procedural Requirements for Recognition

Chapter 15 of the Bankruptcy Code was enacted in 2005 to implement the Model Law on Cross-Border Insolvency (the "Model Law"). The Model Law had been formulated by the United Nations Commission on International Trade Law ("UNCITRAL"), in a process in which the United States was an active participant. The language of Chapter 15 tracks the Model Law, with some modifications that were designed to conform the Model Law with existing United States law.

In order for a petition for recognition to be granted, the petition must meet several requirements. Section 1517 requires recognition of a foreign proceeding if: (1) such foreign proceeding for which recognition is sought is a foreign main proceeding or foreign nonmain proceeding within the meaning of section 1502; (2) the foreign representative applying for recognition is a person or body; and (3) the petition meets the requirements of section 1515.

Recognition under Section 1517 of the Bankruptcy Code is not a "rubber stamp exercise." *In re Basis Yield Alpha Fund (Master),* 381 B.R. 37, 40 (Bankr.S.D.N.Y.2008). The Court can "consider any and all relevant facts." *Id.* at 41. Although Sections 1515 and 1516 are designed to make recognition as simple and expedient as possible, the court may consider proof on any element. The ultimate burden of proof on each element is on the foreign representative. *See In re Bear Stearns High-Grade Structured Credit Strategies Master Fund, Ltd.,* 389 B.R. 325, 335 (S.D.N.Y.2008) (noting that "the ultimate burden of proof as to each element is on the foreign representative" and citing H.R.REP. NO. 109-31, at 112 (2005), *reprinted in* 2005 U.S.C.C.A.N. 88, 173 ("House Report")). * * *

Neither a Foreign Main nor Nonmain Proceeding

The Israeli Receivership Proceeding is neither a foreign main proceeding nor a foreign nonmain proceeding. Section 101(23) of the Bankruptcy Code provides a statutory definition of foreign proceeding, as follows:

The term "foreign proceeding" means a collective judicial or administrative proceeding in a foreign country, including an interim proceeding, under a law relating to insolvency or adjustment of debt in which proceeding the assets and affairs of the debtor are subject to control or supervision by a foreign court, for the purpose of reorganization or liquidation.

Thus, for the petitions for recognition to be granted, the Receivers must prove that the following elements exist with respect to the Israeli Receivership Proceeding, as follows:

(i) a proceeding; (ii) that is either judicial or administrative; (iii) that is collective in nature; (iv) that is in a foreign country; (v) that is authorized or conducted under a law related to insolvency or the adjustment of debts; (vi) in which the debtor's assets and affairs are subject to the control or supervision of a foreign court; and (vii) which proceeding is for the purpose of reorganization or liquidation.

In re Betcorp Ltd., 400 B.R. 266, 276-77 (Bankr.D.Nev.2009). ... [T]his Court has determined that the Receivers have not met their burden of proof in either of the Chapter 15 Cases.

The Receivers have demonstrated that all of the following elements are met here in both Chapter 15 Cases:[15] (i) a proceeding; (ii) that is either judicial or administrative; (iv) that is in a foreign country; (v) that is authorized or conducted under a law related to insolvency or

---

[15] Although several of the reported chapter 15 Cases discuss the requirement of §1502(a)(4) that a foreign main proceeding is a "foreign proceeding pending in the country where the debtor has the center of its main interests," this is not an impactive issue here. Center of main interests ("COMI") is not defined in the Bankruptcy Code or in the Model Law. To aid courts in simple or uncontested cases, Section 1516(c) states that, "[i]n the absence of evidence to the contrary, the debtor's registered office ... is presumed to be the center of the debtor's main interests."; *see also In re Bear Stearns,* 389 B.R. at 335-36 (quoting House Report at 112-13); *c.f.* FED.R.EVID. 301 (explaining that a party's rebuttal of a presumption does not shift the burden of proof; rather, the risk of nonpersuasion remains upon the party on whom it was originally cast). This Court need not and does not reach the determination of GH LP's or GH Ltd.'s COMI.

Moreover, a foreign nonmain proceeding is "a foreign proceeding, other than a foreign main proceeding, pending in a country where the debtor has an establishment." §1502(5). An "establishment" is "any place of operations where the debtor carries out nontransitory economic activity." §1502(2). Here, again, this Court need not and does not reach the determination of where GH LP and GH Ltd. have an establishment under § 1502(5).

the adjustment of debts; and (vii) which proceeding is for the purpose of reorganization or liquidation.

The Receivers, however, have not met their burden of showing that the Israeli Receivership Proceeding is collective in nature under Section 101(23)(iii). In addition, the Israeli Receivership Proceeding should not be recognized by this Court for two (2) additional reasons as to GH Ltd. and GH LP … . The … reasons are: the Receivers were appointed in violation of the automatic stay; and recognition of the petitions would have an adverse effect on public policy, pursuant to Section 1506 … .

Receivers Were Appointed in Violation of the Automatic Stay

The appointment of the Receivers in Israel was a clear violation of the automatic stay. It is axiomatic that when the Chapter 11 Cases were filed, the automatic stay went into effect. The stay automatically enjoined the continuation of any litigation against GH Ltd. and GH LP, and automatically enjoined continuing lien enforcement against GH Ltd. and GH LP to enforce a prepetition claim against the debtor. Bankruptcy Code §362(a)(1), (3), (4), (5), and (6).

Moreover, here, FIBI proceeded in the Israeli Receivership Proceeding in spite of and in the face of this Court's Stay Order. FIBI knew and was specifically told that the stay applied to all property of GH Ltd. and GH LP wherever located and by whomever held. It would fly in the face of the Bankruptcy Code for this Court to recognize the petitions here and authorize the post-petition appointed Receivers to proceed in the United States when they were appointed as the result of a knowing and willful violation of the stay by FIBI. Although on January 7, 2009, FIBI did file its Lift Stay Motion seeking, inter alia, relief from stay retroactive to the petition date of the Chapter 11 Cases, retroactive relief has been denied.

As previously noted, the Israeli Court entered the lengthy and thorough October 30 Decision, in which it determined that FIBI could proceed in Israel in spite of the automatic stay and this Court's Stay Order. After reviewing the background of the parties and their respective disputes, the Israeli Court first discusses whether the Stay Order had been properly registered in Israel as a foreign judgment under Israeli law. The Israeli Court determined it had not been. The Israeli Court then discussed cases regarding whether it should recognize the Stay Order under principles of comity, and discussed relevant cases on comity and recognition of foreign judgment.

With respect specifically to the events of the October 6 Hearing, the Israeli Court noted that this Court expressed concern at that hearing as to whether the Israeli Court would give effect to the Stay Order. The Israeli Court agreed that it and this Court should provide reciprocity for properly registered United States federal court orders and recognize comity between them. The Israeli Court also noted that, in spite of the broad, worldwide grant of jurisdiction given to United States federal courts over a debtor's assets wherever located, a United States court cannot control the actions of a foreign court, nor can it exercise control over assets in a foreign country without the assistance of the foreign court.

The Israeli Court then noted that GH LP's and GH Ltd.'s center of operations are in Israel, not New York. Ultimately, however, the Israeli Court decided to proceed, noting, in part, that while it had jurisdiction to recognize the Stay Order, "in the present case no process of rehabilitating the respondent [GH Ltd., GH LP, and Lucky Seven] has begun in the court in New York" and that "it is desirable that only one court should control the overall rehabilitation or winding up of the company."

The Israeli Court did not give effect to the instantaneous imposition of the stay, which arises by operation of law and without the need for an order to impose the stay. In essence, the Israeli Court made a decision to lift the automatic stay. Whether this Court would have granted stay relief in October 2008 is an unanswerable question and moot because no one sought such relief.

Further, FIBI continued to prosecute the Israeli Receivership Proceeding even after this Court orally ruled on December 10, 2008, and again by written order on December 12, 2008, that the stay prohibited FIBI's actions in Israel, and that "the automatic stay applied to the Israeli Receivership Proceeding to the extent property of the bankruptcy estate is involved." * * *

Once the Chapter 11 Cases were filed, the Bankruptcy Code contains a number of provisions which FIBI could have invoked prior to proceeding in Israel. FIBI could have requested this Court to determine that the filing of the Chapter 11 Cases was not legitimate, and sought stay relief under Section 362, abstention under Section 305, and/or dismissal or conversion under Section 1112. FIBI failed to do so. However, it is for this Court, with jurisdiction over the Chapter 11 Cases, to decide whether and when to grant relief from the stay, but respectfully, not for the Israeli Court to decide to not recognize and apply the stay.

Israeli Receivership Proceeding Is Not "Collective in Nature"

The Israeli Receivership Proceeding is not "collective in nature" and the affairs of GH Ltd. and GH LP are not subject to the control of a foreign court. The Israeli Receivership Proceeding does not meet the requirements of being "collective in nature." A proceeding that is "collective in nature" is one that "considers the rights and obligations of all creditors."[16] *Betcorp,* 400 B.R. at 281 (holding that a voluntary Australian winding-up proceeding was collective in nature because any attempt by a creditor to undermine the orderly, cooperative system that accounted for the rights of all creditors was outlawed); *In re Bd. of Dirs. of Hopewell Int'l Ins., Ltd.,* 275 B.R. 699, 707 (S.D.N.Y.2002) (holding that a "scheme of arrangement" for creditors to estimate and file claims was collective in nature because all creditors had a right to object to the proposed schemes and the court was involved in approving all plans). The *Betcorp* court noted, "This is in contrast, for example, to a receivership remedy instigated at the request, and for the benefit of, a single secured creditor." *Betcorp,* 400 B.R. at 281.

As the *Betcorp* court also noted, a receivership proceeding, as opposed to a "collective" proceeding, is generally regarded as more prejudicial to the creditor body as a whole than federal bankruptcy proceedings. *Id.* at 281.

The Receivers rely on *Bear Stearns* for the proposition that a foreign decision certified by another country is presumptively a recognizable foreign proceeding, and that all requirements within Section 101(23) are thus presumptively met. However, recognition is not a "rubber stamp exercise," and any such presumption is rebuttable upon the Court's examination of "any and all relevant facts." *Alpha Fund (Master),* 381 B.R. at 44-45.

The Israeli Receivership Proceeding is not simply collective in nature. It does not require the Receivers to consider the rights and obligations of all creditors. The proceeding was commenced under the Israeli Companies Ordinance. As GH Ltd. and GH LP contend, the Receivership is more akin to a individual creditor's replevin or repossession action than it is to a reorganization or liquidation by an independent trustee. The Israeli Receivership Proceeding is primarily designed to

---

[16] The proposition that a foreign proceeding must be for the general benefit of creditors is also embodied in Section 1501, which lists the "fair and efficient administration of cross-border insolvencies that protects the interests of all creditors," among its primary objectives. §1501(a)(3).

allow FIBI to collect its debts, and is not a scheme of arrangement or a winding up proceeding, both of which are instituted by a debtor for the purposes of paying off all creditors with court supervision to ensure evenhandedness. Although Bankruptcy Code Section 1502 does recognize that a foreign proceeding may be for the purpose of reorganization or liquidation, the proceeding must still be collective in nature.

The Bartov Declaration acknowledges that there is a distinct difference between a "receiver" and a "liquidator" under Israeli law. [T]he applicable Israeli law utilized by FIBI to commence the Israeli Receivership Proceeding identifies, *inter alia,* that a "liquidator" and "receiver" under Israeli law serve separate and unique functions. [The relevant Israeli law] also elucidates the difference between an enforcement proceeding and an insolvency proceeding. By way of further contrast, Israeli law does provide for collective creditor functions under the Israeli Bankruptcy Ordinance, which models some provisions of the Bankruptcy Code. However, the Israeli Receivership Proceeding is not proceeding under the Israeli Bankruptcy Ordinance. This conflict is another example of the singular as opposed to collective nature of the Israeli Receivership Proceeding.

The Receivers do not dispute this material difference between the ordinances, and instead rely upon an article from Standard & Poor's Rating Services that merely recites that a receiver generally must act as an officer of the court and thus impliedly owes a duty to all creditors. The S&P article, however, is neither legal authority nor persuasive.

Further, the Israeli decision appointing the Receivers heavily examines the loan contract of GH LP and GH Ltd. with FIBI in order to determine whether FIBI had the grounds to demand immediate repayment of the debt. The Israeli Court declared that such grounds existed based on the contract of the parties, inaccurate declarations by the borrowers, admissions of insolvency, and changed ownership. Thus, the Israeli Receivership Proceeding does not meet the Bankruptcy Code's requirement that a foreign proceeding be "collective in nature." Bankruptcy Code §101(23). * * *

[Recognition would be] Contrary to Public Policy

A petition for recognition should be denied if recognition would be manifestly contrary to the public policy of the United States. Bankruptcy Code §1506 Recognition of the Israeli Receivership Proceeding as a foreign proceeding would be manifestly contrary to the public policy of the United States because such recognition would reward and legitimize FIBI's violation of both the automatic stay and this Court's Orders regarding the stay. * * *

[C]ondoning FIBI's conduct here would limit a federal court's jurisdiction over all of the debtors' property "wherever located and by whomever held," as any future creditor could follow FIBI's lead and violate the stay in order to procure assets that were outside the United States, yet still under the United States court's jurisdiction. *See* 28 U.S.C. § 1334(e). Because of the serious ramifications that would ensue in derogation of fundamental United States policies, this Court should not recognize the Israeli Receivership Proceeding as a foreign proceeding.

TECHNICAL AND OTHER CORRECTIONS

Since the publication of the Fourth Edition of the casebook, there have been changes that are not reflected in the book. Dollar amounts in a variety of provisions are updated for inflation periodically under Bankruptcy Code §104. Also, The Statutory Time-Periods Technical Amendments Act of 2009 extended the time limits for some required actions to facilitate judicial administration. And the Technical Corrections Act of 2010 made other changes that were, unsurprisingly, technical in nature.

There are also errors in the Fourth Edition:

On page 11, a sentence reads: "When your assets exceed your liabilities, the assets are not truly yours." The sentence should read (though even as corrected it is, of course an oversimplification): "When your liabilities exceed your assets, the assets are not truly yours."

On pages 48 and 84, it is stated that a decision on case dismissal under Bankruptcy Code §305 is unreviewable. More precisely, however, the provision states that such a decision is unreviewable by a court of appeals or the Supreme Court. The provision does not preclude review by a district court of a bankruptcy court's dismissal decision.

On page 86, at the end of Exercise 3C(4), the reference to "§1104(3)" should be to "§1104(a)(3)" and the exercise should be deleted in that §1104(a)(3) has been repealed.

On page 126, a sentence provides that Bankruptcy Code §362(b)(19) added by the Bankruptcy Reform Act of 2005 "permits an employer withholds a debtor's wages and contribute them to specified pension plan." In addition to the grammatical error in this sentence, the explanation is incomplete. The provision in question grants an employer an exemption from the automatic stay to withhold and replenish from wages money a debtor has borrowed from a retirement fund.

On pages 309-352, chapter 8C of the book on Fraudulent Conveyances incorrectly contains references to a one-year statute of limitation under §548 rather than the current 2-year period.

On pages 388-89, references to §553 need to reflect the current version of the statute.

On page 410, Note 9A.1 should reflect the Supreme Court's opinion in Central Virginia Community College v. Katz, 546 U.S. 356 (2006).

On page 583, the introduction to Problem 11A and the Problem itself present an outdated issue of a Chapter 7 discharge followed immediately by a Chapter 13 case. This problem is now solved by the rules against successive discharge in §1328(f).

On Page 610, the first sentence of the first full paragraph should read: "A discharge in Chapter 13 will not be granted in a case the order for relief in which is not at least four years after the debtor's most recent discharge in Chapter 7, 11, or 12 and at least two years after the debtor's most recent discharge in Chapter 13."

On page 647, in Exercise 12B(1), a debtor with a "high-paying job" likely would be required under §1325(b) to have a repayment plan that covers five years rather than three.

These (and no doubt other, yet undiscovered) corrections will be made in the Fifth Edition, which will follow shortly.